PENGUIN B

T0290306

HEROES
OF THE
SKIES

Actor, writer and broadcaster Michael Veitch began his
career in television comedy programs before freelancing
as a columnist and arts reviewer for newspapers and
magazines. For four years he presented *Sunday Arts*,
the national arts show on ABC television, and has
broadcast regularly across Australia on ABC radio. He
has produced two books indulging his life-long interest
in the aircraft and airmen of the Second World War,
Flak and *Fly* as well as *The Forgotten Islands* in which
he explores the little-known islands of Bass Strait.
In 2015, he began touring a one-man stage version
of *Flak* nationally.

MICHAEL VEITCH

HEROES OF THE SKIES

PENGUIN BOOKS

PENGUIN BOOKS

UK | USA | Canada | Ireland | Australia
India | New Zealand | South Africa | China

Penguin Books is part of the Penguin Random House group of companies
whose addresses can be found at global.penguinrandomhouse.com.

First published by Penguin Group (Australia), 2015
This edition published by Penguin Random House Australia Pty Ltd, 2016

Cover design by Nada Backovic © Penguin Group (Australia)
Text design by Samantha Jayaweera © Penguin Group (Australia)
Typeset in Janson Text by Samantha Jayaweera, Penguin Group (Australia)
Author photograph by Gina Milicia
Printed and bound in Australia by Griffin Press, an accredited ISO AS/NZS 14001
Environmental Management Systems printer.

National Library of Australia
Cataloguing-in-Publication data:

Veitch, Michael, author.
Heroes of the skies / Michael Veitch.
9780143574033 (paperback)

Subjects: Australia. Royal Australian Air Force–Airmen.
World War, 1939-1945–Aerial operations, Australian.
World War, 1939-1945–Personal narratives, Australian.

940.544994

penguin.com.au

CONTENTS

PREFACE

Looking back at it now, I remember – at least I think I remember – in the moment before it happened, that I was laughing.

Surely not.

Laughing?

Yet that's how I recall it, in as much as I recall anything of that day with any clarity.

The images, after all, are blurred; the timeline unclear. A year later, the whole thing now seems distant, remote; a series of images sealed inside their own dream-scape, but inchoate, like paragraphs rearranged by a toddler, or a jigsaw puzzle with missing pieces. But which pieces?

The harder I close my eyes and try to coerce my sluggish memory back to that cold, clear early winter's afternoon amid the tall trees and the bluish light, the more the moments scatter before me like moths. And after doing what I can to bend them into some kind of order, I am simply left, once again, to contemplate the strange and disconnected pictures of that memorable but unremembered day.

Yet, is this perhaps what memory is? No convenient metronomic timeline, but moments, flashing vividly for an instant in the brain's electric palette, connected, ultimately, to nothing but themselves?

* * *

After several years interviewing men who fought in the air during the Second World War, I have developed a pattern in my self-appointed task of recording their experiences. The start is always the same: an exchange of pleasantries, the settling-in to a living room or retirement unit; accepting the cup of tea which is almost always offered. Then I begin. 'Tell me, where were you born?' Always the same question. Let them know it's all about them, that I am there to listen, and hungry to learn.

He doesn't suspect it, yet, but I'm searching him out. Sifting for his story, gambling on how much of it he is prepared to share with me. Will I be given a dispassionate narrative of facts and dates, or will this former pilot, bomb aimer or flying boat navigator take me back seventy years to the maw of war?

Sometimes, I will be privy to memories that have not stirred for decades, long-dormant terrors that will break both of us into a sweat. Some of the men I speak to become reluctant and elusive; others open up like time machines transporting my imagination with a phrase or a recollection. Perhaps it's the description of a colour, or the nuances of a conversation brought back to life after seven decades. Or even a smell, as in the case of one former bomber pilot who speaks of his aircraft being hit by lightning one night over Holland. It left, he says, 'a strange, tingling, stale milk kind of smell'.

Sometimes I must gently cajole, drag the record needle back to the part he seemed to skip, or hide. At other times I will push it forward a little when the timeline wanders. Many times I will check the recorder lest – God forbid – I should lose a moment of what I am hearing.

It seems I have been indulging in other people's memories all my life. Certainly, at least, since before the writing, when the hidden purpose of a lifetime's obsession – for years clumsy and unformed – finally showed itself. As a kid, I would forgo normal childhood interests, preferring instead to engage in conversation with some of the tens of thousands of men, then barely out of middle age, who had taken part in the Second World War. Particularly the airmen. I would appear to them, this strange child, solemn and inquisitive, boldly intruding into the violent events of their youth, eager to extract some flavour of their war. Perhaps my age to them was a little disarming, but they spoke to me, and I learned to ask the right questions.

* * *

Could I really have been laughing? Surely not. Yet, that's how I remember it in the perfectly framed half-second before the fall of the tree, before the tall messmate – *Eucalyptus obliqua* – with all its springy kinetic energy and twenty metres of height, tilting on its severed base which I had cut – badly as it turned out – came crashing down on top of me.

Perhaps not so much a laugh, but a moment of clarity. An instant in which I foresaw the whole thing: the mistake in hastily cutting the wrong tree, its fall, the ambulance, the hospital, the metal, the scars, the crutches and the rehabilitation. As if the whole thing had already played out from start to finish and I was there merely to observe, an audience to a macabre piece of theatre.

The images, though disconnected, are clear: the trunk of the big tree passing me on its way to the ground a mere hand's width from my face. Why so close? Why this odd angle? I still recall the exquisite details of the tree trunk – mottled grey spots with a touch of pink, framed in my vision like a photograph – just as it fell, catching my left thigh, pile-driving it into my bursting ankle, ramming my shattered tibia and fibula into the soil, and pinning me under its ton of weight.

Of the actual break, however – I mean the moment of it – I have no memory at all. No thud, no sickening crack, certainly no shock of pain. Not yet anyway. I was simply on the ground, under a tree, wondering how on earth my boot had managed to come off my leg, before realising my foot was still inside it. Then, suddenly, I was very, very cold.

It certainly doesn't sound like much to laugh about. Perhaps in the hospital under the long and lingering bouts of anaesthetic, or the deranged morphine haze in which I remained, seemingly, for weeks, everything became warped, overcooked, like dreams in a fever.

* * *

The most physically traumatic event of my life took place barely a year ago, and already my memories of it are confused and fading. How then will I remember it should I be around in, say, another thirty years, or forty? If I live to be the age of Jeff Perry, a Wellington bomber pilot who survived his tour of thirty operations at a time when it was almost a statistical impossibility to do so, I will have carried the memories in my head for forty-eight years. How will I recall them then? Will the drama of my little injury, caused by nothing but my own foolish misadventure, diminish across the wider landscape of my life, or will it amplify, its colours more vivid?

The quiet generation that fought the Second World War are, finally, heartbreakingly, leaving us, and taking their memories with them. As we farewelled – so recently it seems – the last living remnants of the First World War, so we will soon mourn those from the Second. It is a parting I have anticipated, and dreaded, all my life.

They leave us at a time when the world has rarely seemed more uncertain or more neurotic, and we will soon be left to simply speculate on how much their courage, their modesty and their humour might have assuaged the runaway anxieties of early twenty-first-century life. We will soon – all of us – be orphans in their wake.

But they are not gone yet. Not quite. As the years 1939–45 continue to emerge from the cocoon of shock and silence that enveloped the early post-war decades, more and more books, television shows and films on the subject are voraciously consumed in the furnace of popular culture. The incomprehensible scale of the events themselves are slowly digested, but the remaining men who saw it with their own eyes are largely ignored. Perhaps it is assumed their stories have all been told, and it is now up to the scholars and film-makers to make sense of the catastrophe. But they have not all been told.

Like a volcano exploding somewhere over the horizon, the

booms of the Second World War continue to echo down the decades. If the French Revolution could prompt one historian, when asked to comment on its legacy two hundred years later, to reply, 'Well, it's a little early to tell,' the reverberations of the Second World War are set to buffet us for a long time to come. And yet still today, we are fortunate enough to have a few of those who can tell us what it felt like, sounded like, smelled like.

Now in their ninth decade, how do the extraordinary events of their youth stand out against the landscape of a long life? To those lucky ones who are, for the moment, beating the odds of time, and whose faculties have remained intact, have the memories become more vivid, or faded to a kind of sepia? How were these men's lives shaped by the war? What did it mean?

It is somewhere close to midnight of the day when the men of the Second World War will still be with us. I have met just a few of them, and the following are just a few of their stories, snatched from the darkness in the nick of time. Often, having closed up for decades, they spoke to me with a sense of urgency, as if keen to unburden themselves of the responsibility of history, lest these adventures and these tragedies be lost to future generations of enquiring minds.

On more than one occasion, some of these brave, remarkable and modest men would themselves seem amazed at the memories rising up like ghosts from their past, uttering, with a shaking of the head, 'It's hard to believe I actually went through all that' – but they most certainly did.

GEORGE SMITH

Role: Wireless operator / air gunner
Aircraft: North American B-25 Mitchell
Posting: 180 Squadron, 2nd Tactical Air Force, RAF

You'd look back and think,
Good God, have we just come through that?

George has always appreciated the value of a good education. Perhaps that's what happens when you grow up with not much of it – nor anything else – to go around. 'I grew up in Collingwood,' he says. 'When I was a kid, our backyard was as big as this room. No bathroom – once a week Mum would put us in a copper and wash us on the kitchen floor.' It's a far cry from those days as we sit in the elegant, sun-filled front room of his modern unit, surrounded by frames, prints and a small but interesting library.

George sets the scene by telling me about his father – originally an entertainer who enlisted for the First World War and served in France. 'I've never smoked,' George announces – an early decision brought on by his disgust at having to roll his dad's cigarettes from the wads of moist, cloying tobacco shoved into his hands. 'The smell of it was revolting. The only way my mother could get rid of it was to rub a tablespoon of dripping and sugar into them.' Enough, surely, to put you off the fags for life.

When war came, George was drafted not into the air force but the army and enjoyed a brief career as 'Trooper Smith', which, to his surprise, he rather liked. But all young George had ever really wanted to do was hang around aeroplanes, so when the RAAF offered him a ground job as a guard at Laverton, with hints of it evolving into aircrew training, he didn't need to think twice. It was here one afternoon that the importance of a good education was again driven home to him when a US Flying Fortress made an impromptu landing and taxied up to a hangar. A hand slid open the big bomber's side cockpit window and the face of a young officer appeared.

'Say, guys, is this East Sale?' he enquired in an accented drawl.

George gave his chief flight sergeant a glance.

'Close that window and come down here,' said the chief. 'You've only missed it by 200 miles!'

I've known George for some time. As co-founder of the delightfully named Odd Bods Association for those Australian airmen who served with RAF units and who therefore found themselves detached from their squadron associations, George has introduced me to many former flyers, but I've known very little of his own career until now. Sharp, engaging and with an almost youthful outlook, he also possesses a baritone voice that could easily have furnished him with a successful career in radio. It's perfect for painting me a picture of operating as a B-25 Mitchell wireless operator / air gunner in the 2nd Tactical Air Force (2TAF) during the Battle of Normandy.

'We had a porter,' he recalls of a morning stopped at a rail siding on a train loaded with fellow cadets on their way to wireless and gunnery school in wintry Canada. 'An absolutely delightful man.' Pulling back the curtain next to his bunk, George was amazed at the very new sight of snow. 'Well, gentlemen,' the porter announced, 'we're waiting here for a train to come through. Permission has been given to get off if you wish.'

'So there we were,' George says, 'all these young men from Australia, running around like four-year-olds having snowball fights and carrying on like ratbags; none of us had seen snow in our lives.' The question of just how many of those young men would return home hovers unanswered.

He tells me of a crew lost on a night-training flight in England. 'The pilot's name was Monty,' he says, 'from around Tatura in central Victoria. Flew into a hill in Yorkshire. He was one of those men we'd glorify today as a typical Australian man: tall, good looking, just a delightful chap.' In the old church in Tatura, he tells me, you can still see the stained-glass window put up as his memorial. 'They reckon the window's worth more than the church,' he says.

After his destiny being decided – somewhat bizarrely – by the drawing of his name out of a hat, George was sent to Pennfield Ridge in New Brunswick, Canada, from where he would eventually operate not in the 'heavies' of Bomber Command, but with Sir Basil Embry's quick-striking army-support aerial thunderbolt, 2TAF.

'When we arrived at 180 Squadron based at Dunsfold in Surrey,' George explains, 'we were told we'd be operating in daylight, flying tight formation, concentrating on small targets at low level, and that we could expect to be doing more than one mission a day.' Formed out of Bomber Command's No. 2 Group in 1943, 2TAF was a far cry from the blunt, area-blasting instruments of the Lancasters and Handley Page Halifaxes of Bomber Command. George would instead be part of a precision instrument, where accuracy could never be over-stressed, surgically removing targets at the advancing army's request. More soberingly, his tour with 2TAF would constitute fifty operations, not the thirty flown by Bomber Command. 'At short notice we'd have to hit a concentration of tanks or a bridge or an ammo dump, and from never higher than 10 000 feet, so we'd cop both the light and heavy flak,' says George. 'Our trips were much shorter than the heavy bombers' – one or two hours mostly – but much of their flying time was over friendly territory. We could be over the enemy in ten minutes.'

The only Australian among his crew of four Englishmen – pilot Ted Burn, navigator / bomb aimer Dave Kirk and fellow air gunner Jim Freeman – George began his eventful tour in early August 1944, approaching the terrible crescendo of the Battle of Normandy, when the German armies were being gradually encircled, worn down and destroyed, prior to the breakout from north-west France. His logbook, written in black ink in an unusually large, almost bold hand, catalogues his trips, beginning with, 'August 4, Ops 1 – Bombing. Marshalling yards at Montfort-sur-Risle; August 6, Ops 2 – Bombing. Ammunition dump at Livarot.'

'We had some flak on those first two but it wasn't terribly

bad,' he says. 'When we came back from that second trip in the morning – it only lasted two hours – we were stood down. Then at around two, things started to liven up again.'

The warning that he might be called upon to fly twice in a day was already proving true, as an officer announced, 'The following crews will be available for an operation this evening,' and George's was among them. 'That third trip,' and here he pauses, shaking his head with a low laugh, 'well, it turned out to be our baptism of fire.' The logbook records it: 'August 6, Ops 3 – Bombing. Panzer Division in woods near Thury-Harcourt. Starboard motor hit by flak. Force landed at B1[temporary landing strip] in Normandy.'

Intelligence from the French underground indicated a large number of German tanks, moved up from the south of France to join the Normandy battle, were being concealed in wooded country near the village of Thury-Harcourt, roughly equidistant between the two crucibles of the Normandy campaign, Caen and Falaise.

'I think we took off at about six-thirty in the evening,' remembers George, 'but at that time of year it's bright as day until about ten.' Sitting in the Mitchell's top turret on the approach to the target, George turned it around to see what he was flying into, and was confronted with the sight of hundreds of exploding puffs of dark, angry smoke, 'black balls of smoke with a hard centre, we used to say'. He was about to get his first taste of the dreaded German 'block barrage'.

As the aircraft started the target run, it was knocked and buffeted by the explosions. George listened as the navigator began a crucial dialogue with skipper Ted Burn, calling up the target as it moved towards the centre of his bomb sight. 'Left,

left, steady . . .' then to his horror, the words, 'Sorry, skipper, round again!'

Oh my God! was George's silent reaction. 'It was drilled into us, you see, that you had to be absolutely accurate, that there were no second chances.' Not confident their bombs were exactly on the money, Ted wheeled the aircraft to port and around to the back of the six-aircraft box formation, for another crack at the target. This time, the German gunners had their range.

'You can't escape the smell, Michael, the *smell* of that smoke,' says George. But the stench of cordite was the least of his worries. 'We ended up with a huge hole in the starboard motor nacelle, one engine gone, a shredded starboard tail fin and one rudder useless.' After dropping their bombs and turning for home as best they could, Ted found it impossible to keep with the formation and began to lose height. 'All right, Burn, do what you can' was the less than encouraging reply over the wireless from their flight commander.

Believing they had no chance to make it back over the English Channel, Ted began to look for somewhere to put the Mitchell down, when Dave called out, 'There's a landing strip down there, Ted.' It was one of the rather small-looking forward strips recently carved out of the French countryside, 'a very home-made looking thing', says George, 'a Typhoon strip, in fact'. Fine for a single-engine Typhoon, but for a twin-motor, battle-damaged medium bomber such as their B-25 Mitchell, it looked awfully short. It would have to do.

Then, in stark contrast to the gravity of the situation, George was surprised to hear the sound of laughter from his pilot and navigator over the intercom. 'The Belgian wing commander in charge of this place was standing up in a jeep, waving frantically, racing down the runway to stop us coming and tearing up his strip!' Needless to say, he was ignored.

The wheels touched and the aircraft sped down the runway. Its damaged brakes could do little to stop it. Reaching the end, it kept on going, hurtling through a fence and coming to rest in a wheat field. 'Ted did a great job,' says George. 'A French farmer was soon on the scene and was as angry as hell. None of us spoke much French but we all decided he was making certain aspersions concerning our parentage.'

It was a surprisingly light-hearted ending to a near-catastrophe, and after a couple of days of hitching a ride back to England, George and his crew were back at Dunsfold and, twenty-four hours later, straight back on the battle order. On their next trip, number four, there would be nothing to laugh about.

With their original aircraft written off, lying somewhere in a Normandy field, George's crew were given another B-25, this time a J-model variant of the famous bomber in which the top gun turret had been replaced with twin half-inch machine guns in the tail. It was not a pleasant place to be. 'You had to crawl into this tiny cramped Perspex blister and sit on a sort of bicycle seat which you drew up behind you,' he says. 'The only way to get out was to drop the seat down and crawl out backwards. Besides, your guns were virtually useless.' Offering barely a 45-degree field of fire both vertically and horizontally, these rearward firing guns were, says George, 'absolutely ridiculous. The only way you could hit anything was if it happened to be attacking from directly behind and dead level.' German fighters were rarely so obliging.

On Wednesday 9 August 1944, the target was an ammunition dump located in Lyons-la-Forêt, south-east of Rouen,
towards which the B-25s of 180 Squadron set off just before
half past ten in the morning. It was a trip lasting two and a half
hours, and every minute of it would remain vividly etched in
George's memory.

'We were hit with some very intense flak before we'd even
reached the target,' he says. From his coffin-like position inside
the tapering confines of the rear fuselage, George rode the
ghastly, heaving explosions of an intense flak barrage, when
Dave, his navigator / bomb aimer, called out suddenly over the
intercom, 'I've been hit!'

Then, the voice of Ted, his skipper, 'George, will you come
forward and tend to Dave?'

Dave, he knew, was in the nose – right at the other end of
the aircraft – requiring a journey over the bomb bay to the main
spar, then through a small tunnel that ran under the pilot's seat.
Taking his parachute – there being no room to actually wear
it – George began extracting himself from the tail and squeez-
ing through the equally narrow space between the Mitchell's
bomb bay and the top of the fuselage.

Looking down, he noticed with alarm that the aircraft's
bomb doors were wide open. 'We hadn't begun the bomb run
yet, so I knew the hydraulics which powered the bomb doors
must have gone.' Reaching an open area between the cockpit
and main wing spar, George then pulled himself through the
small accessway to the damaged nose to reach his wounded
man. 'I got to Dave and looked around – tangled wires, broken
Perspex, jagged aluminium. I could also see there was a hell of
a mess on his left leg above the knee, and he was losing blood.

I said to him, "Dave, the only way I can get you out properly is if I back into the tunnel and draw you out by your shoulders."' Looping his arms under the man's shoulders, George hauled the wounded man to the tunnel's entrance where Dave gave out a yell, 'My foot's caught!' Crawling back over Dave's body, George freed his foot from a piece of damaged cable, then crawled back over him once more, finally dragging him into the small space in front of the main spar, where George reached straight away for the first-aid kit.

'The first thing I noticed was that the tourniquet strap wasn't there,' he says. 'I ripped his strides, opened the sterilised shell packs and packed them onto his wound – he was starting to lose a hell of a lot of blood – then used his intercom cord for a tourniquet and gave him a shot of morphine.'

Just as he'd settled Dave onto a stretcher, the skipper called up again, 'George, can you help me for a minute?' Ted also had not been unscathed by the flak, a shrapnel fragment having struck his buttock, and he was bleeding. Crawling into the cockpit beside him, George decided he would try to hold the aircraft straight and level while the skipper attempted to slip a shell pack dressing under his seat, keeping it in place with his own weight.

With two wounded crew members and an aircraft unable to maintain formation, the mission was now well and truly abandoned. As they approached the French coast, Ted announced he was about to jettison the bombs. Then came an enormous *thump* underneath the tail, and the voice of Jim, the second air gunner, 'Shit, that was close!' They all felt it, and that it was indeed close, but the Mitchell, always a sturdy aircraft, kept flying. Ted released the bombs, then asked George to go aft and check they had all dropped. 'Sure enough, there was one hung up,' he says. It was not their lucky day. Grabbing an axe, and with somewhat unimaginable nerve, he belted away at the recalcitrant 500-pounder until it finally fell away. And still the drama was not yet over.

Calling up Dunsfold, the aircrew were immediately diverted to their sister station at Hartford Bridge in Hampshire, near the south coast of England, home to their fellow 2TAF squadron, No. 226. Here, better medical facilities awaited the wounded men. But first they had to get down.

On approach, Ted hit the lever to lower the undercarriage. 'The starboard wheel came down only slightly out of the nacelle,' says George, 'the port wheel didn't move, and we had no idea about the nose wheel at all.'

'See if you can wind them down manually,' said the pilot. Making their way to the emergency handle at the back of the bomb bay, George and Jim, the two gunners, began the agonisingly slow job of winding the wheels down by hand. At this point he brings to mind the man so inured to troubles, all that is left for him is to laugh. 'We broke the bloody thing!' he says with a desperate chuckle. 'I always think of that saying about fear giving you greater strength. The ratchet mechanism just came to pieces.' The wheels had barely moved.

Now it was up to Ted to steer the damaged aircraft towards the ground for a belly-landing. The crew took up their positions: Jim in the co-pilot's seat to assist Ted if need be, George on the floor, his feet pressed against the main spar, back against the bomb bay, cradling the wounded Dave between his legs, with his arms held tightly around him to shield him as best he could from the impact of the crash.

Ted lined up the Mitchell with the grass strip along the right-hand side of the tarmac, and touched it down as gently as he could, but then, as George says, 'The old dear appeared to have a mind of her own and suddenly swung to port.' With one wheel just slightly lowered, the aircraft drunkenly lurched to the left, careering across the runway, crashing through the complicated array of fog-dispersing troughs and pipes known as 'Fido', eventually coming to a stop in a massive cloud of dust, amazingly, still in one piece. George's first thoughts were for his friends. 'The right wheel being slightly down meant we could access the forward hatch,' he says, allowing the medicos to extract Dave quickly and put him into a waiting ambulance.

Then came a slightly surreal moment when a voice from 'somewhere above' enquired nonchalantly, 'Can I be of some use down there or will I just be a bloody nuisance?' Looking up through a top hatch, George was greeted by the face of Wing Commander Jock Campbell, the commanding officer (CO) of 226 Squadron, standing on the wing and peering calmly down into the chaos. 'Wonderful bloke,' says George, and describes how the senior officer personally oversaw the care of the wounded navigator, Dave, noticing also the limping pilot, Ted, and insisting he too be taken to nearby Aldershot Hospital. 'Ted was patched up pretty quickly,' says George, 'but Dave lost his leg.'

I give out an audible, exhausted sigh.

Wing Commander Campbell, George mentions with sadness, was soon after shot down and killed.

Dave, however, survived, even thrived, progressing – artificial leg and all – to a long desk career with the RAF and later, NATO. On retirement, he and his wife emigrated to Australia, where he and George renewed their friendship for a decade or so, until Dave passed away. 'It was wonderful having him close by for those years,' he says, handing me a perfectly typed letter, which he seems keen for me to read. It is dated 9 August 1994 – fifty years to the day from that most dramatic trip number four. In it Dave apologises to a secretary of the Odd Bods Association for his inability to attend a function at which George was to be guest speaker, and also gives a brief description of the crash. 'Had it not been for George's initiative and actions, I would not have been around to even consider attending any Odd Bods function; I would not be functioning at all!'

I suggest to George that he most likely saved Dave's life.

'Yes, but he also saved mine,' he says, curiously. Surely there cannot be yet another twist to this tale?

From its place of final rest on the far side of the runway at Hartford Bridge, George's heavily damaged Mitchell was brought over to a hangar and parked just outside. Jacking it up and managing to lower the undercarriage, the chief flight mechanic carried out an inspection. George and Jim, meanwhile, were waiting in the mess. Just as they were no doubt reflecting on their extraordinary luck at still being alive, the ground crew chief walked in.

'Were either of you two fellas in the tail today?' he asked.

'Yes,' said Jim, nodding to his companion. 'George was up there until Dave got hurt.'

'Hmm,' said the chiefie knowingly. 'Just come and have a look at this,' and led them out to take a look at what remained of their aircraft.

'Seriously, Michael,' George tells me, 'the tail looked like a bloody colander. There were holes everywhere.' The single burst of flak the aircraft took as it crossed the French coast peppered the tail section with shrapnel, but George had already vacated it to attend to Dave. 'I crawled back up inside the plane and the chiefie poked this steel rod he was holding through the holes. Every time he hit me.' But for Dave's cry for help from one end of the aircraft, George would have almost certainly been killed at the other.

George and his crew – with a replacement navigator – completed an extraordinarily intense tour of forty-four operations, finishing on 3 December 1944, with a ninety-minute trip to Venlo, in Holland, close to the German border. The entries in his log continue to paint small but vivid portraits of air combat: 'December 3. Ops 44 – Bombing. Road and rail bridge at Venlo. Heavy flak. A/c hit (no holes).' His target list – Clermont-Ferrand, Abbeville, Roermond, Oldenzaal, Mönchengladbach – follows the gradual, painstaking progress of the Allied advance out of Normandy and France, through Holland, until the war was eventually taken into Germany itself.

One addendum to an entry draws my attention. 'September 8. Ops 13. Bombing. Enemy gun positions near Boulogne. Heavy flak.' Then, in blue ink, George has added in small, neat writing, 'B-Beer 98 Sqdn blew-up on landing.' His shoulders sink slightly as I draw his attention to it.

'We'd just come in from that trip and had turned off the runway when *B-Beer* landed,' he begins. 'It was a Canadian crew, 98 Squadron. Loveridge – that was the name of the skipper. The wireless / air gunner was a chap named George Churchard, I knew him quite well.' He pauses here for a moment, picturing the faces of the men whose names I suspect he has not uttered in a long time. 'You know they always told us, "Never, ever bring a bomb back." Well, we don't know what happened – perhaps they hadn't checked, or couldn't shake it off – but they had decided to take the risk and land with it.'

As the Canadian Mitchell hit the runway at Dunsfold, the hung-up 500-pound bomb shook free, fell through the bomb bay doors, skidded along under the aircraft for a moment and detonated. 'All of them were killed except George Churchard,' George says. 'He hung on till later that evening with no arms and no legs. Then he died, thank God.'

He remembers also a large ground-staff sergeant they simply called 'Tubby' ('a huge man', George says), 'he was standing by the control tower, watching the aircraft come in and a small piece of shrapnel from the explosion struck him in the chest and killed him. Just like that. Just as he was standing there.' He shakes his head, still somewhat disbelieving. 'We were taxiing at the time and were facing it front on as it went up,' he says. 'The skipper saw it all. It really shook him up.'

Having completed their fifty trips, George's crew were considered 'tour expired', and one day in December were summoned into the wing commander's office, to be quietly reclassified as 'spares'. Then, turning to George, he said, 'Smith, to be quite honest, I think you've had enough.' Despite being one trip shy of his fifty, George had flown his last operation.

In a twist of truly terrible irony, George's pilot, Ted Burn, having survived the flak and crash landings, not to mention bringing back his crew after each trip of his long and dangerous tour, was nearly killed soon after – asleep on his bunk bed. George tells the peculiar story of an airman in an adjacent room inadvertently firing his pistol through the thin plywood wall when using the butt of the service revolver to – of all things – hammer a nail into the wall to pin up a picture of his wife! The wayward bullet struck Ted in the side of the head, but he survived, albeit with lasting consequences.

After cooling his heels far longer than he'd anticipated, George set sail for home in April 1945 and heard the news of Germany's surrender while still on board. His parents even lashed out on hiring a taxi to meet him as he came down the plank and set foot once more on home soil.

He went back to an office job, started to play football and met the love of his life, but his return to civilian life was not an easy one. There were nightmares, there were anxieties and then, well, 'the sheer bloody absurdity', after what he'd seen and been through, of sitting in an office doing paperwork.

'I had a recurring dream of bailing out of an aircraft and my chute not opening and just tumbling, tumbling,' he says. 'My brother and I slept in a sleep-out at home out the back. Eventually, he asked for a room of his own so he didn't have to sleep with that "raving bloody lunatic out the back".'

George admits that his wife and children also suffered the consequences of his war. 'I don't believe I was as bad as some of the fellows that I knew, but I've had psychiatric treatment from Vet Affairs, which has helped.' The two factors which, in his estimation, helped him recover were the strong bond with his crew, most of whom he remained in contact with, and the strength and understanding of his partner. 'She'd lost a brother in the air force in Malta and so understood what it was I was going through,' he says.

Around Anzac Day in 1946, George was listening to the plans of the former servicemen in his office, and how they intended to spend it with their mates from their old unit to reminisce. 'There were a couple of other blokes who, like me, had been in RAF units in Europe. We just looked at each other and thought, Where do we fit into all this?' And so the 'Odd Bods' was born, and for seventy years or so, has provided thousands of men like George with a focal point of friendship, belonging and remembering.

As a man with a natural gift for speaking, George has frequently done so to schoolchildren, telling them not just about his own experiences, but impressing on them firsthand the awful nature of war, and the importance of tolerance and understanding, which starts, he says, 'with your family, with your community, with your nation'.

He seems just as full of vitality at the end of our afternoon as he had been at the start. I, by contrast, am exhausted. I ask him if, knowing the odds, he thought he would survive his tour.

He takes a long pause before answering. 'You know, Michael, I couldn't afford to think that I wasn't going to get through, otherwise I couldn't have done the job. But after a trip, when we seemed to be in flak absolutely all the time, you'd look back and think, 'Good God, have we just come through that?' I remember one occasion – one of the attacks at Venlo, I think – when I looked ahead at what was coming, turned off my intercom and let out one enormous long scream, then switched it on again and just carried on. When we got down, Jim, the other air gunner, quietly said to me, "I've only ever heard you do that once. You obviously haven't been hearing me."'

CLIFF SULLIVAN

Role: Navigator
Aircraft: Bristol Beaufort, Bristol Beaufighter
Posting: 39 Squadron, 47 Squadron, RAF

You could be called out at any time to attack
ships or a convoy. And you had the shakes too.

'What happened there?' asks Cliff, waving towards the obvious evidence of my injury. He listens patiently as I explain then lets me in on what's been happening in his world lately, medically speaking. 'Yes,' he says, casually glancing at his own foot as we settle in. 'Been in hospital and rehab for the last ten months. Blister between the toe got infected, which poisoned the foot, then the entire leg. They were wanting to cut the whole thing off at one stage. What else? Oh yes, then a stroke, then a heart attack under the knife – I was clinically dead for eleven minutes – oh, and two months ago I had a seizure. On the mend now, though. Cup of tea?' and springs up from his recliner to make me one.

This obvious robustness, as well as his utter lucidity, belies his tale of woe and eases my concern for his immediate mortality. Not bad, I think, for a man enjoying his ninth decade of life. Obviously he was cut from the same cloth as his father, decorated in the First World War.

'He was gassed in France, received the Military Medal and was Mentioned in Despatches. Lived to eighty-six,' he tells me.

Cliff has now well exceeded his father's longevity, but on several occasions as a navigator in Beaufighters in the Mediterranean, he nearly didn't make it out of his twenties.

'I actually joined the army first,' he tells me. 'The old man had a motorbike and I thought I'd be a despatch rider. Then after a while I thought that was a bit stupid so I put my name down for the air-force reserve.'

The night-school courses he took, getting to grips with Morse code and trigonometry while waiting to be called up, eventually gained Cliff entry into a very special group of airmen, the astonishingly multi-dimensional second crew member of the magnificent Bristol Beaufighter heavy fighter.

Really a fighter-bomber, the Beaufighter was a hit right from the get-go, its robust twin-engine configuration and quiet sleeve-valve Hercules engines seeing it deployed all over the place: stalking German bombers over the night skies of Britain, tank-busting in the desert, torpedo-bombing in the Mediterranean, harassing Japanese shipping in the Pacific. There was hardly anything the Beaufighter couldn't do. The engineers at Bristol stuffed it full of all sorts of weird and wonderful weapons and equipment – radar, electronic counter-measures, rockets, bombs, cannons, depth charges and, in Cliff's case, torpedoes. It had more than a dozen marks and variants and was even built under licence in Australia at a time when, just a couple of years previously, we'd barely been making bicycles.

And yet, the Beaufighter was meant to be only a stopgap, something for Britain's Air Ministry to fight with until the glamorous and highly secret Westland Whirlwind fighter came on-line. In desperation for something, anything, to throw at the Germans during the Blitz, the Beaufighter was cobbled together out of bits and pieces from its far more ordinary stablemate, the Bristol Beaufort medium bomber. Grabbing a couple of incomplete Beaufort airframes off the production line, they bolted on a new fuselage, found some better engines, test-flew it, and presto, the Beaufighter was up and fighting in record time, just over a year from the flight of its first prototype in 1939. They didn't even give it a proper name, simply taking the first part of the Beaufort's moniker and sticking 'fighter' on the end of it. It was the Japanese who supposedly gave the Beaufighter its famous 'Whispering Death' epithet, on account of its quiet sleeve-valve engines, although the title was probably made up by imaginative British journalists; regardless, the name stuck and has become part of the Beaufighter folklore. This remarkable aircraft was still operating in the 1960s, far outliving both the machine that was supposed to replace it, the Whirlwind, which turned out to be a dud and was abandoned on account of its overly fussy Peregrine engines (which Rolls-Royce just couldn't get right), and its mother, the Beaufort, which had plodded on, never exceeding average, and completely outclassed by war's end.

But being the genuine fighter-bomber hybrid it was, the Beaufighter had particular requirements when it came to its crew.

Having to perform multiple roles, it probably could have done with a dedicated navigator, air gunner and wireless operator, as in a conventional aircraft of its size, but in the Beaufighter's sleek configuration, there just wasn't the room. That meant the second crewman had to do everything the pilot couldn't. In fact, Beaufighter navigators / wireless operators / gunners were probably the most highly trained, multi-skilled aircrew in the British and Commonwealth air forces, and were usually not permitted to fly any other aircraft type, not even when a Beaufighter squadron was re-equipped with another aircraft type. Hence, people like Cliff were pretty special. Not that he had any idea of this when, after a six-month wait, he was finally called up into the RAAF to start his training, in December 1940.

Unusually for most young men eager to take to the air at the time, Cliff sensed early that the role of pilot was not one suited to his quiet and thoughtful temperament, and so nominated instead to be a navigator, a role described by just about anyone who flew at this time as the true 'brains' of any operational aircraft. Although the role was one requiring mastery of trigonometry, calculation and map-reading, all under extraordinary pressure, with the lives of others depending on your accuracy, Cliff is characteristically modest about what it all entailed. 'Just using instruments to plot a course to fly and telling the pilot what to do. It's not hard once you learn it,' he says.

Cliff's nine months' training was nothing if not extensive, involving initial training at Somers in Victoria, then a move to New South Wales for three months of navigation at Cootamundra, a stint in air gunnery at Evans Head and a crash course in how to find your way home using nothing but the stars and a sextant at No. 1 Astro-navigation School at Parkes.

Finally, with a hundred or so other young men in blue uniform, and sporting a half-wing brevet on his tunic, Cliff boarded the very fast American liner *Mariposa* in Sydney just a few weeks before Pearl Harbor.

Via America and Canada, and after an Atlantic crossing in the middle of a storm with snow, ice and 60-foot waves, Cliff arrived in the United Kingdom in mid-winter 1942 to begin training, not on the Beaufighter yet, but its sturdy and less glamorous stablemate, the Bristol Beaufort. 'It wasn't good,' he tells me. 'We lost so many guys due to bad weather and accidents. Learning to fly in outback New South Wales was ideal compared to what it was like in England. Sometimes aircraft would head out on a training flight and simply disappear.' He and his crew survived, however, and, remarkably, were given a choice in joining either Coastal or Bomber Commands. In the end, they would serve with neither. Besides, all Cliff wanted to do was get back home.

'It was a few weeks after Pearl Harbor, and I thought knowing how to attack ships would give us a better chance of being sent back to Australia, which is where we felt we should be with the Japanese in the war.' The RAF agreed wholeheartedly, and sent Cliff and his crew to Scotland to learn the fine art of dropping a torpedo from a plane. Expecting to be sent home soon to fight the Japs in the tropical islands north of Australia, Cliff instead received his papers to travel forthwith to the deserts of the Middle East.

In a stripped-down Beaufort, Cliff made the highly risky seven-hour flight – way beyond the aircraft's normal endurance – to Gibraltar. 'The Germans were onto what was happening and sent out patrols. Some just never made it, including two

Beaufighters. They just never arrived.' Then he made another long flight at roof-height to Malta, avoiding the German and Italian radar stations which dotted the North African coast, for an overnight stop en route to Cairo.

'Malta was under siege day and night at this time. It was considered so dangerous that we had to spend the night in a cave. A bomb dropped just outside the entrance in the middle of the night. It frightened the daylights out of me,' Cliff remembers. The next morning they discovered the huts they were to have stayed in had been blown to pieces by German bombs. 'If we'd been in them, we'd have been killed,' he says. After this sobering introduction to war, and a dawn stint holding brooms to clear the runway of pieces of anti-aircraft shells in order for them to take off without destroying their own tyres, they headed for Cairo to join No. 39 Squadron, RAF.

Having been based in the Far East, then the Middle East since before the war, 39 was close to its nadir at the time Cliff and his crew joined them in early 1942, suffering terrible losses in attacking German and Italian shipping in the fast-moving Mediterranean campaign. But in a stroke of what can only be called luck, Cliff came down with a bad bout of appendicitis soon after beginning operations, laying him up in a Cairo hospital for six weeks. 'During that time,' he says, 'half the guys I knew were sent to operate from Malta and killed.'

Attacking a ship from an aeroplane, he points out, was a particularly dangerous occupation. 'It might sound easy, but usually they're in convoy, and escorted by destroyers, or even cruisers. And that's what you have to fly through to get at the ship you're trying to attack. We had no fighter escort at this stage, none at all,' he says. The pilot was expected to survey the target ship from around a thousand yards, approach at low level, then come up from wave-top height to a very visible three or four hundred feet above the water, before throttling back and carefully lining up the ship, giving the defending gunners a nice, fat, slow-moving target travelling towards them in a very convenient straight line, beautifully silhouetted against the open sea and sky. The bravery required defies comprehension.

'That's what we did,' says Cliff. 'Here, take a look,' and he reaches beside his chair for a large, old-fashioned green photo album, worn but still in good condition. Opening it, he looks intently at the images on the page and, for a moment, falls silent. 'Yes . . .' he resumes eventually. 'This is the end of a 6000-ton Italian ship.' He turns the album around, revealing a series of amazing black-and-white photographs, taken from the air, showing a huge column of black and oily smoke billowing from a ship on a calm sea. 'We hit it near the stern, and one of the other pilots hit it in the middle.'

I take the album from him and turn the pages in amazement. Actual flight combat photographs from the Second World War are incredibly rare, as airmen were usually not permitted cameras, but for a time, Cliff bagged the role of official station photographer and these souvenirs were apparently perks of the job. Watching him, I sense he has not looked at them for some time, years perhaps, and the memories inside his head seem to stir. 'Yes,' he says quietly, looking at the burning vessel on the bloody wartime sea, 'we did our job that day.'

His first attack using torpedoes, in July 1942, was a memorable one. 'We'd been told there was an Italian supply ship tied up near Mersa Matruh. Five of us went out. We found it easily enough and made our attack dropping our torpedoes successfully, but when we peeled away and waited for the explosions, nothing happened.' As he explains it, their weapons had been set to run at a particular depth, impacting as low as possible on the ship's hull to maximise the damage. What had not been accounted for, however, was the fact that the ship had already unloaded and so was now riding higher in the water. The bewildered Beaufort crews looked down as the torpedoes passed harmlessly under the hull. 'No explosions, no nothing,' says Cliff. Anticlimax, however, soon gave way to something far more dramatic. 'As soon as we turned around and headed out to sea, we were attacked by nine fighters. Nine Italian Macchi fighters.'

At a mere 20 feet above the sea, Cliff watched the formation of extremely nimble single-engine Macchi 202s from Mussolini's Desert Air Force swarm above them, two of them latching on to Cliff's aircraft, but hanging back menacingly. 'I remember sitting next to the pilot, Abe Hanway, looking back out the Perspex window and seeing these two aircraft just sitting there above us and behind, waiting to pounce . . . which they did.'

Down they came on the Beaufort's stern. 'Our turret gunner and side gunner were firing at them, all the while telling the pilot what was happening.' All Cliff and Abe could see out the front were neat rows of splashes as the Macchis' four machine guns – two each in the wings and nose – did their best to send the Beaufort into the sea. 'I could see two lines churning up the water, either side of the aircraft right in front of us. First hitting the water on one side of the aircraft, and then the other.' It was the aircraft's two gunners who saved the day that afternoon, watching carefully for the puffs of smoke emerging from the Italian fighters' guns, as they took turns to open fire. 'Left, left' or 'right' or 'steady' were the instructions, delivered coolly, allowing Abe to yaw the aircraft, just a fraction of a second ahead of the deadly crash of bullets.

Although Abe's frantic manoeuvring undoubtedly saved their lives, it was an incredibly risky strategy as a drop in speed could have brushed off what little height they had, and sent them crashing into the surface of the Mediterranean as if it were concrete.

It became a waiting game, as the Italian pilots, frustrated at being denied their kill, were also running out of petrol. 'The longer we headed out to sea, the shorter the Italian pilots had to follow us,' says Cliff. Eventually, they broke off the attack and turned back towards the Libyan coast. 'We continued out to sea for another ten minutes and then went home.' It was now, when things had calmed down somewhat, that Abe remarked, 'What's wrong with your arm?'

Cliff, for the first time, noticed blood streaming down it. 'A bit of shrapnel had come up from the ship, we think, smashed through the front window and a bit of Perspex or metal became lodged in my right shoulder. I didn't even know it had happened.' Back at the aerodrome, the squadron doctor was philosophical. 'Look, there's no point in trying to dig it out, it'll just make things worse. May as well just leave it in there.' Cliff's logbook tells me he was flying again the very next day.

'And it's still in there,' he tells me. 'About the size of my fingernail. It shows up on X-rays. It's never given me any trouble. Well, once, soon after, I was swimming in the Suez Canal, and my whole arm seized up. But after a while it loosened up and it's been all right ever since.'

All five of the squadron's Beauforts returned that day, but Cliff is under no illusions as to how lucky they were. It was the perfectly timed information of their air gunners that got them back, but the gunners also paid the biggest price. 'As we taxied past another aircraft which had just landed, I could see one of their gunners, dead, hanging out over his turret which was all smashed to bits, and the man's brains dripping out of his head. They really should have got us too. There were two of them, faster and better armed. Luck played a big part in all this.'

I try to glean some of the atmosphere inside the aircraft during those extraordinary few minutes out over the sea under the gun sights of the two Italian fighter pilots. Surely it was terrifying? I try to put myself in such a situation, and cannot imagine being able to function. But, as is so often the case when talking to men such as Cliff about the white-hot edge of battle, his response is simply one of having a role to play, and an almost bland acceptance of the consequences. 'No, you don't get scared,' he says. 'It's all part of the job. You just do what you have to do, which in my case at that moment was nothing but wait to see what was going to happen.'

After a few months, 39 Squadron was split in two, one half being sent to suffer badly in Malta, the other, including Cliff, to become part of another veteran RAF unit of the desert, No. 47 Squadron, also flying the reliable but unremarkable Beaufort. From their various bases along the northern coast of Africa and eventually Tunis, 47's role, from late 1942 to '43, was to do battle with the vessels of the Italian navy supplying Rommel's Afrika Korps. Cliff was also to fly with a new, all-Australian crew piloted by Ron Whitington, with whom Cliff spent the remainder of his tour and whom he still speaks of glowingly.

Life on the various desert airstrips of Cliff's squadron, which followed the flow of the campaign, was frugal to say the least: tents, poor food and mile after countless mile of the great North African desert expanse. The local population, sparse in this part of the world at the best of times, made only fleeting appearances. Cliff, unusually for the time, was a non-smoker, and would sometimes swap his small issued packet of Capstans for examples of the local food, usually a solitary egg from a visiting Arab! 'In our tents, we'd dig out about two feet of sand for the floor. That was the only way we could stand up in them. There were no towns nearby and we were hundreds of miles from places like Cairo. But the beaches were beautiful around Misurata, which is where we were based.'

I wonder out loud at this odd life of flying and fighting in such an alien place, and marvel at the almost universally neglected feats of the squadron mechanics, whose job it was to keep these immensely complicated machines flying. How was it done, day after day? What about spare parts? How was battle damage repaired?

'I wonder about that too,' says Cliff. 'Although we did have a lot of engine failures. Not us, but we were lucky. There were a lot of them.'

For the latter half of Cliff's operational tour of 200 flying hours, or thirty sorties, he was finally re-equipped with a comparative thoroughbred, the Beaufighter. ('The Beauforts were all sold off to the Turks,' he remembers with a note of curiosity.) This powerful aeroplane, with a crew of just two, impressed Cliff from the beginning. 'We carried four cannons and two machine guns in the nose. They'd blow anything to bits. We used to go out in tens – five with torpedoes, five as escort.

The escorts would go in first and draw the ship's fire to give the Beaufighters carrying the torpedoes a bit of respite from the anti-aircraft fire. That's the way we operated.'

Now Cliff had to perform the roles of three aircrew: wireless operator, navigator and gunner. He takes me through the detailed layout of his work area, a small desk behind the pilot towards the tail, surrounded by the tools of his trade: wireless, camera and above him the single defensive machine-gun mounted in its clear Perspex dorsal blister. Cliff would now have to operate that too. They of course had parachutes, but at the heights at which they were operating there was not much point in using them. 'You'd forget about them. I never worried about parachutes. Instead, we had our dinghy,' he says. 'If anything happened, we'd be ditching.'

His logbook details operation after operation, some now remembered, others not. Certain brief entries – such as 'turned from formation after heavy flak from destroyer. Results not observed' – tantalise but remain unexplained. Others, though, draw from Cliff his distinctive chuckle of recognition, particularly one entry for August 1943. 'Ah, yes, I remember that day very well,' he says, then pauses. 'Ten of us attacked a convoy of three Italian ships, plus their escorts, hugging the east coast of Corsica, which is mainly mountains so we had to come in from the east.' Cliff's Beaufighter was one of the escorts that day, with the unenviable job of drawing the ships' highly concentrated defensive fire away from the torpedo carriers. On the approach, the weaving of his pilot, Ron Whitington, was violent enough to cause the substantial 10-kilogram Williamson F24 reconnaissance camera to bounce up and down in its holding position on the desk in front of him. 'Every time he went down, the camera would go up. If it hit you it'd kill you!' says Cliff.

Bouncing cameras were the least of his worries. Flak tore into them, the shells from the ships tearing half a metre off the port wingtip and a shell piercing one of the propeller blades, the potentially fatal finger-width hole being discovered on their return. If the blade itself had been lost, the unbalanced engine could have easily shaken off its mounting before the pilot had a chance to feather it. 'On the way back to Tunis,' says Cliff, 'we were flying with another aircraft – about as close as we are to the house next door – at three or four hundred feet above the water. All of a sudden his port motor went up in flames. He just turned over to the left and went down straight into the water. Both of them killed. They were two Englishmen. Bert Temple and Bill Ambrose. It happened so quickly and it could have been us.'

Retribution was instantaneous. Sharp eyes had noticed from where the shots had come and Ron, incensed at the loss of two men he knew well, swung the aircraft down to the water and opened up with the full weight of four 20-millimetre cannons. 'He knew those men well, which is why I think he did his block,' says Cliff. Smoke and shattered debris was scattered across the water after their single pass. 'I think we knocked them off. We got our own back there,' says Cliff without a trace of squeamishness.

I keep Cliff talking longer than I perhaps should. He is visibly tired by the end of our long afternoon. At no point, however, does he slacken off the pace, and he answers my long stream of questions in the same calm and measured tone, correcting my frequent mispronunciation of obscure desert outposts. His two years' operational flying was intense, with the busiest and most dangerous time being mid-1943. 'I've lost track of the number of ships I attacked,' he tells me, as I turn another page in his logbook to read, 'August 1943. North of Corsica. Target – one 6000-ton motor vessel, one small motor vessel, one destroyer. Large motor vessel sunk with two hits. All ships raked by cannon. Intense flak. All okay.'

'It was quite a beautiful part of the world,' he tells me. 'The weather was good in the Mediterranean and it was a pleasure to fly just above the water.'

But not always so. He reflects on coming back to his base at Misurata one time when a massive sandstorm obscured the airstrip completely. Daring to drop lower, the runway could just be made out and the pilot prepared to land. Then, barely a metre away, a Hawker Hurricane fighter emerged from the dun-coloured gloom and flashed by in a near-miss. Cliff shouted to his pilot, who had also seen it, but as Cliff points out with his characteristic matter-of-factness, 'There wasn't much we could have done anyway. There were all sorts of little things like that.'

I turn another page towards the end of the album. One image shows a group of airmen seated in rows in front of a hangar. One of them is a fresh-faced Cliff. 'That's our OTU [Operational Training Unit] at Devon in England,' he points out. Looking closer, I notice that of the thirty-seven figures, nineteen have been marked with a small cross. 'Killed in action, or else in training,' says Cliff. It is a terribly sobering moment, realising that more than half of these young faces did not survive the war. 'Yes,' says Cliff. 'It was pretty dangerous.'

Not long after our final interview in 2014, Cliff's son, Peter, contacted me to tell me that after a short illness, Cliff had passed away. The two men were close, and Peter talked freely about the hole his father's passing has left in his life. I had neglected to ask Cliff about his return from the war and how he found the transition to civilian life. 'It wasn't too hard for him actually,' says Peter. 'I can't really remember him ever suffering much in the way of trauma or nightmares.' Cliff began a career in accountancy, married his life-long partner in 1948, and became president of the Australian College of Manufacturers. 'He wasn't like some of the men who simply didn't want to talk about the war,' says Peter. 'He'd talk about it freely if we asked him, but perhaps we didn't quite ask him enough.'

CY BORSHT

Role: Pilot
Aircraft: Avro Lancaster
Posting: 463 Squadron, RAAF

Looking back at it from this distance,
I feel like it's amazing that it happened to me.

Cy, being Jewish, understood perhaps better than most the nature of what he had joined up to fight. He had only to listen to his mother. 'Mum was from Russia. She would tell horrific stories about hiding in cellars, stifling the cries of the babies, while the Cossacks rode through her town slaughtering whoever,' he tells me in his far more tranquil home on a leafy bend of the Brisbane River one damp Queensland afternoon in early May.

Surviving the pogroms, his father, a shoe salesman, took his opportunity to flee the persecutions of the Old World and boarded a boat in 1915. 'He didn't even know where he was going,' says Cy, 'he just got on and ended up in Australia. That's how desperate they were then.'

Saving every penny working as a navvy on Brisbane roads, Cy's father eventually managed to bring his young wife and some other members of his family out to join him. When Cy came along, his parents raised him in an unfamiliar world of peace, although strictly within the faith. 'Actually, I was a bit of a renegade,' he tells me, knocking against his parents' religious ethics as he grew into his teens.

His parents were a picture of the self-made migrant family: his mother, a brilliant seamstress, made a business selling pyjamas, eventually building a factory which employed more than eighty people. 'She was the main cutter,' he says. 'I remember her cutting layers of flannelette inches thick, with a razor-sharp knife by hand. She had forearms like a bullocky. And she was tough.'

At the beginning of the war, seventeen-year-old Cy, now a draftsman with the Brisbane City Council, was busy converting street shelters to bomb shelters, but his ambitions ran higher. 'My mother was the typical yiddisher momma,' says Cy. 'I was her only son and the apple of her eye. There was no way she was going to let me join the air force.' But with the connivance of his sisters, who couldn't bear the idea of their baby brother being called up into the army, he volunteered for the RAAF in 1941 and, after a night of fierce arguing, managed to wrangle his mother's signature on the dotted line of the form.

Cy was inducted into Course 29 at No. 3 Initial Training School at Kingaroy, but the rigour of military discipline 'didn't sit very well' with him, particularly when laced with old-fashioned anti-Semitism, as by their instructor in rifle drill, one particular sergeant. 'He was a typical English sergeant-major,' says Cy, 'big build, moustache, shiny boots.' When he discovered Cy was Jewish, he'd call him out to the front of the squad, using a typically derogatory term of the day, to demonstrate some aspect of rifle drill. 'I had to take it, but I hated him with a pure hate,' Cy remembers. Years later, upon his return from Europe, Cy, now an officer, encountered the same man again and exacted some revenge. 'Do you remember me?' he asked, throwing in the same term that had been used against him.

'No, sir!' stammered the somewhat trembling man, still in his shiny boots.

While the majority of pilots I've spoken to tell of their easy aptitude for flying, Cy is still slightly bewildered how he managed to get through at all. 'So many blokes around me were being scrubbed,' he says. Cy even survived one particular encounter with his feared instructor Lionel Watters. 'I was a bit hung-over from a few too many beers the night before,' he says. When airborne in their Tiger Moth, Watters suddenly flipped the aircraft on its back and yelled, 'You've got the controls!'

'At this point I was hanging by my straps and my knuckles were just about coming through the skin,' he says.

Then Watters, in the front of the aircraft, pulled the securing pin out of his dual control joystick, removed the stick and started waving it at Cy. 'If you ever bloody well come out on a Monday morning hung-over again, I'll bloody well hit you with this!' From that point on, Cy made sure never to give him the excuse.

With ten hours and forty minutes flying time in his logbook, Cy went solo and the chief flying instructor, who he reckons must have liked him, marked him down as 'average'.

Going via ship to San Francisco then Canada for further training near Toronto, Cy flew Harvards, wearing heated suits in winter and nothing but shorts and boots in summer. After gaining his wings and taking the short trip across the Atlantic to England, Cy fully expected to be put onto single-engine fighters, but was forced to digest the news that the war direction had changed and it was now multi-engine pilots that were needed to take the fight into Germany with the bomber offensive.

'The weather was lousy and the flying was minimal,' he says of his conversion to Airspeed Oxfords in Gloucester. 'I spent half my time playing table tennis and drinking beer with Keith Miller,' he adds, having become pals with the famous test cricketer turned pilot, who would eventually be sent to a Mosquito night-intruder squadron before resuming his spectacular sporting career. 'He was a great fella. Turned up to Lords to play cricket one morning, still in the dinner suit from the party the night before.'

Cy moved from Oxfords to Wellingtons then to a Heavy Conversion Unit at Wigsley in Lincolnshire flying Stirlings, an aeroplane Cy describes as a 'shocker'. At this stage he was forced to let go his flight engineer, who was saddled with the inconvenient habit of becoming violently ill the moment they were airborne. 'I put up with it for two or three training trips,' he says, 'then decided we couldn't really have this happening when we got onto operations.'

Cy's crewing-up process was highly unorthodox. Taking place, as was usual, at his Operational Training Unit, the airmen milled around – in this instance actually outside the hangar – on a fine English afternoon, observing each other cautiously, trying to catch some spark of confidence that might make it easier to risk putting your life in this stranger's hands. Cy, slightly unsure how he had made it thus far anyway, felt anything but confident. 'The smart pilots had already done their homework and worked out who the smart navigators were etc.,' he says, 'and I just stood there, looking around, short of stature and a not very prepossessing figure.'

As he nervously surveyed the mob of airmen gradually forming themselves into crews, a tall and good-looking young man approached him.

'Aren't you Cy Borsht?' said the stranger.

'Er, yes,' answered Cy.

'I'm Glynn Cooper. You know my brother Noel. Hey, have you got any gunners?' he enquired.

'I haven't got anyone yet,' said Cy.

'Leave it to me,' Glynn said and dashed off, to return in a minute with his mate, mid-upper gunner Tom Lonergan. Then navigator Brian 'Snow' O'Connell was plucked out, followed by wireless operator Max Staunton-Smith and an RAF bomb aimer from Newcastle, Tom Laing.

'Bingo! All of a sudden I had a crew,' says Cy.

A little while later, however, as the new crews dispersed, Cy happened to be walking within earshot of a party of wireless operators, one of whom was his own newly acquired Max. 'How'd you get on, Max?' Cy heard one of his mates ask.

'Buggered if I know,' he said. 'I've got this little bandy-legged fella. I hope to hell he can fly.'

Later, after they'd been through 'hell and back', Cy took the opportunity to quietly reveal to Max that he'd overheard the remark, but by that stage, he'd well and truly banished any doubt about his capabilities.

In July 1944, Cy and his fresh crew arrived on a plateau called Waddington, overlooking the pretty cathedral town of Lincoln, as the newest members of No. 463 Squadron, RAAF. This pretty patch of Lincolnshire countryside also catered for No. 467 Heavy Bomber Squadron, and should in reality be as indelible a part of Australia's military heritage as Lone Pine, Fromelles or Kokoda. There was no welcoming committee for Cy and his crew, no speech, no introduction by the CO. They were just seven more faces, just like the hundreds who had already come and gone, subsumed as cogs in the machinery of an operational bomber unit.

There was to be little time to settle in. Arriving in one of Bomber Command's busiest periods, during which both the Battle of Normandy and the flying bomb offensives raged, Cy and his new crew were given a series of night cross-country flights to perform, making their way up to the Scottish highlands in atrocious weather. 'One time we got into a terrific thunderstorm,' he says. 'I can remember hitting a particularly strong downdraft which we couldn't get out of.' Even with the throttles at full power, pushing through the 'gate' to extract extra boost and pulling back on the stick as hard as he could, Cy's Lancaster continued to fall. 'Fortunately we came through the other side before we got too low, but it gave us a hell of a fright. I remember thinking, Jeez, am I going to have to go through this every night?'

Nearly two years since being called up for training, Cy was close to beginning his operational tour. First, though, he was sent aloft on his obligatory observational, or 'second dickie' trip, with an experienced pilot, Wing Commander Bill Forbes. This 26-year-old from Charters Towers was already on his second tour, and wore on his tunic the ribbons of both the Distinguished Service Order and Distinguished Flying Cross. The target was Kiel and what Cy saw that night both impressed and concerned him. 'I remember being amazed at the utter ease with which they carried out the operation,' he says, 'responding to any emergency with great skill and coordination. It was a tough trip, but they made it look easy.' He also could not help reflecting on how his 'rag-tag mob will never be able to do this'. He would soon find out, as a few nights later, his crew appeared on the morning battle order.

In the briefing, they learned the target was to be Stuttgart, with Cy flying Lancaster *G for George*. Cy describes the long flight of nearly eight hours as 'uneventful', except for his throwing the aircraft into a violent 'corkscrew' manoeuvre on the return trip over Holland. This, he says, was purely a safety precaution after a full moon suddenly made them stand out to any marauding German night fighter like a giant moth in the moonlight. Cy kept up the manoeuvre all the way back to England, a task he found exhausting.

His tour now evolved thick and fast with night and daylight trips, mixed in with attacks on special targets such as V-weapon launch sites, as Hitler's flying bomb campaign against England reached its zenith. One such target was Siracourt, a flying bomb site in France. Three hours into the flight, the group received the signal to abort and return to base, but, most unusually, were given discretion to attempt to land with their bomb load rather than the usual practice of dumping them at a specified point in the English Channel. Cy tossed a coin and, feeling confident, decided to try it. Approaching the runway, however, he was greeted with the sobering sight of fire tenders and ambulances lining it on both sides. They apparently sensed the danger of what he was attempting, even if he didn't.

On many occasions, the jolt of the landing would be enough to shake an undelivered bomb free of its harness in the aircraft's bomb bay and explode it. Cy, however, at least had his crew for support as he came in to touch down the extremely heavy aircraft on the runway. A chorus of voices from the crew counted his bounces down the intercom, 'airborne . . . landing . . . airborne . . . landing . . .' etc. But he managed to get them down in one piece, as well as having saved His Majesty's government the cost of several thousand pounds in high explosives.

One trip stands out as memorable, if only for one of those moments of wartime black comedy. After attacking, on consecutive nights, Bremerhaven and the twin towns of Mönchengladbach–Rheydt, Cy's crew were once again put on the battle order for the next night, 23 September, the target being the aqueduct of the Dortmund–Ems canal. On the way out, however, Cy lost an engine and suggested to the crew they return to Waddington. Knowing that an aborted trip was not counted as part of the tour, his crew managed to persuade Cy to continue, since otherwise they would simply have to come back on another occasion to make up the trip. Anyway, the aircraft appeared to be flying well enough on three engines. 'I was a consensus sort of bloke,' says Cy, 'so we decided to continue.'

'Limping along' on three engines well behind the main force, Cy arrived over the target long after the raid had finished. 'It was surprise, surprise,' he says, as his lone Lancaster suddenly appeared over the target, dropped its payload right on the aiming point then turned around and headed home without a shot being fired in protest.

Returning to Waddington so late, however, meant that the aerodrome's 'Drem' lights to assist landing had been turned off and basically everyone had gone to bed. Cy and his crew were already posted as 'missing'. 'Everybody was crook at us for keeping them up late,' he says. But rather than being congratulated for 'pressing on regardless', Cy, extraordinarily, received a severe reprimand from the 463 group captain. Not merely had he 'irresponsibly' endangered his aircraft and crew by deciding to continue on alone, but he had also committed the unspeakable crime of inconveniencing the kitchen!

'The group captain didn't hold back on his language when dressing me down,' remembers Cy. For doing exactly the same thing, he reminds me, other pilots had been awarded an immediate Distinguished Flying Cross (DFC) for bravery. Such were the vagaries of wartime.

Only gradually, Cy tells me, did he and his crew begin to know and trust other, each slowly breaking away from the bonds formed during the long training with their fellow navigators, wireless operators and gunners to meld instead with each other. 'You live and train with these fellas for months and in some cases a couple of years,' he says, 'whereas when you join a crew, you're among a group of strangers. It wasn't till you were well into your tour, after copious visits to the pub and talking together, that you'd finally find some rapport and become good friends.'

The daylight operations of Cy's tour gave him a rare chance to witness firsthand the terrible weapon into which Bomber Command had evolved by late 1944, with enormous concentrations of aircraft being sent into France and Germany on an almost daily basis. 'We used to rendezvous over Reading. Don't ask me why, but it was always Reading,' he says. 'Can you imagine *a thousand* bombers – Stirlings, Lancasters, Halifaxes, and the American Fortresses – formating en masse and turning as one towards the target? And above us was an umbrella of a thousand fighters as well. It was an incredible sight.'

How these massive groups of aircraft came together still astounds Cy. The B-17s of the American 8th Air Force flew in strict, staggered 'box' formations, but Bomber Command's night flying had seen their pilots evolve as individuals, foregoing formation flying to find their way to the target and back again, almost always alone. But in these daylight trips, skills needed to be improvised. 'We used to fly in "gaggles", which really only means that we had to have fifty feet of air between us and the next aircraft,' he says. All that separated this untold mass of aircraft was fifty feet vertically and fifty feet horizontally. 'Vertically, you could use your instruments, but sideways, you just had to look out. It was dicey. Very dicey.'

Engine troubles seem to have been a regular feature of Cy's tour, and on one occasion he lost not one but two of his Rolls-Royce Merlins in a short space of time. The target this day was the V-weapon storage site at Trossy St Maximin in France, but Cy's troubles began at the rendezvous point over Reading when the exhaust on his port inner engine overheated and suddenly 'blew apart'. Instructing his engineer to feather the motor, he decided to carry on to the target on three engines, as the bomb load for that trip was relatively light. 'The next minute the starboard outer did the same thing,' he says. 'We were then no longer happily airborne.'

Powering up as much as he could, his bomb load suddenly didn't seem light at all, and the aircraft began to gradually fall from the sky. The trip, needless to say, was now aborted, but not before Cy dumped the bombs, which they could only do having reached the safety of the English Channel. 'Luckily, Reading wasn't too far from the sea so we headed out and ditched the bombs, then turned for home.' Flying as low as fifty feet off the ground, Cy made his way back to Lincolnshire. Being on a plateau, Waddington's runway was virtually level with the top of the twin spires of Lincoln's thirteenth-century cathedral, and Cy needed to take care to avoid them as he approached.

Lining up on the runway, Cy was once again presented with the sight of ambulances and other emergency vehicles waiting in anticipation of his fiery demise. 'It didn't seem they thought much of my flying,' he says, but he proved them wrong with a safe two-engine landing. A servicing issue, it was later discovered, was the cause of the engine failures, a not uncommon consequence of the often-rushed maintenance of complex machines, which themselves pressed the margins of the technology of the day, in hurried wartime conditions.

Cy came close to finishing his tour of thirty operations, but in high drama, his twenty-eighth proved to be his last, and so nearly the last of him. The target was Walcheren Island on the seaward side of the large and complex Scheldt estuary in the south of Holland, where, in October 1944, Montgomery's 21st Army Group were stalled on the southern bank of the Scheldt River by five massive gun emplacements that the Germans had installed around the town of Vlissingen (Flushing), and which commanded everything that moved on the southern bank and its approaches. The stand-off had already dragged on for weeks when, in an atmosphere approaching desperation, Bomber Command was requested to go in and act as flying artillery to take the German positions out. 'Our squadron got the job,' says Cy.

The Battle of the Scheldt was a drawn-out, controversial and bloody affair for which the 1st Canadian Army – and large numbers of Dutch civilians – were to pay a high price. The Germans had reinforced the entire area and were resisting fiercely despite a raid two weeks earlier, which had attempted to flood them out by breaching one side of the island's sea walls. For Cy, however, the greater enemy for the moment was the weather. Five times he and his crew had been ready to go, and five times they were scrubbed at the last minute. 'Finally, they got desperate and decided to send us anyway,' he remembers. He took off on 23 October in a daylight attack and was told to expect heavy cloud cover over the target. The crews were instructed to bomb only if they could break base cloud at 4000 feet, otherwise they were once again to abort.

Over a hundred 5 Group Lancasters were sent in, with 463 Squadron led that day by Cy's friend Flying Officer John Dack DFC from Melbourne, who'd been given the honour because it was the last operation of his tour. It was to be a short trip, just an hour each way, and they were scheduled to bomb at exactly 1600 hours on a bleak and overcast afternoon.

'I was the second aircraft flying next to John,' says Cy. 'He broke cloud at 4000, and I did the same almost directly beside him.' Suddenly, the whole vista of partially flooded Walcheren Island, together with their target of the gun emplacements, lay before them. 'Of course, the moment we broke cloud, the dozens of quick-firing Bofors guns the Germans had all over the island opened up on us,' he says. Instantly, continuous streams of orange tracer fire started coming towards them in glowing lines, 'just like someone pointing a hosepipe'. It was all over quickly. John Dack's Lancaster was hit first and began going down, then Cy felt the vibrations of violent thuds everywhere. His inner port and outer starboard motors were hit, as was the bomb bay, the doors of which were already open for the attack.

'My engineer, Eric Leigh, was standing beside me,' says Cy. 'A shell hit him directly. It blew a hole in his gut. It went right through him.' Cy's Lancaster was now on fire in two engines as well as the bomb bay, and he gave the order to abandon the aircraft. Trimming it as best he could, he managed to keep it level enough for the two gunners to make it to the side door and jump, quickly followed by the wireless operator. The navigator, stepping over Eric, went past Cy 'like a shot', down the few steps to the nose compartment and out through the bomb aimer's hatch, leaving only Cy and the mortally wounded Eric on board. 'We were going down fast and I knew he had to get out. Eric kept saying, "leave me, leave me", but I couldn't.'

Hauling Eric down the narrow passage to the bomb aimer's hatch, all Cy could do was put the ring of Eric's chest-mounted parachute in his hand and hope he still had the strength to pull it. 'I couldn't pull it for him because the chute would have filled the aircraft,' he says. 'The worst part of it was that I had to stuff him out with my boot. I immediately followed him, naturally.' Cy reckons he was at about 900 feet, and it was his first ever jump.

With no time to adopt the standard practice of counting to ten, Cy pulled the cord as he was leaving the aircraft and immediately felt a violent jerk, which for a ghastly second he believed to be his silk parachute catching on the aircraft's tail-plane. He was momentarily relieved to find that this was simply the unfamiliar sensation of an opening parachute, but the view below was alarming. 'Right underneath me were these terrible metal anti-invasion spikes on the beach,' he says. Grabbing, by luck, the correct shroud, he yanked it furiously and managed to manoeuvre himself to land on the beach. 'Running and falling, running and falling', he gathered up his cumbersome, flowing silk chute and staggered off the sand, 'looking around desperately for somewhere to hide'. Then he noticed, not more than a hundred yards in front of him, one of the great concrete gun emplacements. He was struck by the sudden and appalling realisation 'that there were about a hundred aircraft above me about to hit this very position'.

Seeing a large culvert, he threw himself into it, doing his best to burrow into the concrete, then suddenly, as he says, 'it started to rain bloody dirt', as the bombs of his own squadron began to fall around him. Cowering, hands over ears, he felt the thump of high explosive, and even managed to reflect on the irony. Don't tell me after all this, he thought, I'm going to be killed by my own bloody bombs!

After it finally stopped, Cy waited about twenty minutes before he slowly backed out from the culvert and heard a voice behind him, deep and threatening, *'Für Sie ist der Krieg beendet'* ('For you the war is over') and found a German soldier standing behind him pointing a rifle. It's always intrigued me that this phrase, far from being a cliché, was in fact used time and again, and was, for Cy, the first realisation that he was now a prisoner of war. 'And that was it,' he says.

Marched to a barn, Cy was reunited with the four of his crew who had also been lucky enough to survive the jump, although Snow O'Connell, the navigator, was missing. It was later learned that he had been hidden by a Dutch farmer and two weeks later, when the Canadians finally arrived, he was handed over, 'missing out', says Cy, 'on a free eight months' vacation in deepest Germany'.

The body of 38-year-old Eric Leigh, Cy's English flight engineer, was later fished from the river, his parachute still unopened, Cy suspecting – hoping – that he was dead before he hit the water.

Having recently had the pleasure of inspecting the inside of a superb example of a Lancaster in the Bull Creek museum in Perth, I tell Cy how surprised I was by the small confines of the cockpit. The access forward of the pilot to the bomb aimer's compartment and escape hatch in the nose, I particularly noted, was narrow and tiny. Difficult enough to squeeze yourself into, I suggest, but dragging the prone body of a dying man must have been a mammoth task.

Cy is reflective. 'Well, we were young and lithe and fit,' he says, 'and it's amazing what you can do when you're saving your life.'

John Dacks, Cy's leader on the raid, shot down seconds before him, also survived, and his story is in no way less remarkable. Bailing out with seconds to spare in much the same manner as Cy, Dacks had in the panic only managed to secure one of the two parachute clips of his harness, and when it opened, the uneven jolt was enough to knock him out, also breaking his two sets of false teeth! Coming down in the water, Dacks was supported only by his inflated 'Mae West' life jacket, but was several hundred yards off the beach and drifting out to sea. His plight happened to be witnessed by a German corporal on the shore who, remarkably, requested permission from an officer to take a rowboat out and rescue him.

The officer was dismissive. 'Leave him to drown,' he snarled in reply. The soldier nevertheless persisted, once again seeking permission to row out and save the man's life. 'Oh, do what you like,' said the officer, walking off in disgust. So John Dacks was hauled out of the sea by the kind hand of an enemy, to join Cy Borsht as a POW for the remainder of the war. Sadly, however, four of his crew perished in the crash.

I ask Cy to reflect on what he was feeling at the time, prisoner of the enemy, having survived being shot down and witnessing the awful death of a crewman. Was he, I ask, in shock? Terrified? In despair?

He thinks carefully before answering. 'I don't think we were capable of feeling shock,' he says. 'We'd already seen so much, and this was just another bloody incident. It's hard to pinpoint your attitudes in war because nothing is normal. Nothing.'

Held in a barn overnight, four of Cy's crew and a handful of other downed airmen were the next day marched to the middle of the island and locked in the basement of a deserted school. Glynn Cooper, the surprisingly tall gunner who had approached Cy during crewing-up, had injured himself during his landing, and the others took turns in carrying him. 'He'd landed on the roof of a house and slid into a rainwater barrel, spraining his ankle,' says Cy. 'Tom Lonergan and I were the only ones unin-jured and had to take turns in carrying him on our backs. But he was so much taller than me, his hurt foot would catch the ground and he'd complain bitterly. So I had to try and hoist him up a bit higher.'

So Cy's new journey as a prisoner of Nazi Germany began. After a couple of days they were moved to another part of the island, Dordrecht, then by barge to the coast, eventually crossing into Germany at Gronau. They were moved by train to Dortmund where they were abused by civilians and, ironically, forced to take shelter from an RAF air raid. From here he proceeded to the formidable 'Dulag' interrogation centre near Frankfurt, through which virtually every captured Allied airman passed. It was here that as much information as possible was gleaned before the airmen were assigned to permanent POW camps. While nothing like what occurred in the concentration camps, it was anything but pleasant, particularly if you happened to be Jewish.

Placed in solitary confinement in a windowless 4 by 6 foot cell, Cy was for the next four days 'interviewed' by 'a good-looking Luftwaffe oberfeldwebel who spoke perfect English and who was, at first, utterly charming'. Cy was astonished by how much this man seemed already to know about the squadron – location, personnel, raids etc. – and to be simply seeking affirmation. When Cy refused to divulge anything but the standard 'name, rank and number', his mood quickly turned. 'Then he played the Jew card with me,' Cy says. 'He'd walk around behind me and hit me on the back of the head, gently at first, but harder and harder as he made his point. "You know what we do with Jews here, don't you? All I have to do is pick up the phone and the Gestapo will be here in a flash. Now, let's start again, shall we?" It was a harrowing four days,' he says.

Cy believes he was probably saved merely by the influx of new prisoners, and was simply moved on after his allotted time, before the next batch arrived, expired. Initially sent to Stalag Luft III at Sagan in Silesia – the scene in March that year of the famous Great Escape – Cy was, with the rest of the camp, trained and marched west ahead of the Soviet advance in freezing conditions and with little food into the vast holding camp of Luckenwalde near Berlin. Shuffling through the gate in pouring rain after an 80-mile winter's march, he suddenly heard his name being yelled by men hanging on the wire inside the camp. 'Borschy! Borschy! Cy!' they cried, waving. Peering up, he was greeted by the sight of his crew, from whom, as an officer, he'd been separated. 'It was just delightful,' says Cy. 'Like coming home.'

After more adventures that would fill many more chapters, Cy was handed over at war's end – now by the Russians – to the Americans, taken to a Dutch airfield, packed into a Lancaster with thirty other men and flown back to England. He recalls asking the very young-looking pilot how many hours he had on Lancasters. 'About ten' was the unsettling reply.

Many months later, Cy was, naturally, made a fuss of on his return to Brisbane, picking up life where he'd left it before the war, moving back into the same little house and taking up the study of architecture, eventually becoming a draftsman. The turning point of his life, he says, was meeting his wife, with whom he spent many blissful decades. Post-war, he tells me, 'was a strange era. People weren't interested in talking about the war then. People didn't ask questions, didn't want to know, and I didn't want to tell them. The war was almost a taboo subject, and that lasted a long time.'

Nor does Cy particularly share the rush of enthusiasm of the contemporary 'revival' of military heritage, as expressed in towns and cities around times such as Anzac Day. 'I've marched twice,' he says, 'five or six years ago and I didn't like it. All these people yelling, "good on you" and "well done". That doesn't do anything for me at all. But I'm happy to talk about it now to people who are interested. After all, I've got no other bloody thing to talk about!' I tell him I don't believe that for a second.

I press Cy a little more, trying to get a sense of his experiences as a POW and his being a witness to such gigantic moments in history. He quietly hands me a small, old bound volume. As I turn the pages, I am mesmerised. It was issued to all prisoners, Cy tells me, by the Swedish Red Cross – a blank journal to be filled in at leisure to help pass some of the endless hours of incarceration. Cy, who I realise is a highly gifted artist, turned his into an extraordinary visual record of life in captivity under the Germans. Sketches, maps, brilliantly cartoonish characterisations of his fellow prisoners – even some of the Germans – recipes of bizarre and hilarious imagination and poignant comic poetry, such as his thirteen-stanza illustrated 'Sonnet to a Steak'. But most delightful of all, on page after hand-drawn page, is the long-running tale of a Lancaster bomber, brought to life as Cy's own aircraft – JO-G NF977 (*G for George*):

> *Here is a tale of Georgie Lanc,*
> *Fast as the wind, sure as the bank,*
> *Quadruple power, octuple gun,*
> *Beautiful bomber to battle the Hun,*

And so it continues, page after page, following the progress of the anthropomorphised 'Georgie' as he takes his crew to the target and, worse for wear but safely, home again to England. I scan more pages in silence. Particularly memorable is Cy's portrait of the camp commandant, complete with steel-rimmed glasses and Prussian demeanour, the fence of the camp in the background. 'Pleese, gentlemen, not to sit on the varning vire!'

he hisses in sinister fashion. I have never seen anything like it, and Cy lets me photograph every page. I tell him it should be published separately as its own book, but he laughs at the suggestion.

I have overstayed my welcome with Cy, having for hours wrenched his memories back from across the decades, but although tired, he bears me no ill-will. 'Looking back at it from this distance,' he tells me as I leave, 'I feel like it's amazing that it happened to me. I just shake my head in disbelief, truly. It's amazing I'm ninety-two, isn't it? I should have been dead long ago.'

ED CRABTREE

Role: Pilot
Aircraft: Consolidated B-24 Liberator
Posting: 380th Bombardment Group,
US 5th Air Force

At the height we were bombing, seven or eight thousand feet,
we didn't really think much about using our parachutes.

'You're going to join the air force? Wonderful! I have a relation who does something in the air force. Langslow's his name. I'll see if I can arrange an interview.' These were words the young Ed Crabtree was more than happy to hear from Mr Barry.

Ed was making his way home from where he worked at his father's grocery shop in the leafy Melbourne beachside suburb of Brighton. It was a sunny afternoon, right at the beginning of the war, and the rather well-to-do Mr Barry obviously liked the cut of the younger man's jib. It's not hard to see why. Somewhat older now, Ed is still a very likeable bloke.

But when, in 1940, he fronted up to Victoria Barracks and innocently asked for a 'Mr Langslow', the sergeant at the desk exploded with indignation. 'You mean *Major* Langslow!' he bellowed, before marching him down a long corridor and standing him before none other than Major Melville Cecil Langslow, First World War hero, secretary to the Department of Air, and one of the most formidable public servants in Australia's history. This was the man charged with the mammoth task of holding the purse strings of air-force expenditure in wartime. Tough, thorough and widely feared, Langslow would hold on to the job with an iron grip until 1951.

'All right, what can I do for you?' he asked of the lad before him. It was a good start. But despite such lofty connections, Ed's path to becoming a four-engine bomber pilot would be a long one indeed. 'Yes, all you young fellas want to be pilots,' said the retired, dark-suited major. 'Trouble is, we haven't got any planes yet. Do you know anything about radios?'

As it happened, Ed did, having spent a year or so building them after he left school. So, with a notion that he might become a wireless operator, Ed was given a Morse code test, which he failed spectacularly. Nothing if not determined, he then began to qualify himself for all sorts of air-force jobs, but none of them involving flying. He spent months learning how to become an aircraft rigger, a fitter, an aerial photographer and an instrument maker. In fact, he became so qualified he risked making himself too valuable for the air force to risk losing as a combat pilot. 'Every month I put in my application for pilot training, and every month they said I was too valuable, tore it up and threw it in the bin,' he says.

So Ed carried on, month after month, reconstituting aircraft spark plugs, rebuilding Hawker Demons for the aircraft and gunnery school, even assembling Spitfires and Fairey Battles straight out of their crates from England. It was while doing this one day that his career nearly ended when the supporting cable of a Spitfire fuselage failed, catching Ed under it while he was helping fit the wings. Two men working alongside him managed to leap out of the way, but Ed caught it square in the middle of his back, causing permanent damage. 'I used to have to sleep in the foetal position because of the pain, but didn't tell anyone about it, or else I would have been scrubbed,' he says.

Finally, in March 1943, after much pleading and cajoling, Ed was at last allowed to begin his pilot training at Benalla on Tiger Moths and Oxfords. 'My instructor reckoned I was his best pupil. The others must have been pretty bad, if that's the case,' he says, chuckling. Ed laughs a lot, the kind of man who seems to take very little too seriously.

Being something of an old hand gave Ed a certain insider status as he trained to be a pilot alongside raw cadets. The instructors looked at him oddly, and seemed to know him. One lecturer teaching the subject of airframes – a topic Ed had come to know all too well over the past couple of years – gave him some unusual instructions. 'Now listen,' he said firmly. 'I don't want you coming to my classes and asking me smart-arse questions I won't know the answer to. Why don't you just go to the library and read a book?'

Even at Ed's wings graduation, the CO couldn't resist a final twist, leaving Ed's name off the list of new pilots and their ranks, which were traditionally read out in public. Oh no, thought Ed, crestfallen, I've been scrubbed. To add to the humiliation, his mother was in the public stands watching the ceremony. It was only after a monumental pause that the CO finally added, with a grin, 'Oh, and Pilot Officer Crabtree.' The wait had been worth it. Out of the thirty graduates of Ed's course, he was one of only five to be awarded an 'on-course' officer's commission. It was also the moment he discovered just what he would be doing with the wings he now had to sew onto his blue tunic. Ed would be given the very rare privilege of flying the American Consolidated B-24 Liberator bomber – not with his own RAAF but with the US 5th Air Force operating in northern Australia against the Japanese.

'I'd put down that I wanted to fly four-engine aircraft,' Ed says, 'so I thought I'd be on my way to England. I never thought I'd get to fly them in Australia.' England, however, would have seemed far more familiar to a boy from the suburbs of Melbourne than the desolate place he was headed for. For the next two years, Ed's new home would be a patch of the outback between Darwin and Katherine called Fenton, home in the middle of 1943 to the US 380th Bombardment Group.

On the advice of George Kenney, the American general in charge of the Allied Air Forces in the south-west Pacific, the RAAF were to receive a couple of hundred B-24 Liberators to relieve the pressure on the US 5th Air Force, which had begun operating them from Australia in 1943. They weren't due to be received by Australian squadrons until the following year, so George Jones, the wartime RAAF boss (in one of the rare moments when he wasn't devoting his energies to a long and very public feud with his subordinate, William Bostock), thought he'd get in early and sneak up a few locals to fly with the Americans and get a headstart. Ed, who had in fact completed his pilot's course brilliantly, was chosen to be one of this lucky handful. But when he arrived at Fenton towards the end of 1943, the Yanks didn't quite know what to make of him.

'I arrived in my blue uniform, which was of course no good in the Top End,' he remembers. 'They wouldn't let me fly in my tropical shorts because of their own in-flight fire regulations. So they gave me a pair of trousers and a few shirts and I'd wear my Australian-issue pith helmet. I looked quite a sight.'

If Ed felt a little eccentric among these well turned-out and provided-for Americans, it didn't take him long to appreciate their largess. 'One of the first things they said to us was, "You're well supplied with plenty of everything, it's up to you fellas to use it. Don't let it sit there."' And they weren't kidding. On his first morning a sergeant pulled up outside his tent. 'Hey, Crabtree,' he said. 'Get your arse down to transportation and draw out your jeep.'

'I dropped everything, screamed down and picked it up,' says Ed. 'My very own jeep!' He was also the recipient of two .38 revolvers and a .45 pistol, which seems to have thrilled him no end, two of which he ended up bringing home after the war.

Despite its shortcomings, the Consolidated B-24 Liberator was one of the great success stories of the Second World War, and still holds the record as the most mass-produced American warplane of all time. More than 18 000 of them were churned out from gargantuan production lines across the United States, including the largest in the world at Willow Run in Michigan where, at its zenith, an entire aeroplane was being produced every hour, rolling out the doors in gleaming metallic silver at a cost to the American taxpayer of just over US$300 000 a piece, or $4 million in today's money. The B-24 served in just about every theatre, from submarine hunting in the north Atlantic and attacking Germany from bases in England, to bombing the Japanese in the jungles of the Pacific. It had a long range, was fast for its size and carried a reasonably heavy bomb load, but was not generally thought of by the pilots as a pleasant aircraft to fly: it was complicated, heavy on the controls and had a high wing which made handling temperamental, particularly in formation. '"Flying Bricks" the Yanks used to call them,' according to Ed, particularly the earlier models. It carried the less common 'tricycle' undercarriage, and due to the position of its fuel tanks, tended to catch fire a little too easily in battle. It was also extremely dangerous to ditch or belly-land, as the large, round fuselage tended to break apart. But it was undoubtedly famous, and Ed Crabtree, finally getting his hands on one after such a long apprenticeship, was delighted. His first flight, however, was somewhat farcical.

The day after Ed arrived at Fenton, an American air-force general turned up, accompanied by Air Vice Marshal Adrian 'King' Cole, the boss of the RAAF for northern Australia, and one of the true legends of the RAAF. 'He wanted to go over and take a look at the airstrip at Corunna Downs, which we also used,' says Ed. 'The general thought it'd be good if an Australian pilot took them, and that was me.' Corunna Downs, the so-called secret airstrip, was set up near Marble Bar in the Pilbara as a close jump-off point to launch attacks on Japanese-occupied Java. Its existence was kept under wraps by the air force to prevent Japanese attacks, and flying some top brass into it should have been something of an honour for Ed.

'Cole sat next to me in the cockpit "dickie seat", and the general started giving me instructions: "Flaps down twenty degrees." They were very complex aeroplanes with hundreds of switches and instruments and things.' Ed hurriedly looked around for the flap control wheel. 'Okay, take the revs up to fifteen-hundred,' came another order from the general. Again, Ed searched around frantically. Where on earth was the throttle?

Somehow they managed to get airborne, at which point the air vice marshal leaned over to him. 'How is it you don't know where anything is?'

Ed gave the only answer he could. 'I only got here yester-day and this is the first time I've ever been in one.' The look on Cole's face was one of astonishment.

To the relief of all concerned, one of the engines suddenly registered a mag drop and they were obliged to turn around and go back to Fenton. Back on the ground, Cole took Ed aside. 'Perhaps you might like to, er, go and learn a little more about this aeroplane?' he asked sympathetically.

Ed nodded in furious agreement, and gladly handed over to someone else to fly the bigwigs wherever they wanted to go.

From Fenton's remote outback airstrip, cut into the spinifex and low gums with barely three metres of red dirt on either side of the runway, Ed began, in March 1944, to do his part in taking the war to the Japanese. With the Liberator's large crew of ten, Ed was to be co-pilot to the squadron commander, Captain Joe Cesario from Florida, a fine officer and excellent pilot accord-ing to Ed, with the two men remaining friends for life. 'He was that good he ended up flying Air Force One,' he tells me. Jim Wright, his navigator, also found fame, becoming Speaker of the US House of Representatives from 1987 to 1989. Their aircraft, the first example of the new J-series B-24, was given the name *Dottie's Double*, with nose art depicting a glamorous young female, named after the captain's wife, a charming lady, according to Ed, whom he would get to know later in life.

From the beginning, Ed liked the Americans, and they liked him, although some things struck him as odd. 'The officers and NCOs [non-commissioned officers] didn't mix,' he tells me. 'In the RAAF it didn't matter so much, but the Americans lived totally separately. Usually the only time you met a sergeant was out at the aircraft when you were about to fly on a mission with him.'

Timor, New Caledonia, Borneo, Surabaya in Java, and a host of obscure, all-but-nameless places dotting the northern coast of New Guinea and beyond, all became targets listed in Ed's expansive logbook. Flights were long, fifteen hours not being uncommon for a round trip to attack a jungle airstrip or headquarters, often at night over the featureless, inky black of the jungle or ocean.

Ed prides himself on his memory, and as I speak with him, reading from his logbook, he doesn't disappoint, remembering an array of names and places.

'Nadzab–Wewak. Searchlights. Night fighters,' I quote to him, reading one of his early missions. It brings on his distinctive chuckle.

'Ah yes, that was a night attack on the Jap airstrip at Wewak. We went in first. Our job was to go in and mark the targets for the others, like a Pathfinder, I suppose.' As the formation approached the target, Ed began to make out small pinpricks, 'like lighted cigarettes', flickering in the jungle below. Leaning over to look straight down through the Perspex cockpit windows, he was instantly blinded by dozens of radar-controlled searchlights fixing on him, quickly followed by bursts of flak. 'I pulled my head back in and tried to readjust my eyesight,' he recalls. 'We knew we were pretty close.' In the nose, the more experienced bombardier had come equipped with dark glasses. 'I had no idea about the lights,' says Ed. They placed their bombs right on the Japanese runway, then headed out to sea to observe the attack by the rest of the formation and, as Ed says, 'amuse ourselves watching them get caught in the lights like we did. We'd see them get lit up and laugh our heads off!' All frivolity ceased, however, when tracer bullets started to shoot past them in the dark. 'We were being attacked by night fighters,' says Ed, 'so we thought it might be time to go home,' and off they snuck into the darkness, unscathed. But the night wasn't over yet.

Halfway home, flying down through the Markham River valley, with the perilously steep mountains of the New Guinea highlands on either side, Ed's captain, Joe Cesario, announced that he was going back to take a nap. Not long into Ed's stint at the controls, however, the automatic pilot cut out. Not a major problem in itself, as he simply flew manually. 'Then all the bloody instruments went,' he says. 'All that was left was the airspeed indicator.' A fragment of flak, they later reckoned, had most likely damaged the wiring to the instruments and over the night-time jungle, they failed completely. 'Joe, wake up, all the instruments have gone!' Ed impressed upon his only recently unconscious captain. 'He took over again and between us, some-how we managed to get back,' he says. The relative safety of his tent and the shallow slit-trench carved into the dirt beside it was a welcome sight. Ed was learning fast.

The Liberator was indeed known for having its bugs and gremlins, but how any of them were able to be maintained for flight in such a remote place as Fenton amazes me. Mechanical problems inevitably occurred. Once, en route to a target, one of

Ed's engines suddenly started revving at full bore. 'I tried every-thing to bring it back under control,' he says, 'but in the end we had to turn back to Corunna Downs and land with a full bomb load. We couldn't dump them because we didn't know what was underneath us. There could have been an army base or something.' Landing with a full bomb bay was one of the most perilous situations a B-24 pilot and crew ever had to face. Not only was the aircraft loaded with tons of explosive, but the added weight made the aircraft extremely difficult to land and almost impossible to stop. 'We came in about ten thousand pounds too heavy,' says Ed. The Liberator touched down hard on the outback strip, and then kept going, and going, right off the end of the runway for about half a mile into the dirt. Their luck and, more amazingly, their tyres, held. 'We just got out and left it where it was and waited to be picked up. And Marble Bar's the hottest spot in Australia. Don't ever go there. Terrible place,' he mutters, then once again laughs quietly.

I had always been under the impression that by the time Ed was operating in early 1944, the Japanese air force had been wrestled from the air and was not really a force to be reck-oned with in the south-west Pacific. 'No fear,' he corrects me, recounting encounter after encounter with Japanese fighters, indicated by the word 'interception', which recurs ominously in his logbook.

'We had a squadron chief executive officer who no-one liked, and who was always complaining about missing out on getting flight pay. So Joe said, "Okay, you can come on the next trip." It was to be a reconnaissance flight, which didn't sound too perilous, so he put his name down to go.' The staff officer was to wish he hadn't. The trip involved taking a look at the

Japanese fighter airfield at Kamiri. 'We were attacked by fifteen [Mitsubishi A6M] Zeros,' says Ed. 'His job was to cart the ammunition boxes to the various gunners. Now those boxes weighed about 130 pounds, and he was carrying them like feathers,' laughs Ed. 'At interrogation he was speechless, couldn't say anything. Walking back to his hut, he just dropped his parachute on the ground. We didn't see him for two days. He said later, "You can have your flight pay!" That shut him up. He was a miserable character anyway.'

But they could hit back, and did. Regular radio messages from 'Z Force' commandos operating inside Japanese-occupied territories informed them of much of the enemy's movements. 'One day they radioed that they'd seen a large number of Japanese fighters travelling down from the north. They didn't know where they were going, but if we were quick enough, we'd catch them as they refuelled at their base at Hollandia, just inside Dutch New Guinea,' Ed recalls. That night the Liberators went out, and up to two hundred Japanese aircraft were caught and destroyed on the ground.

On one occasion, *Dottie's Double* became a fighter herself, with the cryptic entry 'Shot down a Nick' listed in May 1944. My ears prick up as Ed unwraps the story. 'We were coming back from Halmahera,' he says. 'Just cruising along, and suddenly we realised we were coming up behind three or four Jap aircraft, which hadn't seen us. We identified them as Nicks.'

Actual Japanese aircraft names were deemed too difficult to remember for Allied personnel, so each was given an English moniker, the Kawasaki Ki-45 twin-engine fighter being designated 'Nick'. 'We opened up the throttles to put on speed and snuck behind till one of them was about 200 yards in front and slightly above. Our top gunner and front gunner opened up on it, and shot it down. We don't know which gunner got it exactly but we were credited with the kill just the same. It just didn't see us, we think. We tried to catch some of the others but they got away.'

Attacking the former Dutch Braat engineering works in Surabaya, Ed discovered he was over the target just slightly too late. 'Tremendous big engineering works it was,' he says, 'about the size of Holden, but we had ack-ack and bad weather so it was very difficult to see what you were aiming at.' Ed spotted the large industrial complex on the bank of a river slightly too late. 'We missed it, Joe,' he said to his captain.

'Right,' came the cool but somewhat unbelievable response, 'we'll go round again.'

Ed was horrified. 'Jesus! I thought to myself.' Making a second run at a target was often shorthand for suicide. 'By the time you reappeared in the sights of the anti-aircraft gunners, they'd usually found your range and height. They plastered us on the way round,' Ed says, but somehow they dodged major damage.

They were even luckier on a nearly twelve-hour trip to Langgoer when a burst of 75-millimetre flak erupted right over them. 'We knew we'd been hit. I said, "Joe, look out behind!"'

'Don't want to see it!' said his captain. 'We're still flying aren't we?' Back at Fenton, the crew chief was agog. 'Jeez, what did you do to it?' he said, getting up on a ladder and actually walking through the hole in the fuselage. 'Once again, amazingly, it didn't hit any of the control cables,' says Ed.

Many Australian airmen I have spoken to openly disparage their American allies, criticising almost everything about them – their supposed trigger-happiness, their arrogance, their lack of training and navigational skills, and even on occasion questioning their courage in battle. Ed, who actually flew with them, will have none of it. 'Yes, I've heard all that,' he says, 'but it's unfair. We flew seventeen-hour trips to all sorts of places and never lost an aircraft due to bad navigation,' he says. Some he recalls having been lost over New Guinea, but that was due, he says, to faulty maps. 'The maps we were given at Port Moresby told us that there was nothing over 12 000 feet on the way up to Nadzab and Lae. I said, "Joe, that's not right. The mountains go up to 15 000 up there." So we went up higher, but some of the others didn't and we never saw them again. They're probably still up there in the jungle somewhere.'

Nor were the Americans shy in a fight, says Ed. 'The 380th lost 75 per cent of its battle order over the course of the war. I think they were as brave as anyone.' He also reminds me of his captain Joe Cesario's decision to go around for a second run at the target over Surabaya. Not exactly the actions of a shrinking violet.

Ed recalls the losses, the sudden disappearance of a face that had become familiar, but doesn't dwell on it. 'It really wasn't very personal,' he says. 'If one didn't come back, they sold anything that couldn't go back to the States and that was it.'

He also resists the claims of arrogance. In fact, one of the five initial Australian pilots to be sent to the 380th, along with Ed, was returned by the Americans almost immediately, and he sympathises with them. 'He was a very brash egotistical character. The Yanks didn't like him and sent him back!'

After a nine-month tour with the 380th, Ed was sent to train other pilots coming through, completing the circle of his air-force career. His luck still held after the war, when he was accepted to keep flying, this time with airline TAA, chosen from the ocean of qualified ex–air force applicants that swamped the airlines at war's end. He became a life-long friend of many of his crew, particularly his captain, Joe, having made many trips to the United States since the war. 'The loveliest, friendliest people,' as he describes them. 'They always treated us so well.'

Of the many men I have spoken to who survived a combat tour, Ed Crabtree genuinely seems to be one of those not too adversely affected by the experience. And his tour was anything but a joyride. 'I was scared stiff,' he says towards the end of our conversation. 'You couldn't sleep the night before a mission, and then, in the air, for some reason you couldn't use the toilet. The first thing that happened when you finally got back was you formed a queue for the toilet.' And if anything went seriously wrong, there was no second chance. Unlike in Europe, bailing out over the featureless jungle was barely an option, even if evading the Japanese was possible. 'At the height we were bombing,' reflects Ed, still with that laugh, 'seven or eight thousand feet, we didn't really think much about using our parachutes.'

The anticlimactic return to the relative ordinariness of civilian life was aided, he says, by his five-year stint as a civil pilot. He claims never to have minded talking about his war, 'It's just that no-one back then was interested,' he says.

Sometimes, it can all come down to attitude. No doubt it was his cheeriness, still evident today, which helped him through, both during and after, a quality which has sustained him all his life.

DAVID MORLAND

Role: Air gunner
Aircraft: Avro Lancaster
Posting: 467 Squadron, RAAF

*All we could do was keep corkscrewing
and hope to hell he misses.*

I guess it was inevitable that I should eventually meet a former warrior of the air at an RSL club, in a subdued atmosphere of wood panelling and honour boards, medals and memorabilia of conflicts past. But I hadn't quite banked on just how much today's mega-RSLs have evolved from the quiet little suburban clubs I remember from my youth, especially in the place where everything seems larger than life anyway, Queensland. I anticipate a quiet afternoon in some cosy corner drinking a couple of schooners of the Sunshine State's finest with former air gunner David Morland, but we are instead engaged in a running battle with noisy meat tray and raffle announcements, small children on the edge of heatstroke and red-cordial hysteria, and hordes of eager bingo players constantly moving us on like UN refugees, as game after game invades whichever nook of the Tewantin RSL we choose to secrete ourselves. Just as well the place is so gargantuan, as there is always another place to hide. Not that David seems to mind, and why should he? After all, this big airy palace is his second home. And besides, the beer is cold and the steaks are big.

Hailing in fact from bayside Melbourne, David was at school kicking a footy with ten or so of his mates one afternoon when the principal put Prime Minister Menzies' 'melancholy duty' speech over the school's tannoy speakers, announcing the beginning of the Second World War. 'We stood around and talked about it,' David remembers. 'We all thought it would be over by the time we turned eighteen. By the end of the war, there were only three of us left alive.'

At sixteen, David put himself into the Air Training Corps while working in the complaints department of a telephone exchange. 'I devised quite an extensive code for people who complained at the slightest pretext,' he remembers. '"PM" on the complaints card meant "perpetual moaner". The mechanics found it very helpful.'

David didn't get the chance to try out to be a pilot, but was happy enough to be put into the air gunner stream, firing at towed drogues from the back of a Fairey Battle at the air gunnery school at Port Pirie, South Australia, where his rating of 'exceptional' was achieved more by cunning than talent. 'I'd just wait till the towing plane got a bit closer then I'd give it a bloody great burst,' he says. 'The pilot was yelling "open fire" in my headset but I'd just hang back a bit.' The average number of hits the students achieved on the drogue was about four. David scored eleven.

'But did they actually teach you how to shoot?' I enquire.

'The whole thing was a waste of time,' he answers dismissively. 'I couldn't hit a bull in the backside with a bucket of wheat.'

As we're speaking, David places a large folder on the table, bursting with letters, photographs, citations and, inside a clear plastic envelope, a superbly mounted row of medals, with the glistening silver cross and blue-and-white striped ribbon of the Distinguished Flying Medal (DFM) on the far left. I've never actually seen a DFM up close, and I give out an involuntary 'ooh' as I pick it up, making David chuckle a little. The DFM, awarded solely to non-commissioned officers, was handed out far less frequently than its officer-only equivalent, the Distinguished Flying Cross, and those humble sergeants or warrant officers who wore its striped blue ribbon on their tunics usually had to have done something pretty outstanding to have earned it. I'm slightly breathless to discover how David came by his.

In early 1944 David arrived at an Operational Training Unit at Lichfield in the English Midlands, where he made the conscious decision to do all in his power to become the very best gunner he could. 'There were two things that mattered to me as a nineteen-year-old,' he says. 'Girls, and being thought of as an adult.' The former, he assures me, were in no short supply in wartime Britain, but he decided that the respect of his peers and elders was a higher priority, and so set about earning it. 'I suppose I looked at it as a continuation of my schooling,' he says, 'and if you wanted to be a good gunner, you had to study.' While the other young trainee airmen, far from home and still with an air of the war being some kind of lark, spent their evenings at the pub pursuing the local 'skirt', David was in his hut poring over books of tables. 'I learned about bullet drop, angles, what happens with a deflection shot of, say, 5 degrees at 230 miles an hour at 16 000 feet; I learned what happens when you're in a corkscrew; what happens when you roll, etc.,' he says. Then he adds after a pause, 'Actually, I didn't do too badly with the girls either.'

This maturity and determination extended even to time spent in a new type of training simulator, an ingenious-sounding device designed to replicate the experience of firing from a moving turret at night, with shaded Perspex and beams of light simulating attacks by approaching fighters, all contained within a specially constructed concrete dome. 'The others didn't like it and moaned about having to "go down to that bloody dome again".' Not so David, who happily volunteered to take their places. 'One day I'd turn up as Smith, the next as Jones, and so on. We were only supposed to get about two hours a week on the thing. I was getting twelve.'

Eventually a flight lieutenant in charge got wise. 'Who are you today, Morland?' he said, confronting him.

'Smith, sir,' pleaded David, but the officer wasn't buying it.

'Listen, we know what you're doing and it's to stop now. These men need this training and you're putting them in danger.' It was the end of the ruse, but David's keenness – for which he expected to be, though was not, punished – left him far better trained than most of his fellows. And later, in the night skies over Germany, he would need to be.

At the crew-up, where the pilots, gunners, wireless operators and navigators mingled as individuals before coalescing into
six-man crews, David found himself among those who, like him,
had hung back, watching, coolly assessing, politely deflecting
approaches, but not committing. Eventually, they found they
were the only ones left. Before they had even spoken a word
to each other, an organising officer announced, 'Right, you lot
are to form the last crew,' and that was that. Perhaps it was this
common fastidiousness that saw the group of men bond closely
and quickly, living, training and playing together: air gunner
Frank Skuthorpe; Bob Faulkes, navigator; George Hopwood,
flight engineer; Bill West, wireless operator; Bob Calov, bomb
aimer; and pilot Gordon Stewart. 'We lived together like a band
of brothers,' says David without a jot of sentimentality.

During their final training test, a leaflet or 'nickel' raid over
France in a Wellington, an oxygen fault saw everyone save the
pilot pass out when returning home over the English coast. 'At
16 000 feet, we all quietly went to sleep and let the pilot fly us
back,' he says. Apparently none the worse for wear, they trained
further on the Stirling – 'a dog of an aircraft', he says – then
finally on the Lancaster, and in August 1944 at Waddington,
Lincolnshire, joined No. 467 Squadron – one of the four dedicated Australian bomber squadrons which had been operating
in Bomber Command since early in the war, as part of Sir Ralph
Cochrane's 5 Group. Only nominally an RAAF squadron when
formed in late 1942, 467 gradually evolved into a dedicated
Australian unit, with more than two-thirds of its nearly 300
personnel Aussies by war's end.

As we speak and David warms up, I realise that every aspect
of his tour is clear and vivid in his memory, and I'm gripped by

his easy ability to recall detailed anecdotes and quote long passages of conversations, usually complete with times and dates. Some are priceless, such as the failure of his fellow gunner Frank Skuthorpe to turn up with the rest of the crew at Waddington after a few days' leave to begin operations. The story goes that the unfortunate young man had been struck by a lorry when riding his girlfriend's bicycle along a road in Lichfield. Waking up concussed in hospital, he found he could recall nothing save the warning he'd been given concerning English aircrew downed in Germany who, it was said, were placed in hospital alongside English-speaking Germans in order to fool them into thinking they were in England, and so were easily pliable for information. 'He came out of his coma,' says David, 'remembered nothing, assumed he'd been shot down and was in German hands, and for two days refused to give away anything except his name, rank and serial number!' It took the intervention of Australia House to sort out the man's true identity. The squadron's gunnery leader seemed to think David was somehow responsible for the mess and their relationship never recovered. 'Well, I was also a bit lippy,' he admits. 'But I never did get to grips with him. He just didn't like me, found every dirty job he could for me and stayed that way for the next couple of months. Then he went in,' he says, using the dry colloquialism for being killed.

Even before his tour began in earnest, David sensed it was going to be an eventful one. In August, he was sent up as a spare rear gunner to the squadron commander, one of the most well-known and highly decorated RAAF personalities at the time, Wing Commander 'Bill' Brill, Distinguished Service Order, Distinguished Flying Cross and Bar, i.e. awarded twice. 'It was a trip to Kaliningrad in Lithuania,' remembers David. 'I picked up a Messerschmitt 110 about a thousand yards away crossing our tail, but he didn't attempt to attack us. Brilly spoke to me in this calm, steady voice, "I think he's been on a North Sea patrol and is running short of petrol." He was a fine leader.' It was just the start.

By late 1944, the clumsy, inefficient instrument that was Bomber Command at the war's beginning had evolved into a weapon of truly terrible destruction. With improved aircraft, navigational aids and more highly trained crews, the cities which had been barely pinpricked two years earlier could now be all but wiped out in a single night.

On the morning of 11 September 1944, in an office at 5 Group headquarters at Swinderby in Lincolnshire, a finger was run down a list of German cities chosen by various committees years before as places suitable for air attack. After a brief discussion by several high-ranking uniformed men, and a consultation with the meteorologists, a coded teleprinter message was prepared and sent out to the fifteen squadrons of 5 Group, all based at airfields around the city of Lincoln:

AC864 SECRET Action Sheet 11 September
Target: LUCE
8 Group to WHITEBAIT
MONICA not to be used at any time
AIM: to destroy an enemy industrial centre
2359 H Hour
Aircraft to attack between 12 500 and 16 000 feet
Main Force 1 x 4000 lb plus maximum 4 lb incendiary clusters

The 'target for tonight' was Darmstadt.

The accounts of what happened that night in Darmstadt

are so terrible as to be almost unreadable. Just why this pretty provincial town was attacked in the first place is today hard to determine and will never be known. With no port and largely bypassed by the main rail system, it could hardly be termed an industrial centre – an American post-war bombing survey describing it as producing 'less than two-tenths of 1 per cent of Reich total production, and only an infinitesimal amount of total war production'.

A little south of Frankfurt, Darmstadt had almost completely escaped the attacks meted out to larger cities nearby and its population, knowing the Allied armies were just a hundred miles away and sensing the war was nearing its final months, had become complacent, believing themselves, and their lightly defended city, to be somehow immune. But by late 1944, the list of targets still intact and worth Bomber Command's attention was shrinking, and Darmstadt, a 900-mile round trip from Lincolnshire, lay within easy reach of 5 Group's heavies. As was the case with many of the places targeted by Bomber Command, Darmstadt was most likely attacked simply because it could be.

That night, 226 Lancasters operated using a new type of bombing technique, attacking along several lines emanating from the central aiming point, spreading the destruction across the entire town. Fire rather than high explosive would be the principal weapon. The weather was predicted to be clear; the target indicator flares were to be dropped; the 4000-pound 'cookies' would blast down the walls; the clouds of cascading incendiary sticks, with their sizzling, white-hot magnesium cores, would set fire to everything they touched. The wind, and the flames, would do the rest.

Up to 12 000 people – a tenth of the town's entire population – were killed, incinerated in the 1500-degree, mile-high
firestorm or asphyxiated huddling below in the inadequately
prepared air-raid shelters, listening to the ghastly reverberating
thuds of falling masonry and collapsing floors above, too terrified to try their luck and make a dash through the crashing
inferno before the voracious fire sucked the oxygen from their
lungs. Animals went mad; human beings of all ages and conditions combusted, melted, perished. Darmstadt, which had stood
intact for 600 years was, in a single night, two-thirds gone. And
David, from the mid-upper turret of his Lancaster on this, the
most dramatic trip of his tour, saw it all.

He mentions it almost casually, in a rush, shifting slightly
in his pale-blue RSL club shirt as we both pause to let an
interminably long announcement about menus and lucky com-
petition winners pass without comment. 'Yes,' he says, almost
as a mumble, his head tilted, glancing at a line in one of the old
documents in front of him. 'Darmstadt . . . coned, bombed . . .
firestorm . . . five Junker 88 attacks, one claimed – probably
destroyed . . . wounded and awarded an immediate DFM.'

'Well . . .' I ask hesitantly, 'just take me through that if you
could.'

He begins slowly. 'You know it wasn't . . . pleasant going
through flak barrages,' he says. 'There were three big belts of
them defending the Ruhr. We flew through them on the way in,
and we flew through them on the way out.' This, he tells me, is
how the Ruhr earned its grim epithet, 'Happy Valley'. Hundreds
of guns – both the light as well as the heavy 8.8- and 10.5-centi-
metre calibre weapons – and searchlights, often aimed by radar,
created aerial defensive zones half a mile wide and a thousand

feet deep, each one presenting a gauntlet taking six or seven terrifying minutes to fly through. 'So added all up,' David tells me, 'it lasted about an hour.' Even above the engines, he says, you could hear the explosions: '*woomph-woomph*, muffled, like a distant door slamming'. The smell of the cordite, 'pungent, like you've been letting off firecrackers', seeped its way inside the aircraft and into his oxygen mask.

I ask him what he was doing in the turret during all this.

'Trembling,' he answers. 'I kept it moving, all the time, not just looking out for fighters, but other Lancs that might be on a collision course. One of the pilots only had to be off by a couple of degrees. There'd be a sudden *whoosh* and two aircraft had gone in – it happened all the time.'

This is the atmosphere David paints for me on the run-in to the target that night over Darmstadt: flak rocking the aircraft, buffeting his large frame against the cloying confines of the clear Perspex turret; fighters, he knew, were lurking, but 'we weren't worried about them at that stage'. Then, six minutes after they had dropped their bombs, added their contribution to the inferno below and turned for home, a radar-controlled searchlight beam – the distinctive cold purple-blue of the 'master searchlight', upon whose cue dozens of other lights acted instantly – picked them out of the ink, holding them like an insect in a torch beam.

'Suddenly, dozens of lights were on us and we were surrounded by this big circle of light a couple of hundred metres across. There was nothing we could do.' Blinded, the beams of light clinging relentlessly to the black undersides and flanks of the aircraft as it attempted to struggle free with a series of violent corkscrew turns, David worked the bicycle-like hand grips of the turret, eyes straining against the glare. The Lancaster was passed from one searchlight to another as it made its way across the night sky. 'We were up there and in that light for about twenty-two minutes,' he says. 'You could actually see clearly inside the aircraft.' As terrible as the flak was, David dreaded the moment it would, as he knew it would, suddenly cease. 'Once it stopped,' he tells me, 'you knew a fighter was in the area.' And then it stopped.

Moments later, a volley of cannon shells from somewhere out in the stygian gloom sprayed a bright yellow stream over his head. 'That first attack came from the starboard quarter, but we were corkscrewing and it missed us completely.' Now acting as fighter controller, David gave urgent instructions to the pilot, Gordon Stewart, to avoid the German's fire. 'Down starboard, now!' he would shout, and as Gordon repeated David's instructions, the Lancaster would drop like a stone to the right. The flight engineer's voice was also heard in David's headphones, reading out the speeds of the aircraft, '250 . . . 270 . . . 300 . . .' giving him a chance to calculate where to land his bullets in the helter-skelter of the battle. Here now was the pay-off for all the tedious hours spent studying, the endless stripping of the Browning .303 machine guns, the poring over the calculations of speed and height and deflection, the foregoing of the pleasures of youth – all that time spent rehearsing for a moment as terrible as this. But he was acting, literally, in the blind. 'Until I could see where the German's fire was coming from, I didn't know where he was, just out in the dark somewhere.' The aircraft braced for another attack. 'On the second pass he got us with three shells. One went through the starboard tailplane, one through the starboard wing, and one got my turret.'

At this I gasp rather foolishly, 'Your *turret*?'

'Yes,' he assures me. 'It left a pretty big hole.' Tearing through the thin Perspex, the invisible German's shell had struck the mounting of David's twin guns, peppering him with shrapnel. 'Down starboard!' he yelled and the aircraft plummeted to the right. Still coned in searchlights, David knew he had no more than three or four minutes before the German pilot would complete another circuit, line up and attack again. The cannon shell had missed his body by inches but steel fragments had torn through his thick flying suit and boots, puncturing him from foot to thigh. It had wrecked the right-hand machine gun and put out of action the hydraulic operating system, rendering the turret moveable only by way of a small manual crank-handle to his side.

I feel compelled to ask, 'Did it hurt?' and he studies the question carefully.

'You know, in all honesty I think my major concern was, I can't let the blokes down. It's me or we go down in flames and burn to death. You've got no bloody options,' he says. Some nagging missing element to this story prompts me at this point to ask him about his fellow gunner, Frank Skuthorpe, under the Lancaster's great tail, armed with four guns as opposed to David's two. Was this not a coordinated defence? 'Ah yes,' he tells me with the grimmest of chuckles, 'Skuey's guns had completely iced up. Couldn't get any of them to operate. He tried hard but he couldn't move them.' In temperatures as low as minus 40 degrees, the hydraulics and electrics of these battle-worn aircraft frequently failed.

In front of him, David saw his right-hand gun was wrecked, and with the ammunition belt feeding through to the left gun, it too was also quite useless. The Lancaster and its crew of seven were now defenceless.

But now the most extraordinary part of the story unfolds: with the seconds ticking down until another attack and a burst of shells blasted from the dark, David, in sub-zero temperatures, encumbered by no less than three sets of silk gloves, another standard pair, and yet another electrically heated pair, all encased in thick leather gauntlets, still virtually blinded by searchlights and being thrown about the sky by his pilot's evasive actions, somehow managed to detach the right-hand ammunition feed, reroute it to the left and get his remaining gun working, giving himself and the aircraft at least some hope of defence.

'It was like the Michelin Man trying to thread a needle,' he says. 'You couldn't touch the metal with your bare hands, your skin would freeze to it instantly. It wasn't easy, but what were the options?'

Twice more the German attacked, and missed. In David's headphones, the pilot's voice relayed his instructions the moment they were given, throwing the aircraft around the sky like a great black toy, frustrating the night fighter's aim. Then, on the fifth attack, the stalking German pilot, amazingly, made a fatal mistake. He emerged into the light.

'Down port!' David yelled, as suddenly, there on the port quarter, a hundred or so yards away, a twin-engine Junkers Ju 88 was now exposed as starkly as the Lancaster itself in the light of the search beams. 'We dived down to increase his deflection, making it more difficult for him to fire his cannon. I think he realised what he'd done and began to break away.' Leaning the weight of his bruised shoulder on the breech blocks to give his remaining gun some elevation, David, wounded, his blood soaking into his flying suit, fired off a long burst which tore into the German for a hundred yards as it passed over the aircraft. 'Fortunately, I managed to just land everything into him,' he says. Full of incendiary ammunition, the Junker burst into flames above his head and fell to the side.

'With the holes in the aircraft, we'd slowed down to about 280,' he says. 'He was moving fast and just overshot. I had to put him down as a "probable kill" but he was definitely all in flame.'

Flak bothered them again on the two-and-a-half-hour trip home, but they made it back to Waddington in the early hours of 12 September. 'They had to carry me out of the aircraft it was hurting that much,' he says. Taken to hospital, his blood-soaked flying gear removed, the medicos began digging pieces of metal out of David's legs. 'They probed it without anaesthetic, digging for bits, picking out bits. I actually passed out a few times,' he says.

David remembers two things very clearly from the next day in hospital: the pain at attempting to go to the toilet, and the image of the burly warrant officer standing beside his bed.

'You've caused a fine bloody to-do,' he glowered.

'What have I done?' asked David.

'They're arguing whether to give you a CGM [Conspicuous Gallantry Medal] or a DFM.'

David thought this over for a moment. 'DFM would be nice.'

Upon hearing this the warrant officer's visage lightened. 'Oh, that's good,' he said and turned away to begin the paperwork.

'Actually,' says David, 'I didn't even know what a CGM was.'

A few days later, summoned to collect his new DFM ribbon

from the same warrant officer, David was overcome by that time-honoured Australian reluctance to say or do, under any circumstances, anything that might possibly be construed as 'big-noting' oneself. 'Jeez, I dunno,' he mumbled to the big man seated in front of him, fingering the blue-and-white ribbon awkwardly in his hands. 'I feel a bit of a jerk wearing this. I mean . . . it was the whole crew that went through it after all.'

The warrant officer looked at him unmoved. 'Put it on your tunic or I'll charge you,' he said.

David did what he was told. 'Actually, I was scared of him!' he says.

Assuming David's injuries may well have spelled the end of his tour, being honourably discharged and decorated for his not inconsiderable troubles, I ask him how long he was taken off flying.

He turns a page in his logbook. 'Twenty-four hours,' he says. I am disbelieving.

'You're not serious?' I exclaim.

'Darmstadt, 11th/12th – Stuttgart 12th/13th,' he reads. 'Yes, we went to Stuttgart that next night. That's what happened. If you could walk or be carried, you went. And they carried me to the aircraft. I could sit, I was fit. That was the way it was done.'

So, on David flew, completing an extraordinary tour that could fill a book on its own. Once, an incendiary over a yard long dropped from another Lancaster above and lodged in his Lancaster's wing between the engines. 'There was nothing we could do but watch it and hope it didn't burn the wing through,' he says. At the end of October 1944, during the final attack on the strategic German-held island of Walcheren at the mouth of the River Scheldt, light flak exploded near the nose, all but blinding bomb aimer Bob Calov with shards of Perspex in his eyes, requiring pilot Gordon Stewart to complete up to five circuits of the heavily defended island at increasingly low levels until Bob could pick out the aiming point of the large-calibre German naval guns. At a near-suicidal 2000 feet, David at last heard him speak down the intercom.

'I see it, I see it! Steady, steady, left a bit . . . bomb's gone.' They took out one of the last remaining big guns on the island and both men were immediately decorated, adding another DFM and a Distinguished Flying Cross to David and his crew's total. Walcheren fell the next day.

On a daylight trip, it all nearly ended when another Lancaster cut across their flight path from above, shearing off their starboard rudder and elevator with its port wingtip. 'It was over in a flash,' says David. 'Their pilot was weaving in the middle of a tight formation in daylight. Madness. His prop missed my head by a couple of feet.' But they survived.

Walking away from their aircraft (*X–X-ray*), after their last trip, an officer approached them with the news that they'd been invited to join the Pathfinder Force, an undoubted honour, but after an awkward silence among the crew, David spoke up for all of them. 'I think we've done enough,' he said, to the solemn agreement of everyone. 'It was the first time I had the courage to say no,' he says today.

I ask him if he thought he'd make it through, and he laughs.

'No, not at all! When we arrived, we were told we had just four trips in us. Four. Then that was it. But you know, being killed didn't worry me, not ever. Being burned or disfigured and having to be a burden on others, that's what I dreaded.'

Returning to Australia in late 1945, David says he didn't

really 'come back' for a couple of years after that, remaining still in that strange airman's nether world between life and death, with alcohol a ready companion. 'For a couple of years, nothing seemed quite real,' he says of it. 'I suppose I just wanted to write myself off. I hit the grog pretty heavily and went back to the PMG [Postmaster-General's Department] as a clerk. How I didn't get sacked I'll never know. I never talked about it. Not ever. Inside you felt that people couldn't really understand anyway.'

As was so often the case, it was the love of a good woman which guided him back to the land of the living. 'I felt I was coming to grips with life for the first time,' he says. 'Before that, nothing seemed real. One of the first things she said to me was, "If you want to be with me, you'll have to give up the bottle." It was the best thing I ever did.'

Pieces of metal continued to come out of David's body up until the mid-1950s, but he healed, and is now able to look back on his extraordinary tour with amazing clarity, although, he says, he can really only remember it in fragments, with whole sections simply wiped from his memory. I assure him his account seems anything but fragmentary.

As David sees me off at the front door of the roomy, noisy club, I catch him as he turns back inside, on his way to prepare himself for the evening session and the company of the community of friends he has made here. I thank him and wish him well, but something prompts me to ask, only half-seriously, if he held on to those fragments of German shell he carried inside him for so long.

He laughs, surprised. 'Actually I used to have them. In a jar. But my wife threw them out. "You can't live in the past," she said. Very sensible,' and he waves as the big glass doors close.

STAN PASCOE

Role: Wireless operator / air gunner
Aircraft: Bristol Blenheim
Posting: 82 Squadron, RAF

You have a different slant on life
when you're fighting a war.

Late one Sunday September morning, Stan Pascoe was sitting on the ground in the wireless operator's compartment of his twin-engine Avro Anson trainer, picking up what he could on his radio set, when an announcement came over the air, giving him one of those moments in life which remain indelibly sealed inside the memory – the smell, the colour, even the taste of the moment forever time-locked, remaining as real and immediate as the day it happened, even when recalled decades on. It was 3 September 1939. The war clouds he had watched gathering for a year or more had burst, and it was on. For Stan, there was no sense of urgency to join up and get into the war lest it all be over before he was ready to do his bit – at twenty-one, he was already trained up, in uniform and ready to go.

'I don't understand the way it is I can remember some things,' he tells me with a sense of wonder as we sit in his lovely Gold Coast village unit on a warm December day. We leave the front door open and allow the warm sweet air and the screeches of the rainbow lorikeets to accompany us as we talk. 'You see, I can still recall the naps we took at school when I was three or four. At midday they turned the desks upside down and strung hammocks between the legs for our one-hour kip. I can still visualise it,' he says, shaking his head slightly.

'When the war started, everyone had different emotions,' he says. 'Some thought with dread, Oh God, this is it, others were looking forward to it like an adventure. I was somewhere in the middle: Well, you're going to earn your pay now, mate. That was the phrase we all used.'

Born in Cornwall, raised in London, Stan decided to pursue his life-long dream of flying by joining the RAF on 1 February 1938, happily leaving his dreary job as a clerk in a tobacco factory. Arriving home one day, he simply announced to his parents, 'That's it. I've had enough. I'm joining the air force,' and signed on for four years.

Unusually, Stan had no desire to be a pilot, fearing he lacked the requisite education. 'I left school at fourteen. I wouldn't have made it with my education,' he says. 'Not in those days.' So, despite his total experience of radios being confined to having put together a crystal set as a kid using his wire bedspring as an aerial, it was to No. 1 Radio School at Cranwell that Stan was sent, graduating into the permanent

RAF as a wireless operator in December 1938.

He loved every minute of it. Posted to the School of Air Navigation at Manston in Kent, Stan was flying every day, taking navigators under training. 'Sometimes they'd lose themselves on an exercise, and turn round and look at me pleadingly. "Oi, can you give us a bearing?"' But, as the stream of casualties in the air war swelled to a river, it was inevitable that Stan would be required to perform less benign duties and, in the middle of 1941, found himself in Norfolk at a small grass aerodrome called Bodney, home to No. 82 Squadron, 2 Group, Bomber Command, flying the twin-engine Bristol Blenheim medium bomber. It was already a squadron with a history.

'Before I joined them, it had been wiped out – twice,' he says. 'Not that they told us that at the time.' No. 82 Squadron had indeed endured a ghastly war thus far, having taken part in two attacks that have gone down as black marks in the often chequered annals of Bomber Command. First, on 17 May 1940, during the German breakthrough into France, 82's twelve Blenheims attacked the German troops pouring through the gap they'd punched in Allied lines near Gembloux. Flak broke up the Blenheims' formation even before their escort of Hurricane fighters arrived to protect them. Fifteen Messerschmitt Me 109s then picked them off at leisure. All but one Blenheim was shot down, the sole survivor, badly damaged, limping home and crash-landing in England (the crew, amazingly, escaping without a scratch). Then, less than two months later, in mid-August it happened again. The target this time was a German airfield at Aalborg in recently occupied Denmark. Twelve Blenheims were once again sent in over the North Sea, appearing above the aerodrome early on an overcast morning. Tragically for them, a detachment of 109s had landed from Norway, allowing just enough time for the pilots to refuel before taking their already warmed-up aircraft aloft to meet the Blenheims head on. Once again, all but one of the twelve were shot down, with twenty-five out of the thirty-six British airmen killed.

After each of these catastrophic engagements, 82 Squadron was reconstituted with fresh young airmen and was operational again within forty-eight hours. Such is the production line of war.

This was the legacy Stan and his crew were inheriting as, fresh-faced, they began their tour. The morning after their arrival at Bodney, the chief engineer took them out and showed them over their brand-new Blenheim. 'This is your aeroplane – V6445,' he said. 'Look after it.' In mid-1941, that was not going to be easy.

There were more Bristol Blenheims than any other type of British aircraft flying when the Second World War began, and in 1936, when this sleek, all-metal monoplane with its ultra-modern features such as retractable undercarriage, metal flaps and super-charged engines had first taken to the skies, it indeed seemed a vision of military aviation's future. Unfortunately however, at about the same time, the Germans were also developing an aeroplane, the Messerschmitt 109 fighter which, three years later, would render the Blenheim and just about everything else in Britain's bomber arsenal completely obsolete. Blenheim losses in the first years of the war were staggering, with a few rounds of cannon into their unprotected bellies from the German pilots easily enough to send them spiralling into the ground. Their best defence thus became flying at low level, but this in turn made them easy meat for the anti-aircraft gunners on the ground. But without better aircraft to replace them, the

Blenheims flew on. The bravery of the young airmen like Stan, his pilot, nineteen-year-old Dennis Gibb, and navigator / bomb aimer Laurie Cash from Armagh in Northern Ireland is beyond measure.

Anti-shipping patrols were to make up the bulk of Stan's brief tour, and he was blooded on his very first trip. On 19 July 1941, an evening in high summer, Stan's Blenheim was one of six sent to attack a convoy of German merchant ships passing through the English Channel. I ask him if he remembers what he felt before that first operation.

'Well,' he answers deliberately after a thoughtful pause, 'you know what to expect, but you don't know what it's going to be like. Coming back from it, I remember thinking, My God. If that's what I've got to put up with for the next few months, it's going to be hellish'.

And it was. Although describing it as 'short and sweet', Stan's first mission was nearly also his last. Flying at a height he illustrates by holding his hands a few inches apart ('This height,' he says with a wry laugh), the Blenheims tore out from Bodney across the water towards a group of German vessels accompanied by their escorting flak ships. He recalls the atmosphere on board as if it were yesterday.

'Very little is spoken over the intercom. The pilot orientates the plane towards what it is he's going to attack and speaks only occasionally with the navigator. I'm also the rear gunner, so I'm in the turret looking out for fighters. The flak ships open up on us. Beside us another Blenheim is hit in the engine. It catches fire immediately and – bang – straight down into the Channel. No survivors.' Ignoring the flak as much as one could, the skipper approached a merchant vessel and pulled up just in time before releasing his two 500-pound armour-piercing bombs. 'It was no good dropping them on the deck,' says Stan. 'They'd just bounce off. You had to punch them through the side of the hull.' A ten-second delayed-action fuse allowed them time to get clear. Stan then witnessed a terrific explosion and the ship was suddenly at the base of a massive plume of black smoke. 'I simply said down the intercom, "Good-o. Direct hit, Dennis." I didn't see it sink but it was obviously mortally wounded.' Not bad for their first trip. Back at the base, the same flight sergeant who had warned them to take care of the aircraft seemed unperturbed by its condition. 'He took a look at the shrapnel holes from the flak and actually seemed quite pleased. "Well, you lot obviously had a good time!"'

Stan, I'm realising as we speak, is a remarkable find. Possessing not just a memory and an alacrity that utterly belies his years, but also a strong sensitivity, a person who instinctively seems to understand my interest and is at pains to convey the colour, the feeling, the very atmosphere of flying into action in a Bristol Blenheim in the early years of the Second World War.

'We get aboard, check the intercom,' he says, taking me, unprompted, through his crew's pre-flight procedure before a shipping strike. 'I test my guns by firing a burst into the ground, then we take off and rendezvous with the other aeroplanes, then go in over the sea at nought feet.'

As the memories come flooding back, Stan pauses, then concentrates, choosing his words slowly. 'Things can happen quickly, and in any sort of sequence. One moment you could be peppered with flak, one moment you're seeing an aircraft go in. I saw several – shot down, hitting power lines etc., and it's awful to see but – and it's a funny thing, Michael – it's only a passing moment. You register it and then get back to the job you're doing. When you get back it's sad and you realise there's an empty space in the squadron, but you almost accept the fact that someone isn't going to come back. And you feel it about yourself, too. You realise when you take off. The chances of us returning are quite slim.'

How does such fear not prevent you from carrying out the job? I ask him, unable to comprehend myself functioning in such a situation.

'It's a strange thing,' he says, again with that shake of the head. 'There was tension in the briefing room when you found out what you had to do, but once you were in the aeroplane, you were fine. You could do anything. That's how we felt. Even when flak was coming up at you, somehow it didn't mean any-thing, as if you were watching it all happen in the third person. Someone was firing at you, and you just accepted it as part of the job.'

There was a pattern of emotion, he says, replicated with every mission: the initial terror as the job and target were revealed in the briefing, settled by the confidence of the pre-flight procedure in the aircraft; then the steely determination of carrying out the attack; and finally the sense of relief when the wheels came down on a safe return to base. 'It was the same every time,' he says. 'But when you got back it was all over: out to the pub that same night and you forgot about it,' though, I suggest, perhaps allowing yourself a quick glance around to note the absentees. He concurs. 'It was all very strange. You have a different slant on life when you're fighting a war.'

At this, he pauses, passing me a photograph: a superb image of two young airmen – one obviously himself – their faces awash with exhaustion, a Blenheim parked just behind them. 'I remember it being taken,' he says. 'A newspaper photographer was on the base and he took it just after we'd gotten back from Cologne.' The raid Stan recalls is a famous one, flown in August 1941, ordered, some say, personally by Churchill as a morale booster during what was for England one of the grimmest phases of the war. The targets were two power stations near Cologne, Knapsack and Quadrath, and Stan, along with fifty-five Blenheims from 2 Group, would fly deep into Germany, in broad daylight, alone. It was as much a demonstration that the RAF was in fact capable of hitting the Germans, as it was any attempt to inflict serious damage. To Stan and the crews, it all sounded suicidal. 'I can still remember the reaction from the airmen in the briefing room when we saw the red line of tape marking the target. You could audibly hear the groan, We're not coming back from this one!' And many were correct. Flying at low level their escort of Spitfire and Whirlwind fighters could accompany them only as far as the Dutch coast. For the remaining 150 miles to the very well defended target and back, they were on their own. 'I can still see one of those Whirlwind pilots waving as he sped away,' Stan remembers. Streaking across Germany at heights as low as fifty feet, Stan recalls looking around him and feeling safe amid the numbers of this relatively large formation, until a Blenheim beside him failed to clear power lines and exploded fierily on the ground. The whole crew saw it, but nothing was said. Approaching the target, the large chimney stacks of the power stations could clearly be seen from some distance away, and the Blenheim climbed to 400 feet. They let go their two 500-pound bombs and sped away, sustaining some damage from flak but avoiding fighters to make it home. 'It all happens so quick,' Stan tells me. 'You approach the target, drop your bombs and speed away. It's over in seconds, really. It's only afterwards you really start to think about it.'

Back at Bodney, Stan's ground crew were delighted to see them, despite some battle damage and even a 'very well cooked' seagull which was discovered inside the engine nacelle! 'Yeah, we were a bit low today,' replied Stan with nonchalance to their incredulous crew chief. 'In actual fact,' he says to me, 'I think I do remember startling a rather large flock of birds as we crossed the Dutch coast.' The *Daily Mail* photographer snapped the remarkable shot of Stan and his pilot, Dennis, moments after they climbed out of the aircraft, relief palpable in their faces. Twelve Blenheims from five squadrons failed to return, with several more having crashed in training for the raid, representing a loss of 22 per cent of the total force. Five escorting Spitfires also failed to return. The damage to the power stations was minimal, and soon repaired.

It took very little time for the crews, should they survive, to become blooded 'old hands', and one afternoon returning from a 'beat-up' of what German shipping they could find along the Dutch coast, Stan was grateful for the level-headedness of his now experienced crew. Flying home over the Channel, a sole Me 109 emerged from an airfield somewhere along the enemy coast and latched onto Stan's tail. 'It hung off just behind us. It seemed to be toying with us a little, jumping from one side of us to another.' Following the German fighter's every move with his twin .303s, Stan in the turret waited for the fighter to attack. 'It just moved from side to side and didn't fire. I said to the pilot, "I think he's on his first flight, he looks scared." I still think that too.' If the possibly inexperienced German had decided to open up with the twenty-millimetre cannon in his aircraft's nose, Stan is certain they would have been shot down. 'I let off a couple of shots at him as he moved back and forth, but he didn't fire at us. We were flying only just above the waves, and I think he was reluctant to attack us that low. We were just lucky.' After a few extremely tense minutes, the German pilot decided to leave them alone.

As I turn the page of his logbook to 20 August, a few brief lines barely hint at the story of the most dramatic day of Stan's tour: 'Attacked vessel off Norderney. Two ships attacked, one sunk.' It had apparently been an uneventful North Sea patrol with the crew about to turn back, when a couple of vessels were spotted around Norderney, one of the Frisian Islands off the north-east coast of Germany. 'They weren't all that big, but the rule was never to take your bombs back. You always tried to drop them somewhere, to do some damage,' says Stan. Dennis, his pilot, assessed the situation for a moment or two then made a decision. 'Okay, we'll go and attack it.'

Lining up on the vessel, the Irish bomb aimer Laurie Cash was lying prone in the Blenheim's nose, ready to release the bombs at the precise moment. Stan was in the turret facing rearwards, looking out for a sudden fighter attack. Skimming low over the water at nought feet, he sensed they were nearing the target, when he suddenly felt an impact and the aircraft pull up. Then, the back of his clear Perspex turret went dark. 'What's wrong, Dennis?' he called over the intercom.

'We've hit the bloody thing! Come up and help!' was the pilot's urgent reply.

In the split-second timing needed to attack the ship at wave height, Dennis had made a fatal error of judgement, pulled up a fraction too late, and struck the top six feet of the ship's mast dead centre with the nose. The whole front of the Blenheim, containing Laurie, had been smashed in.

'It was Laurie's blood . . . it just . . . sprayed back over the fuselage,' says Stan, quietly. 'That's why my turret went dark.' He immediately attempted to make his way forward, but the damage had blocked the narrow passage to the front of the aircraft with a wall of twisted metal and armour plate, and he was trapped just behind the pilot's seat. 'I couldn't get through. I could see Laurie in the nose and he was obviously terribly injured, but it was just blocked.' Something then made Stan look down, and to his horror he saw the surface of the sea rushing past underneath. Like a giant knife, the mast had ripped through the floor of the aircraft, leaving a long gaping tear from the nose to well past the cockpit. 'God, what's happened, Dennis?' Stan said once again.

'We've hit the mast,' replied Dennis. 'I can't see anything.' Stan's radio, situated near the floor of the aircraft, was smashed to pieces, as was the aircraft's compass, and the shattered windscreen rendered Dennis's visibility almost nil. He also suspected the landing gear was now useless.

'How are you going to get home?' Stan asked.

Dennis pulled up to gain some height. Apart from a few scratches, he appeared to be unhurt, and the two Mercury engines seemed to be undamaged and running well. The intercom, remarkably, was also working, allowing Stan and Dennis to at least communicate. The navigational charts, however, had been sucked out of the aircraft with the impact, leaving them essentially blind as well as deaf, and with a two-metre length of the ship's mast, complete with attached ropes and chains, still lodged inside the aircraft.

'Steer westward,' said Stan. 'It's the only thing you can do. Steer west into the sun. You're bound to hit England sometime.'

And so, in their crippled aircraft, on they plodded over the North Sea into the sunset, Dennis straining to see any sign of a coast ahead, while also closely watching his diminishing fuel reserves, knowing the aircraft would soon be reaching the edge of its endurance.

'Eventually, we saw a bit of land in front of us,' says Stan. After being airborne for six hours and fifteen minutes, they crossed the coast of Northumberland, way to the north of England. They had barely any fuel and there was no sign of an airfield. 'I have to put it down. I'm out of petrol,' called Dennis. In a grassy field near a town called Acklington, not far from Newcastle, Dennis came in for a wheels-up landing. 'The noise was terrible,' says Stan. 'Dirt and dust and everything rushing up through the aeroplane.' But the well-constructed Blenheim stayed in one piece, and Dennis and Stan got out with only a scratch.

Meanwhile, on the ground, a colonel in a small car had seen Stan's Blenheim approach, complete with its length of wooden mast, rope and chain hanging from its staved-in nose like some ghastly appendage. That doesn't look right, he thought, and followed it as best he could to the field behind the beach where it made its impromptu landing, lending assistance soon after it had skidded to a halt.

Laurie, though unconscious, was still alive but, as Stan saw when they were at last able to retrieve him from the shattered mess of the nose, terribly hurt. 'A large part of his face had been simply ripped apart,' he remembers. 'It was a terrible sight.' Stan and Dennis were checked out by the medical officer at a nearby RAF station, given some sedatives and released the next day. Laurie was taken to the local hospital at Acklington but didn't last the night, and was buried a few days later in a local cemetery.

Telephoning their CO back at Bodney, the old man seemed almost amused at their ordeal. 'Ah,' he remarked quite cheerily, 'I thought you must have ditched!' The next day they were back at the squadron, debriefed, sent on leave, and that, says Stan, was the end of the affair. While they were away, the squadron was again almost wiped out during another period of terrible losses.

'I've had this extraordinary luck, you see,' reflects Stan. 'They could easily have had me flying again the next week and I probably would have been killed.' In a sense too, the collision was a lucky one. Dead centre in the middle of the Blenheim's nose is in all likelihood the one and only place the aircraft could have survived such an impact.

Stan returned to operations briefly, but was suddenly diagnosed with, of all things, tuberculosis, taken off operational flying for good, and sent back to finish the war right where he'd started it, at Manston in Kent at the School of Air Navigation, once more flying Avro Ansons with student navigators.

Dennis too survived the war, ending up with a Distinguished Service Order but, according to his children, whom Stan kept in touch with, always blamed himself for the tragedy. 'He was actually a wonderful pilot,' says Stan. 'It was just an error of judgement.'

Stan's post-war life was not an easy one, spent struggling to settle into several civilian jobs, until in the late 1940s he asked his wife how she'd feel about him going back into the RAF.

'Whatever makes you happy,' she replied, and Stan, this time with a commission, was back in, spending another twenty years in uniform, working primarily in photo intelligence, enjoying several overseas postings and, he says, loving it.

Since coming to Australia in the 1960s, Stan has made the odd trip back home, but it was not until 2011 that he visited the grave of his navigator, 916895 Sergeant Eric Laurence Cash – Laurie – in a small but immaculately kept Commonwealth war grave at Chevington, not far from the crash site. It was a difficult and moving experience for Stan, and the family members who accompanied him, standing back, heard him say, just audibly as he touched the headstone, 'Seventy years, mate.'

Unusually for a man of his times, Stan has never felt the need to bottle up his war. 'I was of the opinion that I should talk to people about what happened, whenever they'd listen. I wanted to get it off my chest. Think it's been one of the reasons I've managed to cope with that period of my life,' he says. His memory is remarkable and he remains a cheerful and generous man, still slightly bewildered by his long life and good fortune.

'I'm approaching ninety-six years of age,' he says as we emerge into the warm air after a long afternoon. 'Why is it I have been allowed to live so long, when kids were dying?'

It's a question no-one can answer, least of all me.

JOHN CRAGO

Role: Wireless operator / air gunner
Aircraft: Avro Lancaster
Posting: 622 Squadron, RAF

*You always think of it, it never goes away, it's always there somewhere
at the back of your mind, but you just get on with things.*

John's reasons for joining the air force were straightforward
enough. 'I didn't much like the army, and I didn't know anything about boats,' he says as we sit in his living room, where
the Perth sun, even at nine-thirty in the morning, streams
through in dazzling shards of yellow light.

As a kid, John had heard the stories from his father's experiences in the trenches, and besides, his heroes, as so often with
youngsters of the Depression era, were the great aviators: Bert
Hinkler, Charles Kingsford Smith and Amy Johnson. John had
ideas of being a pilot and would have been happy as a navigator,

but in 1942, the best the RAAF could give him was guard duty, spending hour upon hour watching over bomb dumps and transmitters at the Pearce air-force base in Western Australia. 'It was pretty woeful, actually,' he confesses. Eventually, he got the call to front up to No. 5 Initial Training School at Clontarf. Standing before the three-man selection board, John reckons they'd already earmarked those they wanted to train as pilots and navigators and so stamped his form 'wireless / air gunner'.

After being sent to three different states to complete both the gunnery and wireless-operating components of his training, John embarked for England via the United States on the extremely glamorous Dutch ocean liner *New Amsterdam*, then across the Atlantic on the even mightier *Queen Elizabeth*.

Even before he joined up, John had had the foresight to begin learning Morse code at night school, so at his Operational Training Unit, at the appropriately named Wing in Buckinghamshire, he passed his transmitting test by handling more than the required twenty words per minute with a rating of 100 per cent. At his crewing-up, a friendly young pilot from Shepparton named Frank Stephens asked him if he'd care to join his crew, and his future in Bomber Command was set.

In September 1944, after time on Wellingtons, then a conversion to Lancasters, John and his crew arrived at the permanent RAF base at Mildenhall in Suffolk to his new home, No. 622 Squadron, part of 3 Group, beginning operations a week or so later.

'We did a good deal of daylight trips on Gee-H,' he tells me. 'So we could bomb within a few metres of the target.' Gee-H, introduced in October 1943, was a radar navigation system evolved from the earlier systems of Gee and Oboe, and was at the forefront of technology for its time. It relied on the subtle interpretation of lines on a small cathode-ray oscilloscope carried on board the aircraft, enabling multiple aircraft to bomb with accuracy for the first time. John's was one of many crews who thought it wise to limit the monitoring of the Gee-H screen to half an hour at a stretch, after which his dazzled eyes would be relieved by another wireless / air gunner.

Via his high-frequency 1154/55 Marconi wireless set, John provided the aircraft's only means of communication to the world outside, to their base back in England, or over the target with circling Pathfinder aircraft issuing live instructions in open voice as the raid was progressing: 'Ignore the red flares, bomb on the green,' and so on.

Communication was almost always via the so-called Q signals, pre-determined sets of three-letter codes – always beginning with Q – designed to abbreviate otherwise long and complicated messages. 'I can still remember a couple of the main ones,' John tells me. 'QDM meant, "What is the magnetic course I must steer to reach you?"' On the hour and again on the half, a letter code signal was sent by 3 Group, which had to be acknowledged by all aircraft and recorded in the wireless operator's log, 'But apart from that,' says John, almost apologetically, 'we didn't do a great deal on operations at all.'

He could, however, listen over the aircraft's intercom to the back and forth chatter of a bomber crew on an operation: the gunners reporting the position of an aircraft or a searchlight, the navigator giving course updates to the pilot, and the bomb aimer, up the front, often following a map, calling out features of the passing landscape below, 'I can see what looks like a river down there, Skip . . .' etc.

In this manner, John completed a tour of twenty-three trips, as recorded in what I think is the most meticulously filled-in logbook I've ever seen, set down in the standard colour-coding of all RAF and Commonwealth aircrew: night trips written in red, green for mine-laying operations over the sea and, counter-intuitively, black for daylight ops. Then I notice something unusual beginning to happen after his fourteenth trip, a night operation to Koblenz flown in November. 'Oh yes, on number fourteen we had a mishap,' he tells me, chuckling slightly. The far left-hand column of an airman's logbook required him to enter the name of his pilot for every single flight. The pilots themselves simply put down 'self', and for the crew, it was usually the same name repeated down the page. John, however, after a trip to Koblenz, has entered a different pilot's name for every subsequent operation: 'Sqn Ldr Brignall, Fl Off Albright, Fl Off Arkins, Flt Sgt Malcolm . . .' etc., continuing to the end of his tour.

'Yes, there's a reason for that,' he tells me. But I don't want to get ahead of the story.

'It was a night op,' he tells me, an all–3 Group attack by 128 Lancasters flown on 6 November 1944. On crossing the German front line, a sudden, short but intense burst of flak rocked John's aircraft momentarily. 'It was just before a group broadcast at 7 p.m., so I went off the intercom,' says John. The broadcast done and the requisite codes recorded, John switched it back on to hear the fragments of a tense conversation between the pilot and flight engineer.

'Starboard outer's u/s,' the engineer was saying.

'What shall we do, feather it?' was the response from the pilot, Frank Stephens.

One of the starboard motors was on fire, John now realised, and the pilot and engineer were apparently struggling to put it out. 'They tried to feather it, tried to extinguish it, all no good,' he says. In the end all they could do was cut the petrol to both starboard motors, leaving the aircraft to fly, badly, on the two port motors. 'Then the port outer started to overheat and Frank had to throttle back to nurse it, leaving us running on just one and a half,' he says. There being insufficient power to maintain height let alone reach their target, Frank decided to turn back and make for Juvincourt in north-east France, where an emergency aerodrome had recently been established, recaptured from the Germans after four years.

Suddenly, John found himself having a great deal to do indeed – sending emergency signals, and perhaps more importantly, obtaining a radio 'fix' in order for his navigator to determine exactly where they were. 'I was in a bit of a flap. The main aerial, I discovered, had been damaged, so I had to wind out the trailing aerial and eventually managed to contact base on low frequency.' As the Lancaster began losing height, the rest of the crew tried desperately to buy some time by losing weight. The bombs had been dumped almost immediately, but then out went the guns, the ammunition and everything that was not bolted down and could fit through an open doorway or hatch.

Oblivious to this frantic activity, John, disconnected from the intercom, was holding down his Morse key to transmit, enabling the base operators in England to determine his position and broadcast it back to him. 'Finally, they gave me a set of coordinates and I switched my intercom back on to tell the navigator,' he says. Once again, he caught the tail-end of an alarming conversation.

'Do you want me to jump now, Skipper?' said the voice of his bomb aimer, who apparently then proceeded to do so.

It seems while John had been finding the aircraft's position, most of the crew had decided to abandon it. 'Only myself, the pilot and flight engineer were left on board,' he says.

'Do you want me to go too?' John hurriedly asked his skipper who, realising his wireless operator was still at his station, replied with a note of surprise, 'Er, yes, you'd better go too.'

Although the rear escape hatch provided an easier exit, it was further away from John's position just aft of the cockpit, and involved a climb, in full kit, over the dreaded chest-height main wing spar. John instead made his way forward, past the cockpit to the bomb aimer's escape hatch in the nose.

Approaching the gaping black hole, John briefly reflected that the only jump he'd made thus far was from a 15-foot platform into a sandpit in training. 'I got to the escape hatch and knew I had to go head first but I remember saying to myself, "How the hell do I do that?"'

Eventually, he reasoned the best approach was to sit on the edge, dangle his feet into the violent slipstream and simply lean forward into the pitch-black night. 'The next thing I knew was a rush of air, the aircraft floating away in the distance and me swinging on my parachute harness, thinking, If this keeps up I'll be sick. Then, the next thing I knew, I hit the ground.' John estimates that he must have jumped at a perilously low 1000 feet and was only moments in the air.

He was on the ground but, without having taken note of the position sent to him from England, had no idea where he was. 'I couldn't see a thing,' he says. 'It was completely black. I didn't know whether I'd come down over France, Germany or

Holland.' In the ink, and against a stiff breeze, he did his best to hide his parachute and started walking.

A short time later, apparently in a large open field, John heard the sound of massed aircraft engines overhead. His own formation, he presumed, returning to base, as he knew their route home took them back the way they came. Lucky devils, he thought, They're going to be in their own beds tonight. Meanwhile, on he trudged to heaven knew where.

'Was I now going to be a POW?' he says he thought to himself. 'Was I going to be shot? That's the sort of stuff that goes through your head.' Eventually, he came to a road at the end of a paddock, running in the same direction as the aircraft above him. At least they're going the right way, he thought.

A short while later, a truck came onto the road ahead, but, unable to tell if it was one of his own or the enemy's, John hid behind a tree. A little further on, he was challenged by what he thought was an American-sounding voice. Still unable to see a thing, he could only stammer out, 'I've . . . just happened to . . . to bail out of an aircraft.'

Then, the brilliant beam of a flashlight and a pause. 'Say, are you from those British bombers?' the voice enquired as the light shone across John's face. 'And you wear a tie in combat?'

Heaving the longest sigh of relief of his life, John was led away by his American soldier 'captor' – still impressed with the standard RAF flying kit of battle dress, collar and tie – to a nearby medical officer. 'He poured me half a cup of whisky. I think he thought I must have needed it,' he says. John had come down in Belgium, liberated from the Germans just a few weeks previously.

The story of John's Lancaster continues, however, although it would be weeks before he himself would hear how it had unfolded. 'After I'd bailed out,' he says, 'my pilot and engineer were left flying the aircraft.' It was pitch black, and they had no idea where they were. Managing to keep the aircraft in the air longer than they thought possible, they flew west, hoping their luck would hold long enough for them to arrive over friendly territory.

As they were searching the gloom for somewhere that might suffice as a landing ground, amazingly, the lights of a runway switched on directly in front and immediately below. The pilot, Frank, made a decision to land immediately. 'They didn't even have time to put their wheels down,' recounts John. With no communication whatsoever with this mystery aerodrome, the Lancaster skidded to a safe crash landing adjacent to the runway. The Lancaster was a write-off, but Frank and his engineer were unhurt. 'The aerodrome had apparently only turned the lights on because one of their own aircraft was coming back,' says John. Without this extraordinary piece of luck, the Lancaster would most likely have had to come down, somewhere, anywhere, blind. 'I've never gotten over that,' says John. 'I reckon they would have been goners. No question.'

The crew's ordeal, however, was far from over. The gunners and navigator who had bailed earlier had also survived their jump, and that night, all the crew were reunited at an RAF base and taken back to England. But not to their squadron. 'They took us to a personnel depot near St John's Wood in London, and treated us as evaders,' says John. Interviewed and examined, John says their pilot's motives for turning back were viewed with suspicion. 'We more or less had to be readmitted back into the air force,' he says. And in that, some were more successful than others.

'I was asked how I was feeling about what I'd been through,' says John. 'I told them I felt fine, which was true.' Although not directly accused of cowardice, John has always felt that the implication was there. 'The rest of the crew except myself and one of the gunners were categorised "unfit to return to operational flying",' he says. How he escaped the same treatment remains something of a mystery, but he suspects it may have been his positive attitude in the interrogation. 'I think some of the others said they were feeling a bit shaken up,' he says.

Whatever the reason, John, halfway through his tour, suddenly found himself without a crew. 'They didn't know what to do with me when I got back to the squadron,' he says. After floating around, performing routine tasks such as filling batteries, it was decided John would become the squadron 'spare'. Whenever a wireless operator was for sickness or some other reason unable to fly, in John would be sent to fill the gap in the ranks. 'That's why I've put down a different pilot for every trip,' he explains. 'I hardly had the same crew twice.'

So, a little over a month since he had last flown, John's name was back on the squadron battle order, flying with an entirely new crew. His first target, as luck would have it, was the very same one that had so nearly ended it all on trip fourteen, Koblenz. On this occasion, however, it was in daylight, and once again flak tore holes in the aircraft over the heavily defended target, but they made it back in one piece.

John would survive another nine operations, flown during the endgame of the war in Europe: Stuttgart, Essen and twice to Cologne, flying a day and a night in succession. His last, at war's end, was flown on 22 April 1945 as part of a force of over 700 bombers attacking Bremen. The raid destroyed the south-western suburbs of the city, where the waiting British Army was poised to attack. Several thousand houses were destroyed, along with 176 civilians, 26 of those perishing in a concrete air-raid shelter, which collapsed after a close hit by a 500-pound general-purpose bomb. Five days later, the city fell to the advancing British.

After VE Day, John was still flying, this time repatriating British POWs, some of whom had not seen home for four years. 'Some were sick and all of them were skinny,' he says, 'but they were very happy to be out of Germany.'

Arriving home to Western Australia in late 1945, John settled back into the relative mundanity of civilian life, becoming a junior clerk in the public service. He is quite sure he suffered what would now be termed post-traumatic stress disorder, but such terms did not exist in 1945. 'Actually, I think I suffered it from the time of the jump,' he says.

Even late in the war when John flew, the casualty statistics in Bomber Command were heavy. 'We lost five aircraft in the first month I was on the squadron,' he tells me. 'That's thirty-five men, just gone.' Some, he says, were unable to stand the strain, such as his first rear gunner, an Irishman. 'He went home on leave after three trips, and came back and told them he wanted to be taken off operations,' he says. 'There was no argument. You were treated as if you were dead, and spirited away. We all knew of the chances of getting killed but we didn't talk about it much.'

One incident haunts him still. The only other member of John's crew to be put back onto operations after their return to England was one of his gunners, a Scotsman, Jock McRae, with whom John formed a strong bond. 'I was on my own when

I came back to the squadron because the crews would stick together. They didn't want to have much to do with "odd bods" like myself,' he says. Jock had injured his hand when jettisoning his gun from the stricken Lancaster, so was sent on a period of sick and other accumulated leave. But after his return to the squadron, he and John palled up. 'We shared a billet and did everything together,' John says. A short time after John completed his return trip to Koblenz, Jock was scheduled to fly on a 'gardening' or sea-mining operation to Danzig Bay, a long trip to the German–Polish border on the Baltic in January 1945.

In the small hours of the following morning, John was awoken by a bang on his billet door and the sudden appearance of people in the room, moving about with torches. 'I didn't know who they were,' he says. In fact they were members of the chillingly titled Committee of Adjustment, sent to collect and remove an airman's belongings as soon as he was posted missing. When someone failed to return from an operation, no time was lost in erasing his memory from the squadron, lest his sudden absence serve as too vivid a reminder to the airmen of the awful numbers game stacked against them. 'It was the first I'd learned that Jock was missing,' says John. 'They arrived in the middle of the night, collected all his gear and quietly took it away. That really shook me up quite a bit.'

For a while, there was talk of Jock having landed in neutral Sweden and being interned, or having ended up a POW, but no trace either of him or his crew was ever found. His name is on the RAF Runnymede memorial in Surrey, built to commemorate the more than 20 000 British and Commonwealth airmen of the Second World War who left England, never to return, and who have no known grave.

John spoke to me about his war in a way typical of many of the men I met who flew in Bomber Command: openly, modestly, completely lacking in any self-righteousness, and as quietly amazed by the raw events of his youth as was I. The stress of his tour, he says, lingered with him long after his return. 'I found it affected my confidence, things like that. But there wouldn't be too many people who went through a tour without some effect on them.' For a short time, he enrolled in the RSL, but wasn't really interested. 'It was practically all army men,' he says, 'talking army things.' He found more relevance with the RAAF Association, which he joined in 1980, remaining an active member for years.

Today, he still puts in a regular appearance as a volunteer at the nearby Bull Creek air-force museum, showing visitors over the great black-liveried Lancaster, the interior of which he knew only too well, and which stands as a magnificent centre-piece. But John's war remains with him. 'You always think of it,' he says. 'It never goes away, it's always there somewhere at the back of your mind, but you just get on with things.'

JEFF PERRY

Role: Pilot
Aircraft: Vickers Wellington
Posting: 115 Squadron, RAF

I've never spoken about it in this much detail.

'I'm on my way, Jeff, see you in about half an hour.' I can't recall ever having been to Dubbo, and am taken aback by the size of it, with its low, confusing sprawl of seemingly identical shopping strips, truck and car yards, and outlets boasting a bewildering array of machines destined for various agricultural purposes: gargantuan tractors, wheeled and multi-armed harvesters and other contraptions a determined person might well convince me are actually surplus from the Soviet space program. That at least makes up part of the excuse I give myself when running late to meet Jeff Perry, who flew bombers in the early part of the war. But if he is put out by my tardiness, he doesn't let on, instead giving me an errand. 'Look, while you're out,' he says over the phone as I am on final approach, 'can you pick me up some milk? And make it that low-fat stuff. I'm trying to lose a bit of weight.' Jeff, I might add, is ninety-eight years old.

I meet Jeff at his front door where he shakes my hand firmly and invites me into his modern unit on the main road. It's December and the sun is white and blinding, and makes me think of insects I tortured under a magnifying glass as a kid. The relief of getting inside is overwhelming. Jeff pauses at the door. 'Hmm, looks like rain,' he says, glancing up at a clear sky.

'Really?' I say, expecting him to elaborate. He doesn't.

The first glance into a former airman's home can be telling. Some are crammed with photographs, mementos, squadron emblems, often model aeroplanes of the type the airmen flew. Usually, there is at least something, but not a single item in Jeff's abode in any way indicates his wartime life in the RAAF. He draws me into the kitchen. 'My great-granddaughter's just given me one of these coffee machines,' he says, waving in the direction of a shiny new appliance taking up rather a lot of room on the kitchen bench. I've recently had a go at a similar-looking one, and quickly attempt to reacquaint myself with its function, anticipating soon being called to lend a hand. Jeff watches me patiently as I fiddle with the lever where the cartridges are inserted. 'Would you like a cafe latte?' he says finally. I step aside and Jeff proceeds to make me one, perfectly. I take that as my cue to sit down and jettison all remaining assumptions.

It's not surprising Jeff appears so at home on the western plains of New South Wales. His family have been out here since Europeans first began to hammer fences around the boundaries of sheep stations the size of minor principalities. 'I was born about a hundred miles west of here,' he tells me, throwing a hand somewhere in that direction. 'There wasn't really a town. The nearest railway station was called Mullengudgery.' When later I look it up on the map, I see it's still there but there's no sign of a train station, tracks or anything much else for that matter. When giving me a brief history of his family's long association with Merino sheep, he mentions events that took place in the '80s. I shake my head slightly when I realise he's talking not of the 1980s, but the 1880s.

With an uncle who'd been in the trenches, Jeff wanted nothing to do with the army, so in April 1940, he made the long trip east to join the air force in Sydney. At No. 4 Elementary Flying Training School at Mascot, he took to flying easily and, to the delight of his instructor, was the first pupil in his very early No. 7 Course to go solo in a Tiger Moth. His prowess earned him selection for single-engine fighter training. Being so close to Sydney, they were all given one very particular instruction: never, under any circumstances, fly under the Harbour Bridge!

Almost as an aside, Jeff mentions a name that makes me stop in my tracks, one of his fellow student pilots whom he knew not only on the course but back home, a young man whose father ran a property close to his own. A quiet fellow, with whom Jeff regularly played tennis, but who didn't have much to say for himself. 'You'd hardly get to know him,' he says of Rawdon Hume Middleton who, two years later, for a trip to Turin in a Short Stirling bomber, would win the Victoria Cross, posthumously. Shockingly wounded by anti-aircraft fire, Middleton would complete his bomb run on the Fiat aircraft factory, then, blinded in one eye, in agony and losing blood from lacerations all over his body, would deliver his crew back to England, ordering five of them to bail out once they'd crossed the English coast. He went down with his aircraft in the Channel, and his body was washed up a little later. 'Played a good game of tennis, too,' remembers Jeff.

After various adventures on the long voyage to Britain, including a near-miss by a torpedo in the Pacific (which Jeff, on watch at the time, saw and initially thought to be a swordfish), and colliding with an iceberg in the Atlantic, Jeff arrived in the battered British Isles in early 1941. In Bournemouth, a fortune teller unnerved him by predicting he would fall, 'but not from a great height'. Performing just a little too well on a night-vision test saw him transferred from fighters to night bombers. 'Everyone was rated average or below average,' he remembers. 'I was apparently "exceptional",' so instead of the Hurricanes or Spitfires he'd had his heart set on, Jeff was soon off to the other end of Britain, Lossiemouth in northern Scotland, to transfer onto Wellington bombers.

He enjoyed the Wellington and didn't seem to mind too much his change of mount, but wasn't ready to divest himself of his fighter pilot skills just yet. 'First thing I thought I'd do when going solo in the Wellington was some aerobatics,' he says, obviously noticing my look of bewilderment. 'I thought I'd do a stall turn, and then if that worked okay, I'd do a loop.'

'A loop?' I exclaim. 'In a Wellington?'

'I couldn't see why not,' he says.

So, somewhere over northern Scotland, Jeff put some speed on his heavy twin-engine Mark I Wellington bomber, pulled back the stick to make it climb straight up, stalled, kicked on some rudder and let the nose drift down towards the ground in a dive. So far, so good. But when he tried to pull the bomber out of it, the stick wouldn't budge. 'It was like trying to pull at a tree,' he remembers. In a vertical dive with the speed increasing and unable to make the aircraft react, Jeff suddenly realised he might be in a spot of bother. 'Shit! I thought to myself. The wing commander won't be very pleased when I wreck his plane.'

With the ground fast looming large in his windshield, this, one might have thought, would have been the least of his worries. But he didn't panic. Instead, he decided to reach down and turn the elevator-trim control wheel at the bottom of his pilot's seat. Replicating the movement seventy years on, Jeff unconsciously slides his hand down the side of his armchair and turns an imaginary wheel. With only a thousand feet between him and oblivion, the nose of the Wellington started to rise. Probably for the better, Jeff decided to give the loop a miss. But he'd learned something about the aircraft he was soon to be flying into battle. 'I knew then that if I was ever attacked by fighters, I could put her into a dive and get out of it,' he says. It was knowledge he would need to put to good use.

Jeff joined No. 115 Squadron operating from Marham, in Norfolk on the edge of The Wash, a relatively comfortable pre-war brick-building base, as the captain of an all-English crew. ('They were all from Lancashire and Cheshire,' he says. 'Their accents were so strong I could barely understand them.') Jeff would complete an exceptionally long tour of thirty-seven operations, mostly to targets in the industrial Ruhr valley of northern Germany. Sadly, his logbook was lost in a bushfire in the 1950s (along with, he says, many photographs taken with a secreted camera from his cockpit while actually on operations – I wince at what could have been), so we are unable to go through his tour chronologically, but he certainly remembers a great deal.

'I'm not sure of the target. It may have been Hamburg,' he remembers of one operation. 'An anti-aircraft shell exploded inside the plane. It shattered my instrument panel, wrecked the compass and most of the other instruments.' He reckons the shell went off just behind his cockpit, which quickly filled with smoke. But one of the Wellington's strengths was its ability to absorb punishment due to its unique latticed, or geodetic, skeleton of aluminium ribs, wrapped in doped, shrunken canvas. This allowed the shock of exploding shells to pass through the thin canvas wall rather than be absorbed by the crew. There are many instances of Wellingtons returning to base with so much of their outer covering missing they resembled see-through diagrams. So, with his controls intact, Jeff flew on.

'Was anyone hurt?' I ask him.

'No, I don't think so,' he says, then after a pause, 'although I still have some shrapnel in my leg.' His definition of hurt obviously differs from mine.

With no compass, Jeff had no idea where to fly, so the instructions from his navigator to simply 'head west' were somewhat moot. It was, however, a clear night, and looking to his right, he saw the friendly white orb of Polaris, the north star. 'So long as it was on my starboard side, I knew I'd reach England somewhere.' Eventually, the coast did come up, but his troubles were not yet over. 'Suddenly the anti-aircraft guns opened up on us,' he says. 'The British ones! And they didn't miss by much, either.'

He didn't realise it at the time, but the explosion had also wrecked the IFF (identification friend or foe) device which would have marked him as friendly to the gunners below. Evading the friendly fire, he still had to find his way back home, which he did by checking the two-letter identity codes – flashed by all aerodromes – against the daily changing code list on his destroyable notepaper, the 'flimsy'. Finally, and extremely low on fuel, he found his way back to Marham. 'So, yes,' he tells me, 'that was a bit of an exciting one.'

Jeff's tour, in mid to late 1941, took place during the great nadir of Bomber Command when unsustainable losses were expended for little result. To counter the U-boat threat, the bomber crews had in March of that year been directed to concentrate their attacks on submarine pens along the French coast, but in July they were thrown back into the Ruhr, or 'Happy Valley' as the airmen came to dub the heavily defended industrial centre of Germany's north. The RAF believed that with the bulk of the Luftwaffe now in Russia, the west would be relatively undefended. They were in for a shock. Between July and November, Bomber Command would lose a staggering 526 aircraft to enemy fire, the equivalent of its entire front-line strength in just four months. The chance of surviving a standard tour of thirty operations was at this time considerably less than 50 per cent. Added to this, it was realised that the crews, at night over a blackout continent, were barely even finding their targets, let alone hitting them. The sensational *Butt Report* of August 1941, derived from the analysis of over 4000 aerial target photographs, showed that barely one in four crews had dropped their bombs within 5 miles of the target.

What part experience played in keeping a crew off the casualty list was demonstrated to Jeff on one of his early trips when, nearing the target, his rear gunner called up calmly, 'Skip, there's a plane flying behind us. Should I fire at it?'

A split-second of incredulity gave way to Jeff yelling an emphatic, 'Yes!' down the intercom, then executing a violent turn to port. 'At that moment,' he says, 'a whole stream of yellow and white tracer bullets poured over the top of my port wing.' It was, he thinks, a Junkers Ju 88, which had snuck up behind them in the dark, making itself visible to the inexperienced young man in the rear turret only at the last second. 'I had to tell him afterwards in no uncertain terms, "Don't ask, just shoot!"' There were more encounters with night fighters throughout his tour, but each time he evaded them, remembering the hard lesson he had learned in training over Scotland. His gunner never asked permission again.

The trick with the elevator trim came in handy on another occasion when he was trapped or 'coned' by a series of powerful coordinated German searchlights. 'I'd seen aircraft coned time and time again,' he says, 'and almost invariably they were shot down. And they got me too, once.' When his turn came, he threw the Wellington into a twisting dive, evading the lights and the concentrated flak that invariably came with them, brought it out of the dive with the elevator trim, and got away with it.

This period of soul-searching for Bomber Command – when it was poorly led by now forgotten commanders and its purpose, even its existence, was being questioned – combined with unreliable weather, meant Jeff's tour spread out over many months. Days, sometimes weeks would pass without an operation, but his crew gradually became an experienced one, surviving at a time when so many did not. It was frequently a close shave, however.

One trip, he tells me, still shakes him up to think about. The target was a city on the Baltic, and after a successful attack, Jeff was flying home over the North Sea. Feeling relatively safe, he engaged the automatic pilot, known as 'George', dropped down to the relative warmth of about 600 metres above sea level, and gave permission for the crew to break out their nightly complement of sandwiches and coffee. 'Suddenly, all hell broke loose,' he says, as a massive barrage of anti-aircraft fire exploded all around him. 'What the hell was that?' he said to the navigator, grabbing the wheel.

'I don't know,' was the reply. 'We're supposed to be over the sea!'

Flying carefully home, he checked the map and, to his horror, realised he'd flown low, straight and level over the extremely well-defended German island of Heligoland, a mini fortress not only bristling with guns but also well-equipped with barrage balloons tethered as high as 6000 feet. 'I must have flown between the cables without knowing it,' he recalls, realising that contact with any one of them would have sliced a wing off like a knife. 'That shook me up a bit, actually,' he says, and by the look on his face, I believe him.

He seems to have been shaken too by the visible effects of what he was doing, night after night, to German cities and their inhabitants, and gives an extraordinary insight into one of the most famous raids of the war, the one and only attack on Lübeck, the old Hanseatic League city on the Trave River on the Baltic coast, in March 1942. This was the turning point for the RAF, the first major success against a large German target, and the raid that would set the terrible pattern of area bombing for the next four years. On this clear night, for the first time, everything went right for the bomber crews, with nearly all 234 aircraft reporting successful hits on the aiming point, the *altstadt* – the very heart of the old medieval town. Lightly defended, the bombers ventured down to as low as 2000 feet above the city for greater accuracy. 'We set the whole town on fire,' remembers Jeff, who saw it all from his cockpit. 'There were these bridges over the water on the western side. I remember seeing a whole stream of cars trying to get across them to escape the inferno. It was a traffic jam. For the first time, I felt sorry for them. I hadn't felt a thing for them up till then, but this night I felt sorry for them down there.'

Jeff's mood seems to change a little after this revelation. He pauses for a moment, then tells me that after his first trip, he'd conscientiously told the CO that he couldn't be 'absolutely certain' of having hit the target dead centre. The senior officer was untroubled. 'That doesn't matter,' he replied matter-of-factly. 'Even if you missed the target, you probably would have hit the buildings next to it where the workers lived and killed them.'

'After that,' says Jeff a little haltingly, 'we'd always try to aim very carefully at the target.'

Having reached his tour's designated thirty operations, Jeff expected to be stood down, but nobody said anything and his name appeared on the battle order for the next trip, and then the one after that. 'Actually, I think they lost track of me,' he says casually, as if discussing a misplaced rates notice. 'I thought a lot about this afterwards. They could never find my records and such. I think it was because I trained as a fighter pilot then transferred to bombers. I don't think I was in their system.' Still he went on flying – thirty-three, thirty-four, thirty-five – and surviving, and still no word on when he might be done. 'Finally, I said something to the adjutant who seemed surprised and looked something up. Then, after number thirty-seven, they told me that was enough.'

Jeff no doubt earned the Distinguished Flying Cross several times over – not least for his unofficially extended tour – but being on the wrong side of his old-school CO, who took umbrage at Jeff's lack of concern for such military niceties as saluting and treating said CO with the respect to which he believed himself entitled ('Actually, I used to wind him up a lit-tle,' he admits), made certain that decoration was never going to come his way. After his tour, Jeff spent time as an instructor, and by war's end, was back running his family's property in west-ern New South Wales, having been greeted on his return by the news that his father had been diagnosed with cancer and had not much time to live.

Flying during a period when his chances of survival were slim, did he think his number was going to come up? His answer surprises me.

'I thought it might, but I knew I could handle a plane better than most other pilots. I thought perhaps some of them con-tributed to killing themselves.' Jeff is of the firm opinion that many pilots and crews, through inexperience, simply ran out of skill: failing to recover from stalls and spins, miscalculating fuel or distances, or simply getting lost and disappearing without a trace. There was luck, certainly, he believes, but also the small-est of margins to make your own.

He says he can't recall the faces of the many men who came and disappeared during his dramatic time on the squadron, but one stands out, and he tells me the sad story of Allan Weller, a fellow Australian pilot from Brisbane. Weller had been shot down over the North Sea but survived a raging storm to be picked up in his dinghy by a Norwegian vessel and soon found his way back to the squadron. 'I shared a hut with him,' says Jeff. 'His nerves were shot to pieces. At night he'd yell and make noises, so I told the wing commander that I didn't believe he was fit to fly.' The news got back to Weller, who 'went crook' at Jeff in no uncertain terms. In any case, it made no difference. Weller kept flying. 'The next trip they sent him on, he didn't come back,' says Jeff.

Jeff tells me that he has never spoken of his war in such depth to anyone, which humbles me. 'I'm sure I've been affected by it,' he says. 'We didn't have a name for it back then. Stress disorder they call it now, or something. I'm sure I must have had it. I smoked and I drank. Sometimes even now I wake up in the middle of the night and think of things that happened, what I could have done, what I should have done.'

We wind up our meeting – he was right about the rain, which bucketed down suddenly then vanished, leaving a strange, salty smell in the air as I emerge into a much cooler Dubbo. I ask him, just as I'm leaving, about the prophecy of the clair-voyant in Bournemouth about the fall from a short height. While erecting some electric lights at home, Jeff broke both his wrists when a ladder slipped. 'So that old lady in Bournemouth was right after all.'

MURRAY ADAMS

Role: Fighter pilot
Aircraft: P-40 Tomahawk,
Supermarine Spitfire, Hawker Tempest
Posting: 250 Squadron, RAF

It's only now that fighter pilots like me are becoming an endangered species, that people like you are interested.

'So, what are you going to join?' asked Murray's mate as they headed down the Hume Highway (as it was then named) towards Melbourne, driven by a fervent desire to answer their country's call and get into this newly declared war quick smart. Beyond this vague patriotic notion, however, Murray hadn't actually given it much thought. 'The army . . . I suppose,' he said uncertainly to his companion, who, despite working at Murray's local bank in Mansfield, Murray had only just met – at a party the night before. But at least he had a car.

'Don't be a bloody idiot,' the self-assured young man

retorted. 'You'll be up to your navel in swamp water with a heavy pack on your back, without a dry bed to sleep in.'

'Well what are *you* going to join then?' asked Murray.

'Air force,' the lad replied. 'At least you get a ride.'

This made eminent sense, and so the air force it would be. Not that he gave himself much of a hope of getting in. Apart from the fact that – unlike almost every other keen-eyed young man eager to join the ranks of the dark blue – Murray knew next to nothing about aeroplanes and cared about them even less, he'd also barely recovered from a nasty bout of double pneumonia and rated his chances of simply passing the medical as somewhere around nil. But, as with every fighter pilot the world over, luck would step in to play its part. Luck, and a smattering of cunning.

'One of the things they got you to do was hold up a column of mercury with your lungs,' says Murray. 'Mine were shot at that stage from the pneumonia, but I managed to pinch the length of tubing against the edge of the bench when no-one was looking.' The medical hurdle crossed, there was still the interview to get through, where he would be required to appear in front of a selection panel of officers, one of them a group captain.

'I hadn't so much as sat in an aeroplane, knew nothing about them and had no great interest in them,' he says. 'They asked me about ten questions – all about flying aeroplanes – so I pretty much got nought out of ten.'

I ask him if he remembers what any of them were.

'No,' he says. 'I wouldn't have understood them anyway.' The next stage of Murray's flying career – being shown the door directly behind him – was looming when the leader of the panel, possibly just to fill the awkward silence, happened to ask, 'What games do you play, Adams?' to which Murray gave the answer that turned everything around.

'Tennis and skiing, sir,' he replied with sudden confidence.

At this, the officer paused. 'Did you say skiing?'

As Murray explains, 'There were only a handful of skiers in Victoria at that time, and he was one of them. He became quite excited.' While young Murray and the group captain embarked on an animated conversation about the latest downhill techniques and other gossip around Victoria's then nascent skiing community, the other officers kept silent. But when the subject at last returned to the business at hand, Murray was no less hapless.

'So, what do you want to do in the air force?' he was asked.

'Well, what are my options?' he said.

'Well, you can be a pilot, an observer or an air gunner.'

Murray thought about this for a moment. 'I think I'd like to drive the thing,' he said innocently enough. And in the face of undoubted eye rolls from the rest of the selection panel, his newly found friend with the group captain's rings on his sleeve announced, 'Right, pilot it is.'

'And that was that,' says Murray.

To the surprise of everyone (not least himself), Murray found he in fact possessed something of a natural aptitude for flying and breezed through his course at Melbourne's Essendon Aerodrome, despite running foul of his dreaded chief instructor. His crime? Unwittingly escorting the instructor's ex-fiancée to a dance.

'You'll pay for this, Adams,' said the instructor menacingly in a somewhat ugly confrontation in a lavatory just off the dance floor. And he was very nearly true to his word.

'On my final test, the bastard did everything he could think of to scrub me,' says Murray, remembering the morning well. 'Good morning, sir,' he said to the dark-faced instructor as they approached the Tiger Moth.

'Get in the cockpit,' was the curt reply. For the next hour, he put Murray through the wringer, looking for any excuse to fail him. But Murray's talent shone through, and, reluctantly, the instructor had no choice but to pass him, and he was even selected for the coveted prize of single-engine fighter pilot training – the dream of just about every young man at the time. Except, of course, if you happened to be Murray Adams.

On his final day of training at Wagga, with a pair of brand-new pilots wings on his tunic, Murray decided to make a parting gesture to his home town, and 'beat up' the centre of Mansfield in his Wirraway. It was market day, and everyone, he knew, would be out and about as he roared down the main street at rooftop level. This type of shenanigans was, of course, not in the least bit tolerated, so just in case someone happened to be quick enough to read the number on his aircraft and report him, Murray had a contingency plan. 'The day before, I'd made up a little parachute with a handkerchief and a rock wrapped in a note.' After buzzing the town, he flew out to the family farm, spotted his father on his horse, and threw it over the side. 'Get to the police station quickly before anyone can report me,' read his father as he dismounted. As he was on good terms with the local constabulary, nothing more was heard of the incident.

I ask him how low he went down that main street.

He ponders for a moment. 'Well, the barmaid reckons I flew below her window,' he says, smiling, 'but I don't think that's true.'

Sailing in what must have surely been one of the most spectacular convoys ever to have put to sea, Murray steamed out of Sydney Heads in mid-1941 on board the mighty liner *Queen Elizabeth*, accompanied by her sister, *Queen Mary*, and the great but ageing *Aquitania*. Horrendous seas battered their Australian cruiser escort into early retirement at Fremantle, leaving the big ships to steam across the Indian Ocean unaccompanied to the Middle East. Murray would be joining the ranks of Air Vice Marshal Arthur Coningham's Desert Air Force, supporting the British 8th Army in its seesawing struggle against Rommel's Afrika Korps, currently ranging back and forth across the sands and the wadis of North Africa.

Arriving in Egypt during a relative interlude, however, Murray discovered there were no vacancies for new pilots, so was forced to cool his heels. Taking in some sights and doing his best to acclimatise, in October 1941, he found himself on a featureless patch of clay 20 miles south of the Egyptian coast simply called 'LG [landing ground] 013'. Murray was the newest addition to No. 250 Squadron, an RAF unit, where his flight commander, one Clive Caldwell, was well on his way to becoming Australia's greatest fighter ace. 'A wonderful man,' Murray says, 'once you got to know him.'

This desolate spot scraped out of the sand and the camel thorn would be Murray's new home. 'Our mission was to achieve aerial superiority over the battlefields,' he says, 'which was a hopeless task as we were completely outperformed by the enemy.' Indeed, their American P-40E Tomahawk fighters were slower than the Messerschmitt Bf 109Es they were facing, possessing about half their rate of climb, and their 28-litre, liquid-cooled Allison engines were prone to unreliability.

The Tomahawk had in fact never been intended for use by the RAF, a batch of them having been ordered by the French Air Force, but failing to arrive from the US before France's capitulation to Hitler in 1940. The British then took hold of them but deemed them inferior to equivalent German aircraft and so relegated them to the relative backwater of the desert campaign. The relief the RAF pilots in England no doubt felt at not having to fly such under-performing machines as these was probably of little comfort to men like Murray.

'We didn't have the right aircraft and most of us, like me, were not particularly well trained,' he says. But the Tomahawks did have a couple of advantages. As heavy as they were, they had a wonderful rate of turn, which spooked the German pilots, who avoided mixing it with them in a dogfight. 'They would always be above us and come screaming down in a dive – one at a time,' says Murray. 'And if you kicked over the rudder bar at the right moment, they'd go tearing past and you could sometimes get a shot at them.'

Murray passes his logbook to me. It's covered in a rather wonderful piece of embossed leather (goat skin, I'm told), redolent with character and adventure. I open it and start perusing his brief but potent entries for November 1941: 'Patrol in the vicinity of Sheferzen, Ft. Madalena – terrific dust storm blowing on our return; cover for advancing troops – P/O Masters (N.Z.) killed on 21/11; bomber escort to Gambut area – saw Stukas bombing our troops and big cover of Me. 109s above, but unable to leave our own bombers. Later two 109s made attacks at P/O Ranger but missed' etc.

And for December: 'Vectored onto Ju.88 recco at 19 000 and damaged it in two attacks; played hide and seek with two

109s in broken cloud; chased Me110 until I lost it in cloud. Fired several bursts after it. Sgt Canty (RCAF) killed.'

'Yes, we had our casualties,' he says. 'Some chaps you never got to know, they were shot down that quickly. But our morale was very good.' One of the reasons this can be attributed to is an enlightened innovation introduced by the CO of No. 3 Squadron, RAAF, Peter Jeffrey. At a time when class consciousness was rife within the Commonwealth air forces and a virtual institution in the RAF, Jeffrey instigated the quietly revolutionary notion of the mixed-rank pilots mess. About half the Desert Air Force's pilots were at that time sergeants, but it was experience, not rank, which commanded respect, and for the first time, under Jeffrey, pilots of all ranks were made to eat, sit and talk shop together about how to fight and survive in the desert skies. And it was open all hours. 'Some of the old English officers didn't like it much, having to rub shoulders with these grubby sergeants,' says Murray. But so successful was it that Coningham – another colonial from New Zealand – introduced it to all his squadrons. 'If you'd survived for a while, you'd obviously had some experience, and now you could share it,' Murray says.

I continue to read his logbook. Images of Murray come to mind, fountain pen in hand, hunched over this same volume in a canvas tent on the edge of a makeshift runway in the Egyptian desert seventy years ago. For December, he appears to have flown virtually every day in patrols lasting sometimes an hour, occasionally two. But it's what he's written for the very first day of that month that pulls me up: 'Attacked by Me109s escorting Me.110s & Ju 88s. Cannon shell in oil tank forced me to land, wheels up at Taleb-el-Essem.'

He begins the story slowly. 'Well, they always say, "The one that gets you is the one you don't see," and I didn't see this one till it was too late.' On an offensive patrol at 14000 feet one morning, the first Murray knew of any danger was the sudden sight of German aircraft all round him. A section of Messerschmitt Me 109s, escorting a formation high above, had pounced on them in a classic 'out of the sun' manoeuvre, always the slower Tomahawks' Achilles heel. 'Our practice was not to use our mirrors,' he says. 'In a mirror you only got a small picture that can soon materialise into something bigger. You had to turn and look. That's why we wore silk scarves – it wasn't an affectation, it was a necessity – to prevent your neck chafing.' When Murray turned and looked this morning, he saw a large German propeller hub firing its guns in his direction, followed by the sound of something hitting his aeroplane just behind his head.

With just seventeen hours of operational flying under his belt, Murray, at this stage of his still short flying career, felt 'grossly under-trained'.

'I was still learning to fly the thing,' he says. 'I tried to turn towards the German but it was too late and all I did was flick her into a very nasty inverted spin' (another of the Tomahawk's less pleasant flying characteristics). Down he went, caught in a vortex. The more Murray tried to pull the aircraft out by the standard method of powering on the throttle, the tighter the spin became. Added to this, an increasingly large volume of warm oil began sloshing around the cockpit, covering everything with a filthy black smear – his instruments, himself, and most alarmingly, his Perspex canopy. Blinded and heading towards the ground in an uncontrollable spin, Murray sensed his options rapidly diminishing. He reached up to pull back the hood and bail out, but it was jammed tight, and no effort of his could shift it. 'I remember at this point thinking quite calmly, I don't know where the ground is, but it must be getting close, and soon there'll be a loud noise but I won't hear it!' He had been, he knew, up at 14 000 feet, but how much of that was left between him and, as he puts it, 'the unyielding surface of the planet', he had no idea.

As it turned out, the German bullet in his oil pump almost certainly saved his life, as the Tomahawk's Allison engine, now drained of oil, suddenly seized, stopped and released the aircraft from its deadly torque grip, allowing it to spin out of its death roll completely on its own. And just in time.

'As the oil ran off the Perspex I could see I was about 200 feet off the ground,' says Murray. 'So, naturally I put her down.'

'How did she glide?' something prompts me to ask.

'Like a brick,' he says. Nonetheless, Murray executed a smooth wheels-up landing and slid across the sand to a stop. Although covered in oil, he was intact and, amazingly, unhurt.

Now able to apply a hefty shoulder to the recalcitrant cockpit hood, Murray forced it back and was free. The cause of the jam, he now saw, was a single bullet which had struck the canopy's metal rail, mere inches from his head.

He was, however, in the middle of nowhere, with neither water nor food, and what he estimated to be 150 miles of highly contested desert between himself and his base. In between was the endgame of a tank battle that had been raging for a week. So, doing what any downed fighter pilot would do, Murray started walking.

'Did you know where you were going?' I ask.

'Well, I was in the boy scouts and knew how to use a clock as a compass. I unscrewed the aircraft's clock with a nail file and took it with me.'

'Brilliant!' I spontaneously exclaim.

With the aircraft soon swallowed up in one of the endless desert chimeras somewhere behind him, Murray trudged north-west through the sand. Despite it being winter, when temperatures were not extreme, he knew his only hope lay in coming across a friendly vehicle, preferably laden with a good supply of drinkable water. Eventually, he spotted the unmistakable dust trails of a group of approaching trucks, and threw himself behind a pathetically small patch of camel thorn, camouflaged, however, by his oil-soaked khaki battle dress. 'As they got closer, I could see they had black crosses on them,' he says. Not yet willing to exchange his liberty for survival, he hugged the ground. Despite passing close by, the Germans failed to spot him.

By mid-afternoon, thirst was beginning to tell. 'At this stage I would have taken a lift with the devil himself,' Murray says, but that was not to prove necessary. Soon, a second plume of dust – this time from a single vehicle – approached, revealing itself, to Murray's profound relief, as the friendly outline of a British Morris truck containing a British officer and his driver from the Northumberland Hussars. With no need to conceal himself, the sight of the bedraggled Murray 'hitching' beside a track in the middle of the desert must have seemed odd, but he affected nonchalance as best he could. The relief he felt in seeing the cans of water and food in the back was palpable. But when he enquired of his new escort about their whereabouts, the terribly proper major's reply was, 'Sorry, old chap, we're *lorst!*'

ABOVE: The last of the many. The final of 700 DAP Australian-built Bristol Beaufort, A9-700, on show over Sydney, 1945. (Picture courtesy of Keith Webb)

BELOW: A young Cy Borsht on the eve of his eventful tour in Bomber Command. (Picture courtesy of Cy Borsht)

ABOVE LEFT: John Allen in front of his Fleet Air Arm Hellcat.
(Picture courtesy of John Allen)

ABOVE RIGHT: An 890 Squadron Fleet Air Arm Wildcat pilot fails to lower his arrestor hook and comes to grief on the deck of the escort carrier *HMS Atheling* in the Indian Ocean, 1945. The pilot, amazingly, walked away. (Picture courtesy of John Allen)

LEFT: 463 Squadron Lancaster LM130, Nick the Nazi Neutralizer. This aircraft survived 82 operations, only to be lost, along with her entire crew, in a mid-air collision with a Hurricane over Lincolnshire in March, 1945.
(Picture courtesy of David Morland)

ABOVE: 804 Squadron Hellcats in formation over the Indian Ocean. John Allen is closest to the camera. (Picture above and below courtesy of John Allen)

BELOW: 804 Squadron Hellcats pass close to *HMS Ameer* before forming up over the Indian Ocean, 1945. (Picture courtesy of John Allen)

ABOVE: Cliff Sullivan's 47 Squadron Beaufighter strikes an Italian merchant ship off Tunis, July 1943. (Picture courtesy of Cliff Sullivan)

BELOW: Cliff Sullivan's view from his Beaufighter of an Italian tanker ablaze in the Mediterranean after a torpedo attack, 1943. (Picture courtesy of Cliff Sullivan)

ABOVE: A low-level Beaufighter attack over the Mediterranean, snapped by Cliff Sullivan. (Picture courtesy of Cliff Sullivan)

BELOW: The nuggety all-Australian ground-attack fighter, the Boomerang, as flown by 4 Squadron pilot Ron Benson, New Guinea, 1944. (Picture courtesy of Keith Webb)

ABOVE: David Morland and his crew beside their 467 Squadron Lancaster 'X-Xray' LM686. From left to right: Stewy, George, David, Bill, Skuey, Bob, Blue. Each man poses holding a 17-pound practice bomb. (Picture courtesy of David Morland)

BELOW: David Morland at 21000 feet in the mid-upper gun turret of his Lancaster, taken en route to Bremen, October 6, 1944. (Picture courtesy of David Morland)

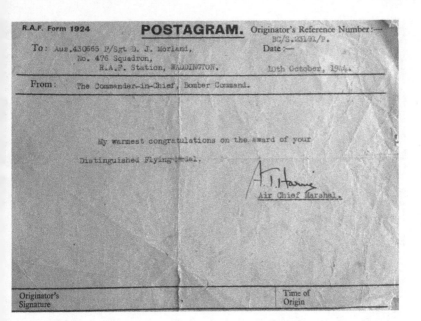

R.A.F. Form 1924   **POSTAGRAM.** Originator's Reference Number:—
BC/S.23191/P.

To : Aus.430565 F/Sgt D. J. Morland,
No. 476 Squadron,
R.A.F. Station, WADDINGTON.   Date :— 10th October, 1944.

From :   The Commander-in-Chief, Bomber Command.

My warmest congratulations on the award of your

Distinguished Flying Medal.

Air Chief Marshal.

Originator's
Signature   Time of
Origin

ABOVE: The personal touch. Bomber Command boss Air Chief Marshal Harris congratulates David Morland on his DFM, which he earned the hard way, over Darmstadt, September 11, 1944. (Picture courtesy of David Morland)

BELOW: Australian personnel at RAF Waddington turn out to see 467 Squadron Lancaster 'P-Peter' take off for a trip deep into Germany, late 1944. (Picture courtesy of Keith Webb)

Date	Hour	Aircraft Type and No.	Pilot	Duty	Remarks (Including results of bombing, gunnery, exercises, etc.)	Flying Times Day	Night
			OPERATIONS — 180 SQUADRON — FROM DUNSFOLD		TIME CARRIED FORWARD	110:15	23:35
4-8-44	19:00	MITCHELL FT 210	SGT. BURN.	WO/AG	OPS 1 — BOMBING. MARSHALLING YARDS AT MONTFORT-SUR-RISLE.	2:30	
5-8-44	15:00	D 225	SGT. BURN	WO/AG	BASE — ODIHAM — BASE	:40	
6-8-44	10:25	U 679	SGT. BURN	WO/AG.	OPS 2 — BOMBING AMMUNITION DUMP AT LIVAROT.	2:10	
6-8-44	18:15	M 199	SGT BURN	WO/AG.	OPS 3 — BOMBING. PANZER DIVISION IN WOODS NEAR THURY HARCOURT STARBOARD MOTOR HIT BY FLAK. FORCE LANDED AT B-14 NORMANDY.	1:35	
7-8-44	17:30	DAKOTA KG 417		PASSENGER	B14 - NORMANDY — NORTHOLT	1:35	
8-8-44	4:00	OXFORD V3741	F.O. BRENFLOE	PASSENGER	NORTHOLT — BASE	:30	
9-8-44	10:20	MITCHELL FT 210	SGT. BURN	WO/AG	OPS 4 — BOMBING AMMUNITION DUMP SOUTH EAST OF ROUEN A/c BADLY HIT BY FLAK. (NOTE 5 - 2-15) NAVIGATOR WOUNDED. CRASH LANDED AT HARTFORD BRIDGE.	2:30	
4-8-44	19:30	L 232	F/O AARNE	PASSENGER	HARTFORD BRIDGE — BASE	:40	
					TOTAL TIME	122:25	23:35

ABOVE: George Smith's logbook, illustrating the first part of his eventful tour with the Tactical Air Force in France. His fourth Op to bomb an ammunition dump near Rouen on 9 August was nearly his last. (Picture courtesy of George Smith)

BELOW LEFT: Wireless/air gunner George Smith. He would complete a dramatic tour with 180 Squadron in B-25 Mitchell bombers in late 1944. (Picture courtesy of George Smith)

BELOW RIGHT: A 180 Squadron B-25 in France, showing the wear of battle, late 1944. George Smith flew a full tour of operations in one of these, all at low level. (Picture courtesy of George Smith)

Fighter pilot Murray Adams with the goatskin log book cover he had made in the desert where he flew Tomahawks with 250 Squadron. He was shot down, but walked out of the desert to fly and fight again. (Picture courtesy of Murray Adams)

ABOVE: US B-24s head out in formation from Fenton to attack
Japanese positions to Australia's north. (Picture courtesy of Ed Crabtree)

BELOW: Ed Crabtree, front left, poses with his American crew in front of 'Dottie's Double'
38th Bomb Group, 530th Squadron, Fenton, 1944. (Picture courtesy of Ed Crabtree)

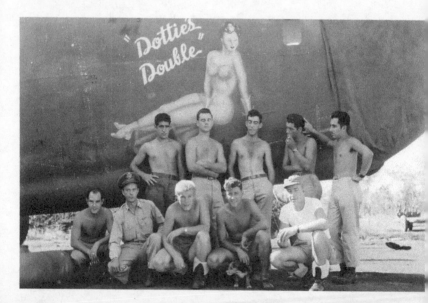

ABOVE: Flying from Fenton, south of Darwin, a US 530th Squadron B-24 attacks Japanese positions at Fak Fak, northwest New Guinea, 1944. A bomb explosion can clearly be seen in the water. (Picture courtesy of Ed Crabtree)

BELOW: A remarkable reconnaissance shot of a Japanese anti-aircraft battery on Halmahera Island, west of New Guinea, 1944. (Picture courtesy of Ed Crabtree)

ABOVE: George Clissold (left) with some delighted local Dutch children after their liberation, 1944. (Picture courtesy of George Clissold)

BELOW: 245 Squadron RAF Typhoons – one of them George Clissold's – line up at Volkel, Holland, to take off for an attack on German armour, 1944. (Picture courtesy of George Clissold)

ABOVE LEFT: George Clissold stands beside his 245 Squadron rocket-firing Hawker Typhoon. Volkel, late 1944. (Picture courtesy of George Clissold)

ABOVE RIGHT: An amazing image of a Japanese Nakajima 'Tabby' transport aircraft, shot down over New Guinea by B-24 gunners of Dick Dakeyne's 319 Squadron, USAAF. (Picture courtesy of Keith Webb)

BELOW: A Japanese destroyer under attack by RAAF Beauforts near Bougainville, 1943. (Picture courtesy of James Boddington)

ABOVE: 51 Squadron Halifax pilot Laurie Larmer's route map to the Frisian island of Wangerooge, his final trip, flown on Anzac Day, 1945. Flak took out one of his engines, and he was lucky to make it home to their base in Yorkshire. (Picture courtesy of Laurie Larmer)

BELOW: Relief on their faces, 82 Squadron observer Stan Pascoe (left) and his pilot Dennis Gibbs make it home to Bodney after the famous Cologne power station trip, August 12, 1941. Twelve other Blenheims failed to do so. (Picture courtesy of Stan Pascoe)

Spitfire pilot Sid Handsaker, in a newly-defeated Germany, 1945. Seeing the plight of the civilian population changed his attitude to war forever. (Picture courtesy of Sid Handsaker)

LEFT: 86 Squadron Coastal Command B-24 pilot Cyril Burcher, suited-up for another anti-submarine patrol in the wild north Atlantic, 1943.
(Picture courtesy of Cyril Burcher)

BELOW: Death of a bomber. A Lancaster with its full bomb load explodes over the target, snapped by wireless operator Ray Jones with a smuggled camera, late 1944. Five parachutes were observed, three of them on fire.
(Picture courtesy of his daughter, Gwynne O'Heir)

'These officers had come out from England the week before with no desert training and no desert equipment,' Murray says, 'so I pulled out the clock and told him I could use it as a compass. He had no idea that such a thing was possible and was very impressed.' Murray was forthwith assigned the role of navigator and directed them back in the direction of – he hoped – the British lines.

After a cold night dining on water and bully beef and sleeping on the sand, the trio set off again the next day. 'At about half past ten, through the shimmer of a mirage we saw a line of tents.' Judging by his calculations, Murray assumed them to be British, but in the moving war of the desert, which at that time was not going well for his own side, things could change rapidly. An RAF Lysander then touched down in front of them, assuaging their fears. 'We'd stumbled right into the 8th Army Advanced Field Headquarters,' he says, still with a note of amazement.

The next day, Murray again hitchhiked back to his aerodrome from where he'd taken off two days previously. 'When I got back to my tent, there was nothing in it,' he says. Having last been seen spiralling helplessly towards the ground, he'd been assumed to have 'gone for a Burton's' (slang for being killed in action) and was posted 'missing believed killed'. Thus, in accordance with fighter-pilot tradition, his paltry personal effects had been divided among his remaining comrades. 'I had to go around with a revolver and get it all back,' he says. 'Their attitude was when you're dead, you're supposed to stay dead! Well, I wasn't prepared to stay dead.'

Despite his unexpected reappearance, Murray's time with 250 Squadron was not to last – a falling-out with the CO after colliding with his boss's aircraft in a landing accident in the middle of a dust storm saw him, probably unfairly, transferred away. But his flying and his war were far from over. After a year or so being 'a bit of a dogsbody', flying training and meteorological exercises, Murray bumped into one of his old flight commanders in a nightclub in Alexandria who happened to be about to take over a Spitfire squadron. 'I'd always wanted to fly a Spitfire and I asked how I applied.'

'You just have,' said his friend. 'And I'd love to have you.'

So it was another RAF squadron, 80, Murray now joined and with whom he remained for the rest of the war. In Italy, then later over Germany, he flew armed reconnaissance patrols, attacking trains, road transport and V-2 rocket sites as the German Reich disintegrated. From the Spitfire, he graduated to the mighty Hawker Tempest, a truly formidable aircraft for which superlatives abound, one of the greatest piston-engine fighter aircraft ever built.

Murray's was a long and wide-ranging war. 'In five years I had fifty-three addresses in ten different countries and flew fifteen different types of aircraft.' At the end of it, however, he was nowhere near Europe. Having begun so early, he had been given a passage home, turning down a job at Hawker as a test pilot. Murray was ready to come back to the family farm. On the ship the captain announced, 'The war is over. We have permission to splice the mainbrace!'

'We got a tot of whisky,' says Murray, 'but realised there were a lot of teetotallers on board, so we got their ration too!'

His treatment on his return, however, somewhat soured his taste for the air force. 'The old permanents who hadn't flown thought the real war had been fought back here in the Pacific, and let us know it,' he says. 'I told people I'd been hearing about the war here, but I didn't really know much about it. It hadn't started when I left and it was all over when I got back.'

I ask him if he always felt he'd get through.

'Buggered if I know. When you're young you feel invulnerable. I immersed myself in work and public affairs, joined things, got on the local council. I think that's why I didn't really have any great difficulty readjusting.'

Murray stayed on his farm for another thirty years, farming wool and beef. He tells amusing stories about using gelignite to blow up dams and trees stumps and such things. Something of the larrikin remained in him then, and still does today. Not a man prone to introspection, I sense it was his time on the land that made his transition back to normal life a relatively smooth one.

'Nobody was interested in what we did back then,' he tells me. 'It's only now that fighter pilots like me are becoming an endangered species, that people like you are interested.' He's certainly right about that.

GEORGE CLISSOLD

Role: Fighter pilot
Aircraft: Hawker Typhoon
Posting: 245 Squadron, RAF

It's the most harrowing thing I've ever been through.
It's hard to believe it happened, sometimes – but it happened.

George, from Kempsey on the northern New South Wales coast, had already had his fair share of drama before he signed up. One afternoon, age sixteen, he and a cousin decided to swim across the local Macleay River. Upon reaching the far bank, George suddenly noticed he was alone. Dashing back, he found his cousin, unconscious and 'quite blue', entangled in the weeds on the edge of the riverbank just below the water. He hauled him to safety, quickly raised the alarm with a local farmer, and the boy was tended by an ambulance but remained in a coma for two or three days. 'There was some talk of awarding me a bravery award,' he says, 'but nothing came of it. News didn't travel very far in country towns in those days.'

When war came, George, with characteristic civic-mindedness, didn't want to join the air force at all. It was in the ranks of the New South Wales Mounted Police that he saw his future. 'I'd studied typing and accountancy and shorthand in order to join them,' he says, 'but it turned out I wasn't heavy enough!' The Mounties back then, it seems, needed men with brawn as well as brain.

But if the Mounties were out, the clean-cut image of the air force seemed to be the next best thing for a boy growing up in a strict teetotal family in 1942. So, a few days after turning eighteen, George put his name down at an RAAF recruiting office in Woolloomooloo in Sydney. 'My father was actually a senior Rechabite,' he tells me. George was, for a while, a 'junior Rechabite' himself, not touching a drop until he was overseas living the life of a fighter pilot. 'At which point,' he says, 'well, let's just say I lost the ability to be a non-drinker.'

George doesn't claim to have found flying easy, but was nevertheless selected for pilot training, and earned his wings at No. 5 Service Flying Training School at Uranquinty, near Wagga Wagga, in October 1942. His unusually long sea passage took him through the Panama Canal to Liverpool. Having survived the journey living mainly on cheese on toast with Worcestershire sauce, his first priority was to make a beeline for the nearest decent restaurant. Choosing the unfamiliar-sounding 'Welsh rarebit' from the menu, George has never quite lived down the dismay of being handed, yet again, cheese on toast. 'I was expecting a nice big piece of rabbit,' he says.

After a long period spent being paid to do little more

than go on leave and tow the occasional drogue in a Lysander, George was finally sent to the first of many Operational Training Units around the country. Learning to fly Spitfires and Hurricanes and entertaining the local girls, he was having the time of his life. The war, however, was getting closer.

'We started training on low-level flying,' he tells me. 'And low means *low*.' When training around the Salisbury area, George was instructed to fly no higher than the top of the spire of Salisbury Cathedral. 'You can imagine,' he tells me, 'we were flying all over these places where the girls of the Land Army were working. People would scatter, horses would bolt, things like that.'

While performing aerodrome circuits in Leicester one morning, he'd heard that the D-Day invasion armada had set sail, and decided, completely against the rules, to break away and go and take a look over the English Channel. 'The sea was completely white with the wakes of thousands and thousands of ships,' he says. 'It's a sight I'll never forget.' Finally, in October 1944, after what he considers the 'curse' of excessive training, George was taken in an Avro Anson to Brussels, then to a recently reclaimed German airfield called Volkel, near the Philips factory close to Eindhoven, Holland, to join the fully operational No. 245 Squadron, 11 Group, RAF. Here, he would be flying the formidable Hawker Typhoon ground-attack fighter. After a surfeit of training, George was finally, suddenly, in the war.

Glancing at his logbook, I can see George's operational tour began with extraordinary intensity. No. 245 had been attached to the 2nd Tactical Air Force (2TAF) since the beginning of the previous year, and was moved onto the Continent to begin army cooperation sorties on 27 June, just three weeks after D-Day. Its losses, as in all the Typhoon squadrons during the Battle of Normandy, were heavy. Six pilots had been killed in August alone. By the time George began flying with them in October, they were already a battle-hardened mob, flying daily sorties of thirty to forty minutes in duration, and usually several in a day.

'We'd attack everything,' George tells me. 'Rocket launching sites, trains, tanks, factories, railway stations. One day we were told there was a German fuel train crossing just south of the Zuiderzee – it was quite a formidable target.' The squadron found their train, a line of rolling stock laden with both fuel and oil, interspersed with protective gun and flak wagons. 'We went in as low as we could and clobbered it,' he says. The fire was so enormous that the smoke was still visible on the ground well after the 245 pilots had landed back at their base at Volkel, over 40 miles away. 'A few hours later in the mess, we were all thrilled to hear the BBC broadcast announcing the attack,' says George. 'It was a lesson in how fast information can travel.'

George found the mighty Typhoon, with its gargantuan Sabre engine, a 'wonderful, sturdy' aeroplane to fly, although at times unforgiving. Having been told never to get it into a spin – as it was nearly impossible to recover – he found himself one day as the number two to his flight commander on a reconnaissance trip. 'We were gaining height and flying up through cloud,' he says. 'I think I was too close to his wingtip because he stalled, went into a spin, and I followed.' The next seconds of George's life are something of a blur, and he says he still doesn't know how, but he managed to regain control of the aircraft and land, where the ground crew said he was 'as white as a ghost.

I climbed down from the cockpit and was immediately sick on the ground.'

Earlier trials of the Typhoon had resulted in serious structural failures, such as tails falling off in dives, and a recurring issue of exhaust fumes leaking into the cockpit (hence Typhoon pilots would usually always be on oxygen, even at low levels), but by the time George began operating, the Typhoon had been refined into a robust ground-attack aircraft, particularly when married with the weapon for which it would become famous, and which, in a way, marked the air war in Normandy, the rocket-fired projectile.

'From the time you start going down for an attack,' George tells me, 'you fire your 20-millimetre cannons on your wings because they're shooting back up at you. Then when you're close enough, you fire off your rockets via a switch on the wheel. You can select to fire all eight at once, but really you never let more than two go at a time.' The rocket was the most elementary of weapons, a simple 60-pound warhead attached to a pipe filled with cordite and a fin for basic stabilisation. They could not be steered, so needed to be aimed with the entire aircraft, lined up against a small illuminated target ring in the pilot's windshield, and fired off. 'When they left the aircraft, it was with a *whoosh*,' says George. A terrible trap, particularly for new pilots, he tells me, was not pulling away fast enough and being caught by your own explosion. 'I'm shuddering myself when I think of these things, but I've seen it with my own eyes,' he says. George tells me the pilots talked about it constantly on the base, impressing upon everyone the need to fire off the rockets and bank away quickly. 'The idea was to let them go at about 1500 feet, and then get away,' he says, 'but still some of them made the mistake of following the rockets in. I've seen so many of my mates following too closely and blowing themselves up.'

One clear afternoon in early 1945, George was part of a flight of six flying at around 400 miles per hour, when from behind, an aircraft unlike anything he'd ever seen flashed by, leaving them stunned in its wake. 'This thing went by close,' he says, 'it just shot past us with a *pwisshh*!' It was his first sight of the world's first proper jet aircraft, the Messerschmitt Me 262. 'I think it was on a reconnaissance trip because it didn't fire at us,' he says. 'All us pilots agreed that if it'd been armed, we could have all been shot down. That's when I realised how far behind the Germans we were.'

After an idyllic-sounding ten days' leave, where George was flown to Lyon, taken by glass-roofed bus to Chamonix in the French Alps, put up in a five-star hotel and given skiing lessons – all on the RAF's tab – it was time to return to the war, and by far the most dramatic chapter of his flying career.

The day of 24 March 1945 was a momentous one in Western Europe. After four and a half years of war, the Allied armies were on the doorstep of Germany itself. All that remained to begin the endgame was to cross the natural barrier of the River Rhine and plunge into the heart of the Reich. Operation Varsity was the largest one-day airborne operation in history, with 15 000 paratroopers and thousands of aircraft involved in getting them across the wide river. It was launched in conjunction with the amphibious Operation Plunder. This so excited Churchill that he commandeered a river launch and sailed across, spending half an hour on the German side of the river before his nervous minders insisted he return. It was also the day George Clissold got himself shot down.

'I'd been flying at low level attacking half-tracks and tanks on the far side of the river,' he says. 'But instead of me shooting them down, they shot me!' He believes it was anti-aircraft fire, but concedes it could even have been small arms. All George knew was a jolt before his engine started running rough, then sudden pain, then smoke and fire beginning to pour into the cockpit. The voice of Cookie, a South African pilot flying alongside, could be perceived, shouting in his ears over the radio telephone, 'Cliss! Get out, Cliss! Get out, get out!'

The art of bailing out of an aircraft might appear simple enough – open the door or hood and simply jump. But in an aircraft such as the Typhoon, it was a more complicated procedure. 'We were told that so many blokes had broken their back by hitting the tailplane,' says George, 'so we were trained to do something else.' Instead of risking it with the Typhoon's large tail, George and his fellow pilots were told to trim the aircraft into a steep dive ('like *that*', he says to me, holding his hand at an angle to explain), then to jettison the hood, throwing it clear with a solid punch. 'Then we had to disconnect everything, release the harness, pull back on the stick then quickly push it forward,' he says. 'It doesn't sound like it would work, but it did!' From an altitude of 3000 feet, as if bucked from a horse, George was suddenly thrown up, head over heels and clear of the tail and the prop of his now flaming Typhoon. 'And that's how I got out of my plane,' he tells me with a shake of the head.

Being George's first ever jump, he fumbled momentarily for the ripcord, but the sound of the parachute opening above him, he says, was 'one of the most beautiful feelings of my life'. His relief was short-lived, however, as he realised he was being fired upon from the ground. 'They shot at me all the way down,' he says. Here, he pauses a moment. 'You know it's funny, people have often said to me, "Isn't it terrible that people would shoot you while you're in a parachute?" Well, why is it so bloody terrible? Five minutes before, I was shooting at them!'

George had come down hard, just inside the German border, but his face was only slightly burned from the cockpit fire. His landing was rough, due mainly to inexperience, and he'd strained both knees, barely being able to make it to a nearby ditch. Not that escape was much of an option, as moments later, a half-dozen German soldiers had gathered around him, pointing weapons.

Being familiar with the terrible stories of airmen who had bailed out over German cities and been lynched, kicked to death, or at the very least roughed up by furious civilians, I fully expected George's treatment to be similar. However, instead of continuing the shooting practice they'd begun on his descent, the only thing the soldiers appeared to be interested in was George's sidearm. 'It really is the funniest thing under the sun,' he says, laughing. 'But all these soldiers wanted to do was take out my Webley & Scott .38 service revolver and see what they could hit with it!' As George sat on the ground, rubbing his knees, his captors seemed content to amuse themselves with a little target practice. 'They couldn't hit a post,' he says. 'The Webley had a notorious kick. They weren't used to it. It was the queerest thing.'

George was taken to the nearby town of Ringenberg, just 7 miles from the Rhine, and due to fall any day to the advancing British. Here he was interrogated, his burns examined but not treated, and the next day taken to the town's railway station where he joined a large group of fellow POWs. Looking at the large open wagons in front of them, all of them reasoned, glumly, that they were heading east.

As the shuffling line of men climbed aboard the wagon in front of him, George noticed a series of painted symbols on the outside: '8 horses or 50 men', it said, George taking it to refer to the capacity of the wagon. It was an odd thing to notice, he admits, but it made him pause before clambering up. There's a lot more than fifty men in there, he thought to himself and slowed to let it fill ahead of him, with a mind perhaps of finding himself a less crowded wagon. Then a familiar sound drew his attention to the sky.

'I looked up into the air and saw six Typhoons circling at about 5000 feet,' he says. A cold feeling came over him. In a dreadful flash of prescience, George saw exactly what was about to happen. 'It was exactly what I'd been doing these previous weeks,' he says. 'I knew those pilots were watching us, thinking we were embarking German soldiers, and were preparing to attack.' George glanced around and, without regard for the consequences, broke away from the group and bolted under an adjacent platform. Hardly had the guard had time to unsling his rifle to challenge him when, as George says, 'All hell broke loose.' He was on the receiving end of a Typhoon attack.

'They came in and strafed with cannon and rockets,' he says. In seconds, the sounds of explosions, tearing of wood and screams turned the railway platform into a place of carnage. 'It's one of the most sickening things I've ever had to see,' he says. When he emerged, bodies, and bits of bodies, were everywhere, and the train was in pieces. 'It seemed I was about the only person left alive in the whole station,' he says.

George's vivid memory is, understandably, a little vague as

to what exactly happened next. It seems that after the attack, he and the survivors were marched away from the station, but put on another train and taken several hundred miles to Stalag 357 at Fallingbostel, near Hanover. But with Germany collapsing around him, he would not be there long.

'We were only there ten days,' he says, 'and then we were told we were going to be marched to the centre of Germany.' This forced mass exodus, ordered by Hitler, of Allied POWs from their camps in eastern Germany to places further west, had begun the previous July. Now, as the most severe European winter in half a century took hold, it continued. Already under-nourished, dysentery- and lice-ridden, thousands would perish from hypothermia or be shot by their guards attempting to escape. It remains one of the ugliest and least known chapters of the war in the west.

George, in a party of several hundred POWs, had been on the road for a week, having befriended a couple of Australian soldiers who had been prisoners since the fall of Crete in 1941 and who at least knew how to scrounge off the land. But his knees, which he had hurt in the jump, were agonising, and during one 'comfort stop' along the road, he and an Englishman decided to chance it. 'I went behind a tree and stayed there,' he says. Amazingly, the column moved on without them.

Hiding out in the Black Forest for a few days, they awoke under their bed of fir needles one morning to the sight of two men standing over them, having spotted their protruding boots! George's dismay at being caught quickly brightened as the men turned out to be Polish farm labourers, who fed them and secreted them in an attic until the booming guns of the advancing Allies came close enough for one of them to venture out and wave down a British tank. 'We were picked up, interrogated and given so much cake and rich food that we were sick,' he says.

Finding his way back to his squadron a month or so after being shot down, George found he was no longer permitted to fly combat missions, as the risk of him being caught again was too great. 'They let me fly the little Auster instead,' he says. Having flown spectacular ground-attack missions in the mighty Typhoon, George ended the war running errands for his CO in a light aeroplane. He didn't complain.

George was in London on VE Day, and in August 1945 was back in Sydney. The evening of VP Day, he met his girl, who he'd kept in touch with all through his tour ('I still have some of her letters,' he says), under the town hall clock, and married her a couple of days before Christmas.

'No-one thought we were going to come out of the war on our squadron,' he says. 'No-one. I didn't think for a second I was going to make it. You'd do the most stupid bloody things.' Both during the war and after it, George counts himself lucky. His marriage and his discovery of carpentry, of which he made a life-long profession, helped him enormously, he says. 'Everything was upside down towards the end of the war,' he says. 'I don't even know what constituted a tour for us, no-one seemed to.' Like many, he simply didn't talk about it, to anyone, for years, and does me the honour of telling me that our afternoon meeting is the first time he's spoken about his wartime ordeal to anyone in any detail. 'You'd tell your kids some things but they didn't really understand,' he says. 'Talking to you like this – it's actually churned my guts up a bit.'

Back in his home town of Kempsey, George was, for a while, destined to be enshrined by having a street named in his honour. 'Then when they found I'd been a prisoner and was still alive, they took my name off the list!' he says.

George has compiled a loose-leaf folder with some fragments of his story, as well as some of the background information of the events he witnessed. I begin to copy some of it by taking phone pictures, but he insists I take it away with me to read properly. 'No, take it, you must take it,' he says. 'It's the most harrowing thing I've ever been through,' he adds as we part, 'and hard to believe it happened, sometimes – but it happened.'

CYRIL BURCHER

Role: Pilot
Aircraft: Consolidated B-24 Liberator
Posting: 86 Squadron, RAF

It's a terrible thing, but that's what happens in war,
you kill people.

Ivanhoe, New South Wales, is a long way from the Atlantic. Though to be fair, Ivanhoe is a long way from anywhere. 'Most people haven't heard of it,' Cyril Burcher tells me of the town where he was born, and it's not hard to understand why once you try to find it on the map. Get yourself to Orange, head west to Parkes, keep on going past Condobolin and, eventually, you'll find Ivanhoe, teetering on the edge of the outback. There wasn't much there in Cyril's day, nor is there now, save for a railway line that goes over to Broken Hill, and a lot of room to grow sheep. Cyril's forebears had been just about the first white people to arrive on these flat western plains, and by the time he came along, their station, poetically named 'Irish Lords', had grown to a 250 000-acre expanse of very little indeed. Fitting then, that, as a pilot with the RAF's Coastal Command, Cyril's job would be to patrol wide open space of a different sort, the endless slate-grey waters of the North Atlantic, hunting German U-boats.

A little older than most of his fellow trainees, Cyril was twenty by the time war started in 1939, but had harboured a notion that he wanted to be a pilot ever since taking a joyride with Charles Kingsford Smith when he dropped in on Bega, all for the princely sum of ten shillings. So in 1941 Cyril left his steady job at the Commonwealth Bank and joined up.

Cyril was selected for pilot training, found it almost embarrassingly easy, and being assessed 'average', was granted his wish and presented with his wings in Canada after learning to fly the twin-engine Cessna Crane, an aeroplane so diabolically awful, it was said that if you could fly a Crane, you could fly anything. His only disappointment – and at the time it was a major one – was being selected for multi-engine aircraft rather than the nimble Spitfires and Hurricanes, which virtually every brash young man in blue at that time longed to fly. 'They chose us by age, you see,' says Cyril, who was by that stage twenty-four. 'They reckoned the nineteen- and twenty-year-olds made the better fighter pilots, and they were right too.'

In England, Cyril came to grips with the far more friendly Airspeed Oxford at No. 11 Advanced Flying Unit at Shawbury in Shropshire before, in the middle of 1942, progressing to Hudsons, then moving to Thorney Island near Portsmouth. Here, he would begin to fly not the black-hued Lancasters of

Bomber Command but American-built B-24 Liberators, with their all-white undersides, designed to merge with the clouds and mists and squalls of the Atlantic. For five years, this vast ocean stage became the scene of the longest battle of the Second World War, the hunting ground of Germany's U-boat fleet, and their nemeses, the pilots and aircraft of RAF Coastal Command.

Liberators served in almost every theatre of the war, including, from mid-1941, the North Atlantic, where the RAF saw their potential in operating against Germany's crippling submarine fleet. No. 86 Squadron took delivery of their Liberators in February 1943, just in time, as it happened, to be joined also by Cyril Burcher.

'They were a lovely, easy aeroplane to fly,' he says of the famous and versatile B-24, itself a testament to the might of American wartime industry.

The system for protecting the convoys from the air during the long Battle of the Atlantic was a three-part affair. The shorter-range Hudsons patrolled the first five hundred miles out from England, at which point the Sunderland flying boats took over for the next five hundred. Beyond this, at ranges of a thousand miles and more, deep into the heart of the Atlantic, it was the turn of the VLR – very long range – Liberators, flown by men like Cyril. These aircraft had been especially adapted for distance by having one of their two bomb bays refitted to carry extra fuel, making take-off particularly hazardous. Several crews were lost on Cyril's squadron alone when aircraft simply failed to get airborne.

'We'd fly five or six hours out to the convoy,' he says, 'another five or six flying around it, then five or six more back to base.' This crucial development in the war at sea meant the so-called mid-Atlantic gap, or 'killing zone' as many of the weary merchant seamen dubbed it, was, for the first time, within range of air power. 'At last we could cover it,' Cyril tells me, 'and with our long-range tanks, we'd cover it for up to four or five hours.'

Flying out of airfields in Northern Ireland as close as possible to Britain's Western Approaches sea lanes, Cyril's days were long, with flight times lasting up to eighteen hours at a stretch. His expanded crew sounds like a fair representation of the Empire's wartime air effort. 'I had a New Zealander second pilot, an Australian observer,' he tells me, 'English air gunners and a Canadian wireless operator.' But the spotting was largely the responsibility of the two pilots, who at the standard patrolling height of 3000 feet had superb visibility courtesy of the Liberator's high wing design.

From the beginning of 1943, Cyril's primary job would be convoy escorts, flying to a pre-determined spot in the middle of the ocean, where, hopefully, beneath him he would spot the weather-battered masts and hulls of ships of all sizes, heading east towards the United Kingdom, laden with the essentials to enable a country with few resources of its own to make war: fuel, food, matériel, sulphur, steel, men. 'Our job was to meet them and fly around the convoy and attack U-boats,' he says simply of his role in the great drama. 'There were quite a few of them at that stage of the Battle of the Atlantic.'

It's a fact that many airmen who served with Coastal Command hunting U-boats went the entire war without so much as glimpsing a single one, but in that there is no shame. The ocean is after all very big, and a submarine very small, and in any case, it was figured the next best thing to finding and sinking a U-boat, which was considered extremely difficult, was to keep them submerged as much as possible, thereby cutting their speed dramatically and forcing them to expend far more fuel. Simply the presence of Coastal Command's aircraft in the skies over the Atlantic was considered a major factor in eventually winning the battle. Cyril's tour, however, turned out to be considerably more dramatic than that, beginning with his very first operation, in February 1943.

'We went out to do an anti-submarine patrol in the Bay of Biscay, looking for them coming out of France and heading for the Atlantic Ocean,' he tells me. 'Cloud cover was down to 100 feet. So, for nine hours, that was the height I had to stay at. It was a very trying experience, and even if we'd spotted a U-boat, we couldn't have turned around to attack it.' As the dusk set in at the end of this exhausting ordeal, Cyril received a wireless communication to land back at Thorney Island near Portsmouth as their normal base was clouded in. The approach and landing were uneventful, but as they were taxiing, Cyril noticed the squadron CO apparently waiting for them at the end of the runway. Thinking he was simply there to greet them, he was taken aback when he was told by the agitated man, 'You and your crew are the luckiest people to be alive. Do you know what you just did?'

Cyril looked perplexed.

'You've just flown straight through the balloon barrage of Portsmouth!'

The site, close to the primary base of the Royal Navy, was, understandably, one of the most heavily defended places in Britain, complete with masses of anti-aircraft guns and a forest of barrage balloons, each tethered by a steel cable designed to slice off the wings of any low-flying aircraft. 'In a Liberator, well, you can imagine the size of it,' he says, still bewildered as to how he blithely managed to avoid catastrophe. But avoiding catastrophe became something of a speciality during Cyril's highly eventful tour, and he has his own theory as to why.

As a child, Cyril was told by his grandmother that a guardian angel was watching over him, and after hearing the story of his war, full of near-misses that many times should have spelled his demise, I'm tempted to concur. Fittingly, Cyril has given the title *On the Wings of an Angel* to his own modestly small volume of the story of his life and wartime experiences, which I have used as a source here.

Over the course of thirty-four operations, Cyril not only sighted but attacked nearly a dozen U-boats, sank at least three, survived storms, lightning strikes and deadly wing 'icings-up', and had several encounters with the great liner turned wartime troopship *Queen Mary*, possibly even, on one occasion, preventing the famous vessel's sinking. In the process, he earned for himself the admiration of his crew and squadron, and a well-deserved Distinguished Flying Cross. Inevitably though, his most formidable enemy was the weather. It seems there was barely a trip in which Cyril did not encounter rain, sleet, monstrous seas and the gale-force winds of the North Atlantic. Often, his crew were sick to the point of incapacitation, but he always knew that no matter how bad it was for them in the sky, it was always worse for the men on the ships of the convoys below.

'I remember going out to a rendezvous to escort the *Queen Mary*,' he tells me. 'They were sending me Aldis lamp messages in Morse code from the bridge, but we couldn't read them because the waves were actually breaking *over* the bridge.' (To give some perspective, the 1000-foot-long *Queen Mary* displaces nearly 82 000 tons and sits 180 feet above the waterline.) 'Eventually, they signalled me to patrol about 10 miles ahead of her, but I was more concerned with the ship as she was leaning over about 50 degrees. I thought she was going to capsize!'

On another trip in similarly filthy weather, the wireless operator wound out the 100-foot-long trailing aerial from its hole in the fuselage to get a radio 'fix' on their position. 'All of a sudden, there was a very loud explosion,' says Cyril. 'It knocked out the entire crew, including myself.' Cyril estimates that everyone inside the aircraft was out cold for up to two minutes. 'When I came to, I was amazed we were still flying,' he says. The aircraft, however, seemed to be locked into a large right-hand circle, and Cyril sent his engineer to investigate.

'Skipper, there's a huge hole in the side of the aircraft, I think we've been hit by lightning!'

His deduction was correct. The trailing aerial, it seemed, had served to discharge the aircraft's current from one cloud to another and the Liberator was hit by a massive bolt of self-generated lightning. The hole created was now causing a lopsided drag on the fuselage, forcing the aeroplane to fly in a continuous loop. To counter this, the second pilot had to apply continual full left rudder to stop the swing. 'But worst of all,' says Cyril, 'we lost our heating, and with over a thousand miles still to go!'

Even the regular test flights could be hazardous. One day Cyril opened up the throttles to take off when, 'Halfway down the runway, I looked down at my instruments and I didn't have any!' he says. 'They were all blank.' Deciding to abort, he hit the brakes, which worked momentarily then failed. With a jolt, Cyril ran off the end of the runway, the aircraft going over on one wing, luckily causing only minor damage. He was, it seems, the victim of two pieces of misfortune, neither of his making. First, the ground crew had neglected to remove the canvas pitot-head cover, blanking out his instruments, and second, a motor used to boost brake pressure, which was only supposed to be switched off once the aircraft was in flight, had been disengaged way too early. 'It was the crew's fault,' he says, 'but I didn't let on, otherwise they would have gotten into trouble.'

A month into his tour, on 17 March 1943, after having flown 900 miles through huge seas and rain squalls to meet a convoy whose escorts were under attack from a wolf pack, Cyril attacked his first U-boat. Through extensive research, he has been able to identify nearly all those he attacked, and all those he sunk. He first encountered *U-439*, captained by one Oberleutnant zur See Helmut von Tippelskirch, on his first command. 'I remember spotting the wake first,' says Cyril. Diving steeply to attack as the boat was submerging, he found his speed was far greater than it had been in practice bombing and he overshot, dropping four depth charges into the swirl of water in front of the boat. It was enough, however, to subdue it, and *U-439* took no part in the attacks on that particular convoy. (Just a few weeks later, in May, Tippelskirch and all but nine of his crew would meet their demise, bizarrely, in a collision with another U-boat off the coast of Spain.)

On 6 April there occurred one of the most dramatic moments of Cyril's tour, when at midnight they set out from their base at Aldergrove, again in appalling weather, to meet a convoy south-west of Iceland. Around dawn, they found the group of ships as planned, but also the 220-foot-long Type-VII U-boat *U-632*, running on the surface. 'That was unusual,' says Cyril. 'I think he thought he was beyond the range of air patrols and was carrying out some maintenance.' Dropping height to attack from cloud cover, Cyril followed the wake of the sleek grey vessel and clearly remembers seeing the German crew on the deck. 'There were about seven of them,' he recalls, 'all running around trying to man the heavy guns fore and aft. I remember one of them pointing directly at me.'

Seared in his memory also is the image of a man with a beard in an officer's cap. 'It was obviously the captain,' he says. 'I distinctly remember him shaking his fist at me as a group of them disappeared down the conning tower to dive.' At just 30 feet, Cyril hit a button on his control column and straddled the U-boat with four depth charges. 'I could see the swirl of the conning tower just as I laid my depth charges right on it,' he says. Quickly circling, he laid another four across the boat, and watched it shudder in the water as he banked away. 'We weren't sure at the time if we'd sunk it, because the weather was so bad,' he says. Later, however, it was confirmed as a kill: *U-632* was lost with all forty-eight hands. The image of the German captain shaking his fist defiantly in the final moments of his life, would, sixty years later, be recalled by Cyril for reasons he could never have imagined at the time.

While some of his fellow pilots were not seeing a single U-boat on their patrols, Cyril was finding them – and attacking them – on a regular basis. He puts it down to luck, and the exceptional eyesight of both himself and his crew. On one occasion, again near Iceland on an uncharacteristically perfect day, they had climbed to 8000 feet when Jack, Cyril's second pilot, called out, 'I think there's a U-boat down there at periscope depth.'

'Don't be silly,' replied Cyril, convinced that nothing so small could be spotted at such a height. Jack, however, insisted, so Cyril gave him the benefit of the doubt and descended. Nothing was seen on or under the water, but Cyril knew that a flotilla of four destroyers was in the area, and he'd been told to call them in if anything was spotted. Half an hour after reporting the possible sighting, they arrived and immediately picked up a submarine contact on their asdic (sonar). Circling above, Cyril watched, fascinated, to see how the little ships hunted in much the same 'pack' pattern as the U-boats themselves, descending on the position from all points of the compass, then attacking with a fury of depth charges. For their efforts, Cyril and his crew were credited with 'half a kill'.

At 0200 hours on 12 April 1943, Cyril's crew took off in Liberator *H for Harry* for a trip they were convinced was going to be a quiet one, once again escorting the *Queen Mary* part-way across the Atlantic as it headed back to America, carrying several thousand wounded and repatriated US servicemen. 'Nothing ever happened when our squadron escorted the *Queen Mary*,' he tells me, and it was considered a milk run. This was due to the great ship's extraordinary speed, up to 35 knots – the rate of an average speedboat – whereas the U-boats, even on the surface, could manage no more than 20. 'The only way they could attack a ship as fast as the *Queen Mary* was if they happened to be directly in front of it,' he says.

In another sense, however, the trip was anything but usual, as they had been selected to carry a new and highly secret weapon, a 600-pound magnetic homing torpedo, together with its American operator who was to evaluate it in a real attack. To accommodate this hush-hush piece of hardware, they had dispensed with all but two of their usual complement of ten depth charges to make room in the bomb bay. But there was a caveat: 'We were expressly forbidden to deploy it against a U-boat on the surface,' Cyril tells me, 'just in case the attack wasn't successful and they reported its details back to their base.' Being armed, however, with just two depth charges was 'next to useless', he says. 'You needed at least four.'

After many hours flying the 1500 miles to their designated rendezvous point in the Atlantic, Cyril spotted a large U-boat running on the surface. It was a new one, another type VII, and as Cyril was to discover, it was in no mood to run and hide. 'We attacked hoping to release our two depth charges before it submerged,' he says. 'To my surprise, it remained on the surface and starting firing at us.' Armed with four 20-millimetre Oerlikon cannons mounted on the conning tower, plus a Bofors and various other machine guns on the deck, the boat put up a tremendous fire, which shocked Cyril and his crew. 'You could see the tracer bullets coming up and shells bursting all around us,' he says. 'It was pretty scary.' He dropped his only two depth charges, which exploded close to the boat, causing it to roll, shudder and even be momentarily tossed up out of the water, but it remained unharmed.

In the face of fierce protests from his crew, Cyril then decided to attack it again. 'They weren't happy and we only really had a single machine gun, which was pretty useless,' he says. Nevertheless, in Cyril went for a second pass. The German fire this time was even more intense. 'They were more accurate with lots more flak. It's a miracle we weren't shot down.'

With his depth charges gone and another attack seeming pointless, Cyril's mind turned to the secret weapon in the bomb bay, which he was forbidden to use while the U-boat was on the surface. 'I decided to try and trick him into thinking I'd broken off the attack and to make him dive,' he says. Banking away into a nearby rain squall, he planned to make a quick 180-degree turn and catch the German in the act of diving, at which point he would deploy the weapon.

Emerging from the other side of the squall, however, Cyril got 'the shock of my life' when the vast grey camouflaged bulk of the *Queen Mary* appeared directly below him. 'There she was, heading straight towards the U-boat, and just a few miles away, the U-boat was heading straight towards it.' Immediately, he ordered his navigator to send a visual Aldis lamp signal to the ship's bridge, 'U-boat on surface six miles directly ahead'. Barely had the message finished sending when he witnessed 'one of the greatest sights of my life', as all 80 000 tons of the great *Queen Mary*, perhaps the most famous ship afloat, executed a sharp 90-degree turn to the right. 'That image will stay with me forever,' he says.

Cyril was never given the chance to use the torpedo. Despite returning to the area where he'd last seen the German submarine, it was now nowhere to be found. They returned to the *Queen Mary* and continued escorting it for another six hours before heading back to Ireland, perhaps just having saved it from a torpedo attack. Certainly somebody high up thought so, as two days later, Cyril was granted an immediate Distinguished Flying Cross.

Years later, Cyril had the chance to meet the man who was the captain of the *Queen Mary* that day, Sir James Bisset, at a lunch in Sydney. Questions were asked and answered, anecdotes exchanged and Sir James was invited to sign Cyril's logbook. 'Thanks and good luck,' was the sum of his somewhat perfunctory gratitude.

Cyril's luck held through all manner of circumstances. One day in May 1943, towards the end of an escort, he sighted and attacked yet another German submarine, dropping a stick of depth charges along its wake as it dived. It escaped, though in all likelihood not undamaged. Cyril was unable to wait and confirm this, however, as his fuel was low and his relief aircraft had arrived. 'I told the relieving pilot of the position where we'd attacked it and turned for home,' he says. Back at Aldergrove, Cyril enquired if the relief aircraft had discovered the German vessel, only to be told that it had indeed found it, and attacked it on the surface but in the process was shot down into the sea. The entire crew was lost. Cyril was shocked. 'It could so easily have been us,' he says.

Not surprisingly, Cyril held his squadron's record for the greatest number of German U-boats spotted and attacked, and remains vague about his final tally. 'We saw thirteen, attacked twelve and as far as I know, I sunk three,' he says. The weather, however, probably prevented that being even higher. 'We attacked a lot of them but usually we didn't know the results because of the weather conditions,' he tells me. 'The waves were so big they just blotted out any evidence of damage.' A sense of the monstrous conditions in which he was operating can be gained from some of the operational photographs he managed to take of his attacks at sea. Thunderous skies, violent seas and, somewhere among it, the white plume of an exploding depth charge.

Cyril's tour took him on to patrols further south to the Bay of Biscay, where his amazing knack of finding submarines, and attacking them, continued. He finished with just over a thousand hours' operational flying time and was promised a bar to his Distinguished Flying Cross, which oddly never materialised. In March 1944, he was delighted to hear that he'd been selected to ferry newly purchased B-24 Liberators from the factory in America to Australia, which meant that he'd be home far sooner than he could have anticipated. But perhaps his guardian angel was telling Cyril that, finally, enough was enough, for soon after his first ferry job was completed, he developed a duodenal ulcer, which promptly ended his flying career. But he was home, and he was safe.

His return to civilian life seems to have been relatively straightforward, save for the ulcer, which he was told had been brought on by the stress of flying, and which took three years to heal. But no nightmares, no depression and few regrets. His book, written in the same open, matter-of-fact style in which he speaks, dwells little on reflection. I ask him if he ever thinks about the dozens of young German sailors who perished at his hands. Does that not haunt him sometimes?

'But that's war, you see,' he says. 'It's a terrible thing, but that's what happens in war, you kill people.'

Sixty years later, however, one of those sailors, in a sense, did come back to haunt him. In April 2007, Cyril was surprised to receive a letter mailed from Reston, near Washington DC in the United States, from a woman he had never met. It began: 'Hello Mr Burcher, it is difficult for me to write this letter to you . . .' and continued for several paragraphs, signed at the bottom, 'Inge Molzahn'. The letter told the story of the captain of

U-boat *U-632*, Hans Karpf, lost in the Atlantic along with his entire crew, on 6 April 1943. Karpf was Inge Molzahn's father, but they never met. 'My father had left home and shipped out on March 15th from Brest. I was born a few days later, but never saw him,' she wrote. Inge had grown up in Germany and Argentina wondering about the father she never knew, and eventually began to put together the story of his life and naval career, even to the extent of tracking down the man listed as having sunk his boat, 86 Squadron's Flight Lieutenant Cyril Burcher from Australia. 'I would like to hear from you. By finding out about you and your plane it closes the chapter.' Cyril, though somewhat taken aback, was more than happy to oblige and wrote back immediately.

Inge had long pondered if her father ever knew of her existence, and after much research, tracked down a signal in the German government archives, sent by the navy to the captain of *U-632*, congratulating him on the birth of his child, 'born without a periscope', so it said.

'So at least he knew he had a daughter,' says Cyril. This remarkable exchange was only the beginning of a story which developed into a firm friendship between Cyril and Inge's family, who have now visited each other in several parts of the world and still keep in touch to this day. 'It even turned out that her father's and my birthday were the same day, 14 May,' he says, giving away, for the first time, a slight touch of emotion in his voice. 'I think that more or less created a bond between us.'

JOE BARRINGTON

Role: Pilot
Aircraft: Supermarine Spitfire
Posting: 451 Squadron, RAAF

I'd been flying every day and drinking at night.
When I got home, it all caught up with me.

Just about every young man who joined the air force in the
Second World War wanted desperately to be a Spitfire pilot,
but very few were given the chance. Joe Barrington told them
he was quite happy to be a navigator, but they made him a
Spitfire pilot anyway.

'We're a close family,' says Joe when I visit him in his
quite large and lovely home overlooking Sydney Harbour.
Then again, it needs to be large, because a few years ago, the
Barringtons did the reverse of what most of us do in farming
out our elders to nursing homes etc.: Joe's entire family decided

to all move in together. Kids, grandkids, parents, the lot. This may account for Joe's charming demeanour, but then it could be also that he hails from colourful-sounding theatrical folk. 'My father, Bernard, was on the stage,' he tells me. 'He had a famous act at the time, *Stanley and Bernard, Two Yiddish Boys and a Piano*.' I wish I'd seen the act. Joe, however, decided to follow a more sensible pursuit and at war's beginning was a nineteen-year-old studying wool-classing. He remembers the night it all started like it was yesterday.

'There was a place called Stone's Milk Bar in Coogee where people could get up and sing,' he tells me. 'I remember they rushed in with a special edition of the papers, saying that war had been declared. I remember that night particularly well.' (I'm not sure what intrigues me more, this intimate memory of the first moments of the war, or the notion of a musical milk bar.)

Joe waited till he'd finished his wool-classing course before joining up, then went onto the reserve to learn Morse code, and, eventually, to Bradfield Park for his initial training with RAAF Aircrew Training Course No. 22. 'When I got there, I thought I'd make a better navigator than a pilot, so that's what I put on the form,' he says. For some reason he's never been able to explain, the man seated behind the table said, 'What about a pilot? I think you'd make a good pilot,' before proceeding to cross out the word 'navigator' and write 'pilot' next to it. So, it was a pilot's job for which Joe would train at No. 4 Elementary Flying Training School at Mascot to fly Avro Ansons. 'Then the Americans arrived and kicked us all out,' he continues. With the US juggernaut demanding the whole of Mascot for themselves upon their entry into the war, Joe was relegated first to Victoria, then Mallala in South Australia. 'You never left the station,' he tells me. 'There was nowhere to go.'

After what sounds like the time of his life sailing to America, then being paid to do nothing in Boston for three months save visit jazz clubs (even on one occasion meeting Louis Armstrong) and wait for a ship, Joe eventually sailed as part of a fifty-vessel convoy on the Australian cargo vessel *Esperance Bay*. On his second night out, they were attacked by U-boats and diverted to the north of Iceland, in winter, taking a full two weeks to arrive in wartime Britain.

Soon after his arrival, Joe received another reminder that what he was on was no holiday. In May 1943, while waiting along with many other young Australian airmen to receive their postings at the RAAF's Personnel Dispatch and Receiving Centre in Bournemouth, Joe and a couple of mates decided one sunny Sunday morning to pass a couple of hours chatting on canvas deckchairs overlooking the sea in what was, before the war, one of England's most popular seaside resort towns. 'Let's have a beer before we go up to the mess for lunch,' said one of the young airmen. Joe still doesn't know why, but his reply was, 'No, I'll go straight on up. I'll see you there,' and his two friends headed off towards the Central Hotel. 'A few minutes later,' says Joe, 'there was a direct hit on that hotel and they were both killed.'

On this May morning, possibly the blackest in Bournemouth's history, twenty-six Focke-Wulf Fw 190 fighter-bombers had taken off from their bases around Caen, just a few minutes away across the Channel, and hit the town in a sudden raid which lasted barely a minute, but which killed 131 people, including the friends Joe had just been sitting with, and nine other Australian airmen. Bombs were dropped over the centre of the town, hitting hotels, garages, children's hospitals and churches, strewing bodies and body parts everywhere, and just for good measure, the fighters decided to strafe the town's Pleasure Gardens, killing more civilians, on the way home. It's been speculated that this lightning attack, Bournemouth's last for the war, was in retaliation for the Dambuster raid of a few weeks previously, but in any event, the Germans' logic was simple and brutal: kill as many Commonwealth airmen as possible on the ground before they can get into the air.

'That night,' says Joe, 'I was helping blokes pull rubble out of the hotel to find my mates, but I never did. That was my first experience of losing someone in wartime.'

Finally, the forty or so pilots in Joe's course received their postings, and with his twin-engine training, he prepared to proceed to his Operational Training Unit to fly Wellingtons. However, when the postings appeared, Joe's name was conspicuously absent, and his CO called him aside and explained why. The problem wasn't Joe's flying, it seemed, but his height. The RAF had apparently decided that it was too difficult for pilots of 'a certain stature' to hold the rudder bar of a twin-engine aeroplane flying on one motor. Joe was taken aback, but was then made an offer. 'You can have day fighters, night fighters, army cooperation, or you can return to Australia,' said his boss.

Joe didn't have to think too hard. 'Well, I've come this far, I'm not going back home now. Day fighters.'

In a short time, Joe found himself converting to single-engine Miles Masters, before being posted to an Operational Training Unit in the Middle East to train on the somewhat rickety Battle of Britain veteran Spitfire Mark Is at a spot in the sand near Cairo named Abu Sueir. In June 1944 he moved to the Australian No. 451 Squadron in Corsica. When he arrived, however, the mood was sombre. The very night before, he learned, twenty-five Junkers Ju 88s had struck with fragmentation bombs, damaging all but two of the squadron's aircraft and killing eight people, including two pilots, who had pitched tents too close to the runway under attack. It turned out Joe even knew the father of one of the pilots, Barney Sneddon. 'He had a shop around the corner from me in Clovelly,' he says. 'I used to go in there to buy cigarettes. I remember him telling me he had a son in the air force. But he was killed the night before I arrived and I never got to meet him.' The CO of the squadron at the time was considered partly responsible for the loss of life, due to his placement of the tents, and replaced.

In a matter of days, Joe's name appeared on the 'gaggle board', and he was 'on'. 'I'll always remember my first operation,' he tells me, and for good reason. Flying from their base in Poretta, Corsica, Joe was equipped with long-range drop-tanks to reach his operating area in northern Italy, and was told they would provide him with exactly one hour of fuel, at which point he was to drop them and switch onto his main tank. Flying as number two to the squadron wing commander, Joe flew north over Italy, keeping a careful eye on his watch, counting off the minutes, fifty-four . . . fifty-five . . . fifty-six . . .

'Suddenly, at fifty-seven,' he tells me, 'the motor stopped, and I'm dropping out of formation, going down with a wind-milling propeller, thinking, Am I going to get out or try and land?' At 10 000 feet, he managed to switch over to the main tank and start the engine.

When he rejoined the formation, the wing commander used his call sign. 'Where've you been, Ab-duck 2?'

'I, er, ran out of gas, sir,' was all that Joe could reply. The response was nothing but a cold silence, and Joe vowed thereafter to always give himself a five-minute buffer for switching tanks.

Joe's journey to operational flying had been a long, and at times delayed, one, but he seemed to make up for lost time, flying escort and strafing missions against the retreating Germans in Italy on a daily basis. 'I did fifty-something trips in a year and a half,' he says, and his logbook tells the story.

On one occasion his radio telephone (R/T) was set to the same frequency as the formation of American Liberators he was escorting below. After bombing, Joe saw one of the aircraft fall from the sky in flames. 'Goddamn,' said an American voice over the R/T, 'there goes my roommate.' At a designated point, Joe, with the squadron, turned and crossed the coast to head home, thinking he'd completed his trip.

'Follow me, Ab-duck 2,' came the wing commander's voice over the air, 'there are some ships in the harbour down there, we'll go and see what we can do,' and he peeled over into a dive from 10 000 feet. Following him down, Joe saw his target, a freighter laden with supplies for the Germans. 'I knew I couldn't sink them, so I selected both my cannon and machine guns and fired, just to make a mess of them,' he says. He's not sure what he hit but remembers the mast of a ship flying past, level with his head. 'That's how low I was. But I was happy. I'd fired my guns for the first time.'

And he would get to fire them a good deal more, marking the parameters of Hitler's shrinking empire as it retreated across southern Europe. Flying ground-hugging strafing missions became Joe's speciality, and at those heights, there was very little he could not see from the cockpit of his Spitfire IX. 'Any movement on the ground, I would attack,' he says. Several instances stand out in his memory, such as once spotting a truck laden with German soldiers. As he dived towards it, he noticed all on board scrambling out and taking cover in a ditch by the side of the road. 'All except one,' he tells me. 'This one man got right down beside the truck and as I came down, started firing at me. I think I blew him away because I had cannon and machine guns and he was right in the line of fire, but I thought, What guts he had to do that!'

On the Aegean side of the European coast, Joe once came across a large Allied POW camp filled with recently surrendered German soldiers. 'There were about 500 of them, all at the beach, standing in the water,' he says. 'It was my first sight of German soldiers so I got right down low to the water and flew right over the top of them. Every one of them dived under the water as I flew along, one after the other, all the way along.' He seems to have enjoyed that one.

For two whole days in August, Joe witnessed what he describes as 'the largest armada I have ever seen', as the assembled Allied invasion fleet made its way from North Africa to begin Operation Anvil, the amphibious assault on southern France, a vast but now little-known military operation quickly dubbed by the soldiers 'the Champagne Campaign'.

Following the Axis retreat, Joe, with 451 Squadron, moved to near Toulon in southern France, where, when not flying off for more strafing trips, he was in charge of taking a jeep and procuring alcohol for the squadron. On one occasion, he decided to duck over to briefly join the party in nearby Marseilles on the afternoon of its liberation. Amid the shouts of *'Americain!'*

(to which Joe cheerfully nodded and waved), he witnessed the sight of girls who had taken German boyfriends being spat on and marched down the middle of the street to have their heads humiliatingly shaved in public.

In September 1944, the squadron was on the move once again, this time all the way back to England, where, from their new base at Matlaske in Norfolk, they were issued with brand-new Spitfire XVIs to specialise in dive-bombing German flying bomb and rocket sites.

'We were the only people ever to see a V-2 rocket in flight,' he tells me. This remarkable sight was witnessed on one of his regular 45-minute trips across from Norfolk to the coast of Holland, sometimes flying several missions a day. 'I was one of six aircraft, and as we approached the coast, up comes a rocket, right in front of us,' he says. 'We were too far away to fire at it, but the slipstream threw us all over the place. I can still see it,' he adds, pausing. 'The sun glinting on it as it went past us. I can never forget it.' His logbook entry for 23 March 1945 records the details, penned on the day: 'First trip with 1000-pound bombs. Squadron bombed launching site which was well plastered then strafed same. Landed in Belgium. On way saw rocket which threw kite around and returned to bomb and strafe target nearby.'

With a single 500-pound bomb carried under the fuselage, and two 250s beneath the wings, Joe would descend on his target from near 90-degree angles, and would need to be very, very careful. 'The "g-effect" would make you pass out,' he says. 'If you'd had a good sleep, it'd be only momentarily, but if you'd been drinking the night before, you'd stay out for longer.' One V-2 launching site had been situated by the Germans in the grandstand of a racecourse in The Hague. 'They told us it was more effective to bomb the railway line leading to it,' he says. 'We'd bomb it one day, and the next it'd been repaired and we'd have to come back and do it again.'

At war's end, Joe could have expected the squadron to be disbanded and him sent home, but instead 451 found itself earmarked for three months to be part of the occupation forces in Germany, stationed first at Wunstorf near Hanover, and later close to Berlin. 'We were given lectures in how to behave as conquerors,' he tells me. '"If you're walking down the road, do not step aside for a German." That's the sort of stuff I had to listen to!'

Taking a tour of some of the cities destroyed by years of bombing, Joe would drive through entire cities that were little more than the sides of buildings. 'There was a strict policy of "no fraternisation" but it only lasted six months,' he says. A rampant black market evolved whereby American cigarettes became the only real currency. 'You could buy anything with them,' he says. 'I know people who bought diamonds with Lucky Strike cigarettes.'

I ask did he himself ever mix with any of the vanquished enemy?

'No, and I didn't want to,' he says, with a touch of bitterness that somehow surprises me. Looking back, however, he ranks his time as a Spitfire pilot as the unquestioned highlight of his life, although he qualifies it by telling me of the difficulty of his homecoming.

Readjusting was, he says, 'Terribly hard, terribly hard. I'd been twenty-one when I left and was twenty-five when I returned, and I'd lost all my friendships.' His tremors were so bad, he couldn't pick up a cup. 'I'd been flying every day and drinking at night. When I got home, it all caught up with me.' Friends advised him to see a psychiatrist. 'I don't know that he did anything,' he says, 'but he did advise me to change jobs.' So, Joe left the wool industry for which he'd trained so hard, and began what was to become a very successful career in finance and insurance. 'No-one was interested in what we'd done after the war and I didn't want to talk about it,' he says. 'But now it comes back to me, and often, such as when I talk about it to people like you. These days, suddenly, people are interested.'

As I'm leaving his lovely home, he apologises – unnecessarily – for some of the noise and the comings and goings of people during our talk, and explains that this coming weekend big plans are afoot with the celebration of his sixtieth wedding anniversary. Then he tells me something I'm certain he hadn't intended.

'After the war, I went to the concentration camp at Belsen,' he says softly. 'I'm Jewish, you see.' His voice becomes almost inaudible as he continues, as if what he witnessed of this ghastly chapter of humanity doesn't bear articulation. 'I was fumigated when I went in, and then when I went out. They'd burned the huts, all except one, but the ovens were still there. They'd forced the inhabitants of the local town to come in and see it, then bury all the bodies. I remember a huge pile of shoes, much higher than this ceiling. Just shoes. They didn't know what to do with them. But every shoe was a person. It was an absolutely searing experience. That's why I didn't want to fraternise with the Germans after the war.'

STUART 'SNOW' DAVIS

Role: Fighter pilot
Aircraft: P-51 Mustang
Posting: 122 Squadron, RAF

You could never forget what we saw there.

A wise man once said that you can tell the best year of a man's life by his haircut. And by that measure, Stuart 'Snow' Davis's would have been somewhere around 1943. Over the course of a long series of chats on his balcony overlooking Port Macquarie, during which much beer is consumed, jokes old and new shared, and a great many memories exhumed, I can never quite take my eyes off the man's magnificent coiffure. His white but full head of hair, which he tells me has been the same since childhood, earning him his life-long moniker 'Snow', is, even in his nineties, flawlessly groomed. Combed into a series of perfect waves, it's more like a rooster's coxcomb or lion's mane than just a simple head of hair. But even more impressive than its meticulous styling is the way it speaks of a very particular moment in time, when handsome young men everywhere wore their hair just so. If you knew nothing else about the man, his hair, loud and clear, tells you, 'This man was a fighter pilot.'

'Luck, just luck, time and time again, that's what got me through,' is how Stuart describes not only his tour in Europe flying Mustangs with an RAF squadron, but also the passage of a long and busy life. Luck, I would certainly agree, but add to that a great deal of charm and, even today, a little bravado. Stuart fits the bill for the archetypal Australian fighter pilot like few I have met: confident, charming, a killer with the ladies, showing a healthy disrespect for authority, and that dash of devil-may-care larrikinism that made them irresistible on the ground and formidable in the air.

Stuart joined the air force for one reason only, to become a single-engine fighter pilot, and an officer at that. The notion that his lofty ambitions might not have been met exactly as he foresaw them simply never entered his head, and he was not disappointed. 'There was just no way I could have gone onto multi-engine planes,' he tells me. 'I was just too quick, too sudden. I've always been like that,' he adds. 'If I decide to do something, I do it immediately and go for it.'

I mention that a former bomber pilot who, in training, was devastated at being rejected for fighters was told by his instructor, 'The trouble is, you think before you act. And a fighter pilot who thinks before he acts is a dead fighter pilot.'

Stuart nearly jumps out of his seat in agreement. 'Yes, that's exactly it!' he exclaims. 'It was all just instinct.'

However, as dashing a former knight of the air as he is, Stuart has no interest in sugar-coating war's reality. 'When I came out, all I wanted to do was forget about it,' he says. 'All the blokes I knew who were in the air force wanted to forget about it. I didn't even start to talk about it until the late 1980s.' Now, though, Stuart is happy to make up for lost time, and he astounds me with a voluminous memory that has recorded the tiniest details: dates, place names, pilots he met but once, and such minutiae as the cost of renting a wireless from the Radio Rentals company in Sydney in 1941. 'Ten shillings and six a week,' he announces proudly.

Not so confident, however, was the CO of Stuart's first posting, 231 Squadron on England's south coast, in early 1944. 'I was waiting outside the CO's office to go in and see him,' Stuart recalls. 'The adjutant went in to tell him I'd arrived. All I heard through the open door of his office was, "Not another bloody colonial! And an Australian at that!"'

Standing before the officer, Stuart gave as good as he got. 'Well, I didn't ask to come here, sir.' It was a bad start to a relationship that failed to improve, and would typify Stuart's attitude to the obstinacy of British military authority, infuriating many a senior officer.

Initially, instead of being a fighter pilot, Stuart would have to sit it out, literally, at 30 000 feet, flying photo reconnaissance missions in a Spitfire over France, Germany and Holland. 'I bloody hated it,' he tells me. 'Flying all by yourself, for five hours at a stretch – no guns, no armour, and no heating.' Even with three pairs of socks, two pairs of trousers and three sets of gloves, Stuart still needed to constantly bang his hands together to prevent them from freezing. 'There was heating for the cameras,' he tells me, 'but none for the pilots!'

And then there was his CO. '"Turn-back Tommy", we called him,' he says. 'He was notorious for returning early from missions claiming there was something wrong with his aeroplane. I flew that aircraft a couple of times and I can tell you there was nothing wrong with it.'

One day, after being chased back to England from a photo recce trip to Germany by four aircraft he initially believed to be German, but which turned out to be American Mustangs, Stuart was accused by this same CO of lacking sufficient 'ticker'. His nerves already frayed, Stuart let him know, in no uncertain terms, what he and the rest of the pilots thought about his own 'ticker'.

'I told him I'd tested that plane he kept bringing back and there was nothing wrong with it.' The other senior members of the squadron present could only gasp. 'I told him he was a coward, or at least I strongly implied it.' A week later, Stuart was told he would be transferred to another squadron. He was delighted. Now he would swap his unarmed Spitfire, an aeroplane for which he surprisingly expresses not a great deal of affection, for the American Mustang, flying ground-attack missions in support of the armies in France with 122 Squadron.

First, however, I feel I need to clarify his less-than-ebullient opinion of the legendary Spitfire, an attitude which in some circles would be regarded as something close to heresy. He is happy to explain: 'The Poms were notorious for building a good aeroplane and then saying, "Shit, we need someone to fly it! Where are we going to put them?"' he says. 'The Yanks, on the other hand said, "Here's a pilot, now let's build an aeroplane around him."' The Mark II Spitfire he flew was so cramped, and the positioning of instruments such as fuel gauges so odd, that he could hardly read them, and the lever to switch over fuel tanks was virtually impossible to reach. The Mustang on the other hand, he says, was far more comfortable, roomier, armed with six half-inch machine guns and, even with the Mark III version he flew, extremely manoeuvrable at low levels.

Flying initially from their forward bases of Ford and Funtington in Sussex, Stuart began his tour just a few days after D-Day, on 10 June 1944, immediately becoming as embroiled in the fury of the Battle of Normandy as it was possible for a pilot to be.

'We would go out with bombs to a target such as a bridge or a rail yard,' he explains, 'but once we got rid of them, it was "targets of opportunity".' This, in reality, meant anything that moved on the roads in France in mid-1944. 'The French were told that they must not be on the road during daylight,' he says. 'If they were, they were subject to being shot up by us.' He and his fellow pilots favoured getting rid of their bombs early, so they could 'have a real good go' at whatever German transport or armour they could find. They hunted, usually in flights of four, looking for a truck on the road, or a river barge, or a tank, disguised by its crew with branches, skulking under a tree. Radio silence, despite what you see in the movies, Stuart says, was strictly maintained until something was spotted and called in to the flight leader. 'Alright, Black leader, send a pair down,' would be the response.

It was a brutal and uncomplicated process. 'You just came down close and at about 100 metres opened up,' says Stuart. 'Then you got out of the way as soon as you could. Strafing blokes on motorbikes was good fun,' he adds, somewhat chillingly. 'The dopey bastards never got out of the way. If they had any sense they would have thrown the motorcycle into a ditch but instead they just kept on going.'

His logbook tells the story of his own Normandy campaign:

Dropped bomb but missed out on strafing behind beach head.

Dropped one bomb. Off target.

29 June Heavy flak over Hun lines. Hit in starboard elevator.

Dive bombing – hell of a lot of flak, south-west of Caen. Bombed bridge.

Fighter sweep Chartres, Argentan.

Armed recce Alcon, Le Mans. Strafed truck, several flamers.

On 25 June, the squadron, now part of the three-squadron 122 Wing, crossed the Channel and based itself at a French airstrip near Bayeux known as B7. They would not remain there long. As the Normandy front pushed further inland, the forward bases would move with it. Between June and September, Stuart would move no less than six times, his logbook recording airstrips at Martragny, Ellon, St Andre de L'Eure, Beauvais, and then into Belgium on an aerodrome coded as B60 near Grimbergen.

In August, with the German army squeezed on three sides by the American and British armies into a long, oval-shaped pocket around the village of Falaise, air power was invited to go in and do its worst. It was a massacre, which no pilot I have met who witnessed it can ever forget. 'At Falaise, they gave us one day to get into the slaughter,' says Stuart, 'and we took it.' Flying over the condensed, chaotic ranks of retreating German soldiers, Stuart's view was vivid and awful. The Falaise battle-field became a tangle of roads blocked with shattered vehicles and body-choked streams. Stuart was particularly appalled by the sight of dead and wounded horses. 'They were everywhere,' he remembers. 'You could never forget what we saw there.'

'At one stage I learned to see through camouflage,' he tells me. 'I was section leader and one day I reported I could see armour down in the timber underneath us,' he says. The squadron leader took the formation around to spot them, but informed Stuart that no-one else in the squadron could see what he was talking about.

'Well I can see them, they're there!' he protested.

'Well take your number two and go down and show us they're there,' was the reply. Stuart peeled off and descended, firing into the trees. 'We swooped down,' he says, 'and jeez, did we leave a stream of bloody fire!' Seeing the mayhem, the rest of the formation, says Stuart, 'came down like bees to a honeypot'.

The next day, he was given not two but four aircraft to command. 'Come on, Snow,' his fellow pilots teased, 'show us the bloody way!'

And he did. 'That went on for about a week. Jeez, we had a lot of fun then!'

In October, the squadron packed up and headed back to England to fly escort duties from airfields in East Anglia, protecting bombers making daylight sorties. For Stuart, it was to be a totally different experience from the low-level work he'd known. It was a two-handed system. Spitfires would leave their bases on the Continent to rendezvous with the bombers as they crossed the coast, then stay with them to the target, at which point they would hand over to the longer-range Mustangs, who had flown over from England and would see the bombers home again. Stuart remembers one particular encounter vividly.

'We picked up some Lancasters and sat there covering them at 25 000 feet as they came up to the target,' he remembers. Lagging behind the formation of several hundred aircraft was a straggler, obviously in some kind of trouble but pressing on to the target nonetheless. 'He probably should have turned back,' says Stuart, 'but he didn't.' As he kept an eye on this aircraft, watching for German fighters, the Master Bomber of the formation also came down for a look. This second Lancaster made wide circles around the slower-flying aircraft, then for some reason dropped beneath it. Stuart watched as the bomb doors of the first Lancaster opened to disgorge its load. 'I saw the bombs come down and knock a wing off that Master Bomber,' he says. Like a falling leaf, the aircraft, to his horror, began to spiral its way towards the ground. Amazingly, a parachute emerged, then another and still a third . . . 'I counted six of them,' he remembers. The remarkable addendum to this story had to wait a decade before being played out on a veranda in rural New South Wales in August 1955.

By this time, Stuart had settled into his post-war career of wool-classing, at which he would excel for the remainder of a happy and productive working life. 'One of the blokes I trained lived in Wagga,' he tells me. 'Bob Coveney was his name. I knew he'd been a wireless operator in the air force and been shot down, but nothing else. I used to go and stay with him when I was in Wagga. Our wives became friends.'

One evening at a country dinner-dance put on by the local RSL, Stuart and Bob sat on the porch, talking about the war. 'So, when did you actually "buy it"?' asked Stuart. As Bob spoke, Stuart sat in increasingly amazed silence as Bob proceeded to describe exactly the scenario he had witnessed from his cockpit one afternoon in 1944. One of those six parachutes he had seen leaping from the stricken Lancaster, he realised, belonged to the man he was now talking to.

'I saw that,' he at last revealed to Bob. 'I was in the plane covering you.' Bob's crew, learned Stuart, were on their second tour, and for their experience had been chosen for the important Master Bomber role. He couldn't remember why they were circling the aircraft at the time, but the pilot had attempted to hold the aircraft steady as the rest of his crew bailed out, and was killed. 'It's amazing any of them got out at all,' he says. 'Bob Coveney. Gee, he was a nice bloke.'

Stuart flew his last trip on New Year's Day 1945. However, when his logbook was examined by his CO, four of his trips were disqualified for not having been strictly flown in the face of the enemy, reducing his tally to ninety-nine, one short of the obligatory hundred. The senior officer asked Stuart if he'd like to do one more the following day to complete his tour. His answer, once again, was forthright. 'I told him, "No bloody way." It was my birthday the next day, January 2, and I've always had a habit of doing nothing on my birthday. Besides, I'd seen too many blokes get killed by tempting fate one last time.' The powers that be let Stuart's ninety-nine operations stand as a full tour.

Stuart believes that keeping himself busy was the key to an easy passage back to civilian life. During the war he had courted an English girl, but having seen his share of young widows left behind, often with young children, when their airman husbands were killed, he would not consider marrying her until it was all over. 'There was no way I'd leave her in that position,' he says. Upon his return home in late 1945, Stuart threw himself into the preparations for her passage to Australia, and took up the job he'd left with the great rural giant Dalgety, rising to the top of the organisation by his mid-thirties.

Having flown with an RAF unit, Stuart was an 'Odd Bod', and saw few from his old squadron. 'I joined the RSL for a while,' he says, 'but it seemed to be filled with blokes who wanted to still fight the bloody war, so I left.' Like so many, he never talked about any of it, simply opting to forget.

As we conclude our talks, some of the bravado wears off a little, and I ask him again what stands out in his tour, flying the mighty Mustangs with 122.

'You can never forget what we saw at Falaise,' he says, in the most reflective mode I've yet seen. 'It was just terrible, just slaughter. Being a country-based bloke, to see those horses being wounded and killed, it was just awful. And you didn't have to worry about those soldiers shooting back at you either. They were on the run, didn't have any ammo. It was just slaughter.'

RON BENSON

Role: Fighter pilot
Aircraft: CAC Boomerang
Posting: 4 Squadron, RAAF

*Just imagine, flying just above the trees over the amazing scenery
of New Guinea, and being paid to do so!*

'Of course,' says Ron, 'you realise that in the Pacific theatre, aircrew serving above the Tropic of Capricorn were only allowed
to do so for nine months before being brought back home.'
I didn't realise, but talking to Ron in his elegant home in one
of Melbourne's oldest suburbs is to be an afternoon of firsts.

'The conditions in the tropics were considered too harsh
for us delicate little blue orchids!' he says. There was nothing
delicate, however, about the low-level, ground-attack operations Ron flew in New Guinea against the Japanese with 4
Squadron RAAF, nor the aircraft in which he flew them, the

Commonwealth Aircraft Corporation's nuggety, all-Australian 'Boomerang'. Ron is the first Boomerang pilot I have ever met.

Before the war, the Australian aircraft industry had barely managed to produce anything more complicated than a toaster. So the fact that by 1939 the 'trainer and general purpose' Wirraway was in production at Melbourne's Fishermans Bend plant, followed two years later by the licence-built Beaufort medium bomber, was a feat of extraordinary industrial genius. The great gap in our air defence, however, was the lack of a fighter, and when Japan entered the war in late 1941, the gap opened to a chasm. The Wirraway was briefly, and foolishly, thrown up against the Japanese Zeros with awful losses, but with that hard lesson learned, Australia had nothing.

Luckily, the head of the Commonwealth Aircraft Corporation, Lawrence Wackett, never one to let protocol stand in the way of a good idea, got wind of a recently arrived Austrian-Jewish aircraft designer with the unlikely name of Fred David, who had worked in Germany under Ernst Heinkel designing fighter aircraft. David was, and remains, an enigmatic figure, but legend has it that Heinkel, concerned for his safety when Hitler came to power, spirited him away to work on some of their Japanese contracts where he designed military aircraft for the Aichi company. When Germany and Japan became allies, David moved once again, arriving in Australia as, of all things, a refugee, where he was promptly interned as an enemy alien.

Snaffling him before he had time to unpack what little luggage he had, Wackett told David to start designing a fighter that could be manufactured in Australia, and to work fast. In what must surely rank as one of the great Australian bureaucratic ironies, David, despite being the chief designer of Australia's only purpose-built defensive fighter aircraft, remained an enemy alien and was required to report to the police on a weekly basis.

A few days before Christmas 1941, just a fortnight after Pearl Harbor, the Boomerang's initial design was drawn, says the legend, on the back of an envelope. Apocryphal or not, what is undisputed is that the first model began test flights in late May the following year – an astonishingly short amount of time, particularly given Australia's lack of aircraft-manufacturing expertise. The RAAF put in an initial order for around 100.

Admittedly, the Boomerang was not much to look at. With its short fuselage of not quite 26 feet, stumpy wings and enormous-looking Twin Wasp radial engine, there's always seemed to me something a little comical about its design. But the Boomerang was well armed with four Browning machine guns and two wing-mounted 20-millimetre cannons, which, as none of these actually existed in Australia at the time, had to be reverse-engineered from a captured example brought home from the Western Desert as a souvenir!

In the end, the Boomerang was not really needed as a fighter, as superior American types began to arrive in numbers in early 1942. This was probably just as well, as indications were that the Boomerang would have been no match for just about any Japanese fighter it was likely to come up against. And as its handling was particularly bad above 15 000 feet, it would probably have been unable to catch them in any case.

Closer to the ground, however, it was a different story, and with its robustness and versatility, the Boomerang found its niche as an extremely effective army-cooperation, ground-attack fighter.

With his father wounded, and an uncle killed in the First World War, Ron, when his turn came, decided on the air force. 'At the time I was interested in cars and ships and girls,' he says. 'I'd never been in a plane, but after I joined the air force, I became interested in those too.'

Joining up just after Pearl Harbor as an eighteen-year-old, Ron took instantly to flying and became a star pupil, being selected for single-engine fighter training and awarded an officer's commission while still on the course. One afternoon, after taking off from No. 2 Service Flying Training School in Deniliquin, however, it all nearly came to a fiery and premature end.

While flying on a cross-country exercise over the flat plains of central Victoria in a Wirraway, a fire broke out in the fuse box beside him in the cockpit, then proceeded to burn its way back along the fuselage towards the tail. 'The normal procedure was to bail out,' says Ron, 'but it was burning slowly so I thought I'd be able to get her down.' Landing wheels-up in one of the innumerable pancake-flat paddocks beneath him, he had failed to notice a shallow irrigation channel hurtling closer as he skidded along the dry ground. With a jolt, the aircraft's nose went suddenly down, and the tail came suddenly up, teetering there for a dreadful moment, before righting itself. 'If it had gone over,' says Ron, 'I couldn't have got out and would have been incinerated.' As it was, he was able to retrieve an extinguisher from a rear compartment, put the fire out and walk to a local farmhouse to get help. (A few years ago, he went back to the farm, close to Benalla. Not much had changed.)

Graduating in June 1943, Ron could reasonably have expected to be put onto Spitfires or Kittyhawks. But, unlike almost all of his fellow young pilots, he had no desire to sail around the skies at 22 000 feet. 'From the moment I went low-flying,' he says, 'I knew it was for me.' So, when the word went out that General Thomas Blamey had called for the formation of two new dedicated army-cooperation squadrons to assist the men slogging away against the stubborn Japanese in the steaming jungles of New Guinea and New Britain, Ron was one of the first to put up his hand. 'Also, my mother had told me, "You can join the air force, but only as long as you don't go too fast or too high." I decided to abide by her wishes,' he says.

Initially joining No. 5 Squadron at Mareeba near Cairns, Ron began acquainting himself with the fine art of low-level combat flying. 'We went out on exercises with the army,' he remembers. 'They'd have two sides and we'd have to report what they were doing, what equipment they were using, drop smoke bombs and practise a great deal of strafing,' he says.

Flying from Townsville in a DC-3, Ron's first impressions of the tropics remain with him still. 'Magnificent scenery,' he says, 'mountains going up to 15 000 feet.' Soon he would himself be flying over those formidable peaks of the Owen Stanley Range. In an attempt to cover some of the vast scale of the New Guinea campaign, 5 Squadron divided itself into two flights, one based at Nadzab in the Markham Valley, the other at an American-built airstrip, Gusap, in the Ramu Valley. Ron, eager to get into action in the Boomerang as he was, had to nevertheless content himself with going back to the old Wirraway. 'New pilots had to spend a month flying the squadron courier service from HQ in Port Moresby,' he says. 'It was magnificent training for flying over those mountains.'

In January 1944, at Nadzab, Ron commenced operations for real. Aviation enthusiasts sometimes decry the little Boomerang, but Ron will have none of it. 'It was a beautiful aeroplane to fly,' he says. 'As fast as a Spitfire or a Mustang, incredibly manoeuvrable, comfortable and with good range and visibility. But above 20 000 feet,' he admits, 'completely useless.' It was 'on the deck' in the thick air of the tropics that the Boomerang came into its own.

Ron's neat and meticulous logbook illustrates his intense few months fighting in the jungle. Operating primarily on the north coast of New Guinea, he and his fellow pilots would have to negotiate the 15 000-foot Finisterre Mountains on an almost daily basis. 'We'd have to take off in the morning before the clouds built up,' he says. 'Sometimes we'd be too late and we couldn't get back over them, so we'd have to fly the long way, all around the coast.'

The weather and terrain, he says, were as dangerous as the enemy. 'In three years,' he explains, '98 pilots went through 4 and 5 Squadrons and 33 were lost,' largely, he believes, through bad weather and impossible terrain. 'But you never thought it would happen to you,' he says. 'Everybody else might get it, but not us.' One of those who did not come home was Ron's tent-mate, Ken Linklater, a married man with two children. 'He was on a strafing mission in New Britain,' he says. 'He got a little bit too enthusiastic and failed to pull up in time and went into the trees. After I got home, I went and visited his wife. She lived in Manly. We were sad about losing Ken,' he adds, 'but we couldn't afford to lose any sleep over it.'

Ron himself could easily have been counted among those missing after taking off alone one morning from Saidor on the north coast of New Guinea, heading back over the mountains to Nadzab. 'It was clear when I took off,' he says, 'but the clouds soon built up around me and I got caught.' At 12 000 feet, he attempted to fly through them, but emerged into a huge spherical pocket of clear air, as if inside a vast white cathedral of cloud.

'I was surrounded,' he says. 'There was cloud all around me, and I knew there were mountains nearby at 15 000 so there was no way I was going to attempt to fly out of it not knowing what was on the other side.' Flying around in ever-decreasing circles, Ron sensed the walls of cloud gradually closing in on him and his fuel was beginning to run low. 'I shut my eyes and said a little prayer, "Please, show me the way home!"' As he opened his eyes in a steep, banking turn, a hole in the cloud appeared directly below him. In the middle of that hole, miraculously, he saw a runway, and on the runway, an aeroplane. 'I recognised it as a little strip I'd flown over a few days earlier,' he says. Putting the Boomerang into a steep dive, Ron emerged from the cloud base, deciding not to land on this strip but hug the ground home to Nadzab and safety. 'It was one of the times I knew I had a charmed life in the air force,' he says.

Ron flew operations on an almost daily basis, mainly as one of a pair. He and his number two would follow the terrain, often below the tree line at the army's behest, directing artillery, finding and marking targets or conducting observations. The Japanese air force had been checked at this stage of the war, but they were there, usually way above them, thankfully being dealt with at high altitude by Australian Kittyhawks, or American Lightnings and Airacobras. Ron, below, would be privy to their chatter over the radio telephone. 'I remember the call sign of one American squadron was "shit",' he says. The various aircraft of this squadron seemed to have expanded on this theme by adding the word 'frighten'. 'I can still hear it coming over the radio,' says Ron. '"Shit-Frighten One, to Shit-Frighten

Two . . ." etc.' He laughs at it to this day.

One of the Boomerang's primary capabilities was ground attack, but with the dense jungle largely obscuring the enemy, Ron had to wait for his opportunities. 'We'd regularly catch them in the open crossing some of the big river deltas,' he says. He and his number two would swoop in, firing their six guns apiece into the wading ranks of Japanese, suddenly and hopelessly exposed and with nowhere to hide. 'It happened about every third trip,' he says. 'I'm not proud of it, but one occasion we must have killed about a hundred of them. It was slaughter, really.'

Barges, vehicles, armour, men, Ron would fire at anything that could be seen from the air. 'Some of our pilots would strafe the local's huts, thinking the Japanese might be using them,' he confesses. 'But I never did that, I thought that was stupid.'

An unusual logbook entry, in faint pencil, can just be made out next to a record of one such low-level attack. It mentions the captured diary of one 'Major Komori'. 'A few weeks after we strafed them,' Ron explains, 'the army found the body of this Japanese officer and Intelligence translated his diary. It spoke about the attack we had made on them.'

'A soldier broke his leg in the attack,' the officer had written. 'He had to be left behind.'

Ron tells me that the greatest fear experienced by himself and his fellow pilots was of being captured. The stories of the fate of downed airmen at the hands of the Japanese were well known, but some of the highland people could not be relied upon either, he says. A Wirraway crew he knew who had bailed out had apparently been captured by some locals. 'They beheaded the dark-haired observer, but treated the blond pilot as a god and let him go,' he says. 'They'd never seen a blond person before.' Consequently, Ron always flew as prepared as he could be, wearing a .45 revolver with a hundred rounds of ammunition, carrying food, water-purifying tablets and a compass given to him by his father. Thankfully, he would not be required to use them.

Having flown thirty-three operations in four months, Ron was brought back to Australia and suffered the relative ignominy of being made an instructor, back on Wirraways and Tiger Moths at Laverton air force base. 'It was a comedown,' he says, 'and complaining didn't do any good.' Eventually, he was given a job as a ferry pilot, flying Spitfires and Mustangs, once again at low level, but in considerably less danger than in his Boomerang over the jungles to the north.

After the war, Ron confesses to 'not being happy', but mainly because he seems to have missed his days in the cockpit, viewing his time in the air force as one of the great highlights of his life. 'Just imagine,' he tells me, with an air of wonderment, 'flying just above the trees over the amazing scenery of New Guinea, and being paid to do so!'

Simply the fact that he'd survived seems to have been a spur for him to get on with the rest of his life. Ron went on to study medicine and spent many happy years as a GP, his course paid for by the air force, eventually running a major repatriation hospital in Melbourne. His book-lined home attests to a long and interesting life. He is still an active man, writing and delivering papers on his favourite topic, genetics, and caring full-time for his disabled wife. 'I met such wonderful people in the air force,' he says. 'Everyone gets counselling these days. Back then, we didn't have any of it. And some of the people I knew needed it.' But not, seemingly, Ron Benson.

JOHN ALLEN

Role: Fighter pilot
Aircraft: Grumman Wildcat, Hellcat
Posting: 804 Squadron, Fleet Air Arm

I came out of that cloud and was virtually
formating with two Japanese aircraft!

John greets me warmly as I walk up to his door on a hot Melbourne afternoon.

'How are you, John?' I ask him.

'I've just got out of hospital,' he tells me cheerily. 'Pleurisy, heart attack, pneumonia – apart from that, I'm fine!' Before getting down to the business of telling me about his days with the Fleet Air Arm of the British Royal Navy flying American Grumman F6F Hellcat fighters in the Indian Ocean, he shows me a couple of wedding photos of him and his wife, Faye. 'Bit better looking then, wasn't I?' he says. All things considered, however, John's not doing too bad.

I continue to look through his collection of brilliantly clear wartime photographs of life on board a Second World War aircraft carrier, perfectly preserved in their heavy, black leather album. 'There was a professional photographer on board,' he says. 'They had to take a photograph of every landing in case something went wrong.' And things did go wrong, a lot. One of his many images is of an American Grumman Wildcat fighter, its back broken, lying completely inverted on the deck of a carrier. Another shows a collision between two Hellcats, one of them virtually severed by the spinning prop of the other. 'His arrester hook broke and he went straight through the barrier,' John tells me. I let out a gasp. 'That sort of thing was pretty common.' He points to another. 'This was the last day of ops in the Indian Ocean,' he tells me. 'I was trying to get a couple of Kamikaze suicide planes. Instead, they nearly got me.' We'll get to that one later.

John was born in Cambridge, England, one of three brothers, all of whom finished up as naval lieutenants serving on British aircraft carriers. 'One was on a fleet carrier, one on a light fleet carrier and me on an escort carrier,' he says. 'My brother Eric stayed in the navy and ended up designing the Royal Yacht *Britannia*. He was a bright boy.'

As a young post-office engineer, John was frequently called to visit some of the aerodromes of the Battle of Britain, servicing teleprinter machines to help keep open the vital lines of communication. Watching the Spitfires and Hurricanes take to the air planted in him a seed of interest in the air force, but it was a moment closer to home, in Cambridge, that sealed his ambition. 'A German plane flew right past the window of the postal exchange,' he says. 'I was at work on the first floor. I can still see the face of the German pilot looking at me. I thought, I'm going to get him.'

Answering an ad in the paper for 'flying duties with the Fleet Air Arm', John travelled to Gosport in southern England for an interview and was accepted for assessment for pilot training. 'I loved it,' he says. Passing through elementary instruction at Yeovilton, then on to the oddly named Royal Naval Air Station Twatt in the Orkney Islands, John joined No. 771 Squadron to properly learn how to fly a naval aeroplane. The ageing types he was given, however, left much to be desired, such as the Blackburn Skua, an example of British aviation best forgotten. This carrier-based dive bomber was an underpowered lemon even in its 'heyday' at the beginning of the war, but the clapped-out examples John was given to fly were particularly grim. 'We had to do a lot of dive-bombing practice over the North Sea,' he remembers. 'The planes were so old that we had to fly with the hoods open or else they could cave and scalp you. Then after every dive I used to carefully have to put my hand around to the other side of the windshield and wipe away the oil that had leaked from the engine. You were lucky if you got to the end of the runway and it hadn't lost all its hydraulic fluid.'

Eventually, in January 1944, John was sent back to the south of England to convert to the rugged American Wildcat, which had already served well with United States forces in the earlier part of the Pacific war and was now also in use with the Fleet Air Arm. 'They were a beautiful little aeroplane to fly,' he says. 'Awful in a cross wind, but perfect for the deck of an aircraft carrier.'

Posted to 890 Squadron, John boarded the cruiser HMS *London* and steamed out to his area of operations, the Indian Ocean, referred to in those imperial days as the Far East, where his base would be the great harbour of Trincomalee in Ceylon. His ship was a small escort carrier, HMS *Atheling*. 'We were met by Lord Mountbatten,' he remembers. 'He gathered us pilots around and said, "Well, chaps, we've got the little yellow bastards on the run now, and you're the first fighter assault carrier out here to help."' John was now officially operational but, he says, 'there were no operations for us to do'. Instead, they went back to training, and then, still more training. For many pilots, however, this was one of the most dangerous parts of their tour.

'In about six months,' he says, 'they managed to kill about five Seafire pilots.' Sharing the ship with another Fleet Air Arm squadron, 889, who were operating the carrier-based version of the famous Spitfire, John pitied the men who had to fly them. 'The Seafires were wonderful in the air,' he says, 'but almost impossible to get them onto the deck. You couldn't stall them, they just wanted to keep flying.' On one occasion, a New Zealand pilot had crashed just prior to John himself landing. 'He'd panicked,' he says. 'He was a small man, probably shouldn't have been flying at all. He'd lost his nerve, missed the arrester wires and crashed through the barrier. He killed three other blokes as well as his best mate. As I got out, they were squeegeeing blood off the deck. Later I remember one kid crying as he tried to pack five of his mates' kit bags.'

Such accidents were understandably common. The concentration required to place an aircraft on the deck of a moving aircraft carrier can scarcely, I suggest, be imaginable.

'When you see the carrier,' says John by way of agreement,

'it looks like a matchbox. Then when you get closer, it looks like a short plank.' Applying high throttle but at just above stalling speed, the pilots would approach the deck in a tight curve, right foot hard on the rudder to counteract the prop torque, and keep an eye on the all-important batsman. 'The feeling is that you're going to end up on the front end of the plank,' he says, 'but the ship is moving away from you, so you end up on the rear. At least, that's the idea.' When practising circuits, he says, the strain on his right leg holding the rudder was immense. 'Sometimes I'd get such a cramp in it, I'd just have to go around again and fly for a bit to get it out.'

The rise and fall of the deck could be as much as fifty feet, which, combined with a corkscrew motion, could make a safe landing seem impossible. 'I can remember trying to get down eight times before I got the lucky combination of rise and fall, when I didn't either slam the aircraft into the deck or just bounce off again,' says John. Eight steel arrester wires were in place on the deck for the hook at the rear of your tail to grab, and if you missed them, you *might* still be stopped by the barrier at the end of the deck.

John recalls his first realisations of the dangers of deck landing. 'We were in a small boat being taken out to the ship,' he says. 'There was a Wildcat hanging over the side, its nose almost submerged, the arrester wires stretched out to the water and the pilot scrambling up the wire back to the ship. Turns out it was the second time he'd been over the side *that day*! Many blokes went over the side. There was usually a destroyer following us to pick us up if we went in.'

Flying back and forth between the ship and airstrips on Ceylon, John experienced the tropics in all its colour and movement. 'Once a herd of wild elephants stampeded across the runway and put holes in the new bitumen so we couldn't take off,' he says. Another elephant, this time a tame one named Lulu, acted as a far better tower of aircraft than any trac- tor. 'There were lots of Italian POWs there too,' he tells me. 'Happy as anything to be out of the war. Always immaculately dressed. One even asked me if I could take him up for a flight!'

Ceylon, in reality a backwater of the Pacific war, ended up as the unenviable posting for many RAF Beaufighter and Mosquito crews who, John says, 'were slowly going mad, hav- ing been out there a couple of years with nothing to do'. He could easily have fallen into the same category, but instead, in January 1945, he joined a new squadron, 804, on a new ship, HMS *Ameer*, a small American-built escort carrier of 8000 tons which had been transferred to the Royal Navy under the US Lend-Lease program. Most importantly, however, John would be given a new aircraft, one of the true stars of the Pacific air war, the Hellcat.

Twelve thousand F6F Hellcats were built by Grumman during the Second World War, and their rugged and simple design accounted for the destruction of thousands of Japanese aircraft in the Pacific conflict. Hellcats were so well-suited to their jobs as carrier-based fighters, their design remained virtu- ally unaltered throughout the entire conflict. The Royal Navy gratefully took possession of around 1200, putting them to very good use in the hands of men like John Allen. 'They were won- derful to fly and wonderful to land,' he says. 'You could plonk them down right where you wanted to.'

John would also learn to fly the Hellcat very, very low. 'In training, you could get to know when your propeller was about

6 feet off the ground.' Over the water, John had a rule: when he could see in his rear-view mirror a spiral of spray being thrown up behind him by his prop, he was to go no lower!

In the first month of the last year of the war, John's fighting began in earnest. His logbook describes operations over Burma, Malaya, Thailand, Sumatra and the Nicobar and Andaman Islands, as the Japanese, step by step, were pushed out of the Indian Ocean. All-but-forgotten military operations with code-names such as Sanky, Bishop and Balsam took place in unknown colonial outstations, obscure ports or along sandy, tropical beaches. John's roles varied between providing top cover for bombers, reconnaissance, covering island bombardments, strafing and generally attacking anything Japanese he could find.

February 1945 saw Operation Stacey, a photo reconnaissance task conducted over northern Sumatra and the Isthmus of Kra in Thailand. On this occasion, John was part of an air-to-air engagement, rare at that stage of the war with the decline of the Japanese air force. 'We got three Jap aircraft that day,' he says. 'The first was an "Oscar". He didn't even see us. All we had to do was get in line astern and attack. There was none of this dogfighting business.' Two Japanese aircraft were shot down by John's flight in a matter of moments. His flight commander went in for the first, and did most of the work. 'He just about shot it to bits,' says John. 'By the time I got in after him, it was all coming apart anyway, so we gave the victory to him.' John reckons he was only fifty feet behind the aircraft, and 'the pilot's body came out just as I got up to it. So just to make sure, I followed it down and gave it a few more squirts.'

Remarkably, John tells me that on board his ship were a few 'bright young Intelligence boys from Eton or somewhere', who spoke fluent Japanese. Part of their job was to tune in to the frequencies of the Japanese radio. 'They could hear the Jap pilots talking to their airfields,' he says. The third kill that day was a twin-engine 'Dinah'. According to the Intelligence officers, the last thing the pilot said was, 'enemy fleet sighted, stand-by', before another flight from John's ship shot it into the water. 'Three in one day was pretty good,' he says.

In an attack on Port Blair in the Andaman Islands, he remembers the anti-aircraft fire as 'vicious'. 'You'd dive into it and kid yourself that by standing on the rudder and "skidding" from side to side, you were avoiding it,' he says. 'But more often than not it just made it more likely to hit you.' Overflying a Japanese prison, John remembers, almost surreally, seeing people on the roof who had made out the word 'welcome' in stones. 'I remember seeing that quite clearly,' he says. Two Japanese ships which were loading troops to take back home, he says, were sunk.

In June, John took part in Operation Balsam, a series of naval and air strikes on Japanese forces on the island of Sumatra, in preparation for an eventual invasion. Three squadrons from three separate carriers were each allotted a Japanese airfield to attack, with 804 being given a large one in the town of Medan. Having proved himself as a superior strafing pilot both in training and combat, John's task was to deliver his bombs on the airstrip, then attack a group of four Oscar fighters parked around the control tower.

Reconnaissance had shown there were also aircraft hidden in nearby jungle, as well as significant fixed anti-aircraft defences, which were to be tackled by a Grumman Avenger squadron. 'We dropped our bombs right on the runway,' John says. 'It was beautiful bombing, but of course the next day the Japs could just take off from the grass. That's why we had to hit the aircraft.' He then lined up the Oscars and set them ablaze.

'I had to do a particular circuit that took me below the rooftops,' he says. Flying right down the main street of Medan, he knew the Japanese small calibre anti-aircraft fire was deadly accurate. 'You had to be that low, otherwise the Japs would shoot your head off,' he says. John made three runs and was hit on each of them. 'They had a gun positioned right at one of the street intersections and it opened up on me as I flew past.' He could hear the strikes of the armour-piercing bullets, one even hitting his petrol tank, at which point he had cause to thank the inventor of the self-sealing tank. He tells me he's since wondered if the Japanese hadn't planned the whole thing. 'They'd been attacked there before, and I've often thought if those Oscars out in the open like that weren't dummies,' he says. 'The way they had their guns ready for us right at the cross street, makes you think they knew exactly what we were going to do.'

The CO of another squadron, 808, flying with them that day was not so fortunate. 'He'd come along for experience and was shot down,' says John. 'We thought he'd been killed but we later found out he was kept alive and beheaded on VJ Day.'

Next was Operation Livery in July 1945, a series of naval air strikes off the future Thai resort island of Phuket. John set off to attack a railway junction at a place called Thung Song. Soon after leaving the ship and forming up, however, he discovered a serious fault with his aircraft. 'My number two called me up and when I went to answer him, I received an electric shock!' he says. An electrical short meant that every time he pressed the transmit button on the control column, not only did it not function, but he was hit with voltage. 'I didn't like that much,' John says. His radio useless, John decided nevertheless to carry on. But he was far from happy.

Swooping down over the target, John hit the bomb-release button on the stick, but his number two flying alongside began making urgent hand gestures towards the underside of John's plane. He realised then the fault had also prevented his two 500-pound bombs from parting company with his aircraft and they were still hung up on their racks. 'I had to fly back to the ship with them still there,' he says. A tense half-hour was spent while the ship's officers debated whether John should ditch or attempt to land. Eventually, it being decided that he was, after all, a good pilot, he was told to come in. As if a deck landing wasn't dangerous enough, doing so with bombs attached was an emergency. 'As I came in to land,' he says, 'the only people I could see were the batsman guiding me in and one solitary face on the bridge. Everyone else had taken shelter!'

On 26 July, as the final preparations for the atomic bomb attacks which would end the war on Japan were underway, the battle nevertheless still raged in the Indian Ocean. John remembers it vividly. By this stage, the primary Japanese weapon against Allied ships was the Kamikaze suicide attack, and every vessel in the area was jumpy.

'I was sent up to investigate radar "echoes" of what they thought could have been Kamikaze aircraft,' he says. After searching the skies for two hours with his number two, he had found nothing but open sky and was recalled. Returning to the fleet, it appears that the great battleship HMS *Nelson* had in fact spotted two approaching Kamikazes but had failed to let anyone know, least of all John. Up above, circling the fleet with his own ship directly beneath him, John noticed a large cloud over to his right and eyed it with suspicion. Deciding to inspect the far side of it, he flew into it and emerged right beside two Japanese Kamikaze aircraft preparing to dive onto the ships below. Instantly, a storm of anti-aircraft fire erupted around him, and frantic orders came to him over the radio from the great ship below. 'Get out of it, Red One! Circle! Circle!' He didn't need to be told twice and quickly pulled away.

'I came out of that cloud and was virtually formating with two Japanese aircraft!' he says. 'But I didn't actually see much of it. I was too busy trying to work out what was going on.' He barely managed to avoid being destroyed by his own ship's gun-fire, but one of the Kamikazes then dived towards the *Ameer*. Extraordinarily, it was shot down with a single round from a Bofors gun, fired by an officer, he says. The other Kamikaze chose a nearby minesweeper and sunk it with heavy loss of life. John didn't know it at the time, but it was the final day of oper-ations in the Indian Ocean and the end of his brief but intense war. A few weeks later, he spent the night of VJ Day back in Trincomalee, where fireworks of a strictly friendly nature were enjoyed. Again, he has the photo to prove it.

On the way home, John watched with sadness as the Hellcats which had served himself and his fellow pilots so well were, under the terms of the Lend-Lease agreement, crated up and tossed into the sea.

Months later, John walked back into his office in Cam-bridge, enquiring after his former job. 'I'd advise you not to come back,' were the words of his old inspector. A flood of returning and better qualified men, it seemed, had beaten him to it. It was, however, a blessing in disguise. John once again answered an ad in the paper, this time for Shell Oil, and headed out to Trinidad to begin a new career in the oil industry. 'I'd have found life very difficult if I'd just gone back to work in Cambridge,' he says. The hard work and hard play of the oil game made his return to peacetime relatively easy. Eventually, he would spend a great deal of time back in the Far East, not far from some of the places he came to know from the cockpit of his Hellcat in 1945.

'The only thing I was scared of was being captured,' he says, echoing the sentiments of many of the men I have spoken to who flew against the Japanese. 'We well knew what they would do to you if they caught you. And they wondered why we drank!' John says he always carried a loaded pistol and six rounds with him on every flight. 'Five for them and one for me. I don't know if I would have had the courage to do that, but I would never have wanted to be captured.'

LAURIE LARMER

Role: Pilot
Aircraft: Handley Page Halifax
Posting: 51 Squadron, RAF

It sent a shudder through the aircraft,
and it sent a shudder through me.

As it happens, Laurie and I have quite a bit in common. It turns out he and I spent much of our childhood across the road from each other. The son of a publican, Laurie grew up in a suburban Melbourne hotel opposite a school I myself attended as a youngster. Admittedly, it was forty years later, but who's counting? And besides, right from the get-go, Laurie and I seem to speak the same language. For some reason, I've always wanted to know the price of a pot of beer back in the 1930s. 'Sixpence,' he tells me straight up. 'And a bottle was a shilling. I can remember the day they raised the price a halfpenny. Dad couldn't cope.'

It was sitting in a chair outside the pub's ladies' lounge that Laurie, a sixteen-year-old, heard his country go to war, as Prime Minister Menzies' sombre tones drawled out the famous words '. . . and as a result, Australia is also at war'.

'Pretty big stuff,' says Laurie. And he was right. Dreading the prospect of being drafted into the army, Laurie beat them to it by putting his name down for the RAAF. He still has no idea why, but after a couple of months at No. 1 Initial Training School at Somers in Victoria, his name was simply read out from a list. 'The following will train as pilots . . .' So without even requesting it, a pilot was what Laurie would be.

In England, at his crewing-up in a large hangar in Lichfield, Laurie stood around somewhat vacantly, not seeming to know any of the milling mass of airmen from which he was expected to select a six-man bomber crew. Then a 'funny little fella' approached him.

'You seem like a decent sort of a bloke,' he said. 'I'll be your bomb aimer.' Bill Hudson was a used-car salesman from Sydney, and seemed to know how to close a deal. 'Now, I know this great navigator,' he said, and promptly went and fetched him. 'Just a sec, we haven't got any gunners,' he continued. 'Wait here . . .' and in this manner proceeded to select the entire crew. Laurie didn't have to do a thing.

'It turned out that they were all pretty good too,' he says.

Laurie's tour began in the last few months of the war, and he is the only pilot I have met who flew the Handley Page Halifax, a great aircraft whose legacy has remained somewhat overshadowed by its more famous sibling, the Lancaster. Nevertheless, the 'Halibag' was a significant part of Bomber Command's arsenal in the long and bloody air offensive against Germany.

Air Chief Marshal Harris hated the Halifax. In his view, its slightly smaller bomb-carrying capacity, particularly its inability to carry the 4000-pound 'cookie' blast bomb, rendered it a waste of time, and he gradually relegated them to less important commands and theatres. Nonetheless, 6000 Halifaxes – just a thousand fewer than the Lancaster – were built, and their crews swore by them. This is understandable, as the Halifax was generally regarded as more comfortable than the Lanc, as well as easier to get out of when in trouble.

In early 1945, Laurie and his crew were sent to Snaith in East Yorkshire, the only Australians flying with No. 51 Squadron, RAF. This well-established unit had been operating almost the entire war and had paid a high price in doing so. During an infamous attack on Nuremberg in March 1944, 51 lost almost the strength of an entire squadron, eight of its Halifaxes in a single night. Laurie and his crew's arrival, in early 1945, was inauspicious. No welcome, no guided tour of the base or rundown of what they could expect, just an uninterested glance from his new flight commander, seated behind a desk. 'Oh. Larmer,' he said tiredly. 'You're the new crew are you? Well, there's nothing doing today. That is all,' and dismissed him.

Likewise ignored by the rest of the squadron, Laurie's crew nonetheless were listed on the battle order a few days later for their first trip, a daylight raid to Dortmund. 'They gave us a meal of bacon and eggs, which I thought was a big deal. You couldn't get that sort of tucker in England during the war,' he says. After a minimal briefing, Laurie handed over all personal items for safekeeping and prepared for his first trip.

'Bloody hell!' he remembers saying to himself when seeing

flak for the first time, knowing he was expected to fly into it. 'Once you got into the target area, though, you were too busy to notice it.'

A new pilot was usually required to perform a so-called second dickie trip, accompanying an experienced skipper to get the feeling of just what he could expect on operations himself. The fact that Laurie was sent on the daylight trip to Dortmund beforehand was an exception to the rule. A few nights later, however, he found himself seated beside a veteran to witness night bombing for the first time. The raid itself was uneventful, the return to Snaith anything but.

As they were taxiing to dispersal amid other returning aircraft, Laurie heard a pilot over the radio announce, 'U-Uncle, overshoot!' and a Halifax, too high for a landing, came around again. The pilot of this aircraft was also taking along a newbie, but as they attempted their second approach, Laurie heard a tremendous explosion. 'They crashed just off the runway,' he says. 'All of them were killed.' The cause of the crash was not long in being pieced together. Without a co-pilot, RAF bombers relied on the bomb aimer to partially fill that role, particularly on landings and take-offs, when he would sit beside the pilot with his hands on the throttles, preventing their usual tendency to 'creep' back if not locked in place. On this occasion, however, it was the rookie seated next to the pilot, and bad communication saw the throttles left unchecked. The Halifax lost power on approach, stalled, hit the ground and killed them all. 'That really shook everybody,' says Laurie. 'It was awful.'

The aftermath of this tragedy he found just as unnerving. 'There was never a funeral, no lowered flags, and no discussion about it in the mess,' he says. 'Afterwards, I asked someone about it. They just looked at me and said, "Laurie, there was a war on." That was just the way it was.'

Laurie's crew commenced their ten-trip tour that included an attack on Wuppertal in the industrial Ruhr, a joint attack on Zweibrücken and Homberg near Frankfurt to interrupt German troops – and which also killed nearly 200 civilians sheltering in basements – a long trip to the south of Germany to deliver Bayreuth's only air raid of the war, and on 18 April 1945, a visit to the German naval base of Heligoland in the North Sea. Laurie still has some of the post-raid photos of this trip, which show virtually nothing but a cratered, moon-like landscape. Another remarkable souvenir Laurie has hung onto for seventy years is his own maps for this trip, which rode all the way attached to his knee, the routes marked in still-vivid coloured lines of ink: green for the inbound leg, pink for the return. The target is clearly marked and Laurie's notes and calculations in pencil are still visible in the margins. On this day, nearly a thousand aircraft attacked in twenty-minute waves to allow the smoke to clear for visibility. The only losses were three Halifaxes, and Laurie witnessed two of them.

'One aircraft was directly below another,' he says. 'I watched it suddenly gain height and slam straight into the one above. The pilot or his gunners should have seen it, but they didn't.' From the awful tangle of falling aircraft, Laurie watched five parachutes emerge. Five survivors out of a combined crew of fourteen. 'But they would have just come down in the North Sea,' he says. 'There was no-one there to rescue them. They would have frozen to death in ten minutes.'

Trip number five, flown on the night of 8 April, was a 'diversionary raid' to the northern city of Travemünde, and Laurie was expecting a quiet night. Overflying larger raids nearby, his rear gunner had a superb view. 'Hey, Skip, you oughta see the fires down there!' he reported enthusiastically. Intercom chit-chat, however, was never encouraged.

'Never mind about the fires, just keep a look out for fight-ers,' Laurie rebuked him. Silence, then a minute or so later, Laurie's blood ran cold as his gunner returned to the intercom. 'Actually, Skip, I think there's a fighter on our tail now.'

Suddenly, from the gloom, a ghostly grey twin-engine air-craft flashed past at close range. Laurie thinks it was the very fast and very deadly Heinkel 219 Uhu 'Owl'. This highly advanced purpose-built German night fighter, one of the most sophisticated aeroplanes of the war, had in less than two years already accounted for a staggering number of British bombers in the blacked-out skies over Europe. The Owl was a hoodoo, secret and dreaded, said even to be capable of outclassing the otherwise invulnerable Mosquito. Some have suggested that had this machine been flown earlier, and in greater numbers, it may have had a significant impact on the RAF's night-bombing campaign itself.

'He went past us and then turned around and came in from the side,' says Laurie. Without delay, he wrenched the Halifax into a sickeningly tight turn, straight into the path of the approaching fighter. Laurie knew that if the German was able to position himself for a side-on beam attack, he would rake the Halifax, stem to stern, with cannon and machine-gun fire. His only hope was to present him with the smallest possible front-on target, and ramp up the two aircrafts' closing speed. 'He fired off a couple of shots,' he says. 'I could see the tracer com-ing towards us – but he flew straight under us.' The increased speed had the desired effect. 'Because he was going so fast,' says Laurie, 'it took him a long time to come around again.' But he did come around again, and with his gunners keeping track of the German's position, Laurie once more pulled the aircraft around to face him. 'This time he was actually too close to fire, and went under us again,' he says.

For a third time in this deadly battle of wits, the night fighter attacked, and 'that time he went above us', says Laurie. It was a moonlit night, and they were up above the clouds, with visibility for both pilots good. But unlike the Lancaster, the Halifax lacked a front gun turret, and Laurie's two gunners were unable to get a bead on the Owl. All they could do was keep calling out its position as it prowled, turned and attacked.

With the German passing as close as fifty feet, Laurie could clearly make out the night fighter and its pilot. Eventually, the German, possibly low on fuel, perhaps realising he'd met his match in Laurie, broke off. 'It seemed like an eternity, but it was probably only five or six minutes,' he says. 'It was absolutely stressful and completely exhausting.' As he speaks, I can still sense in his voice an echo of the terror he must have felt that night.

Laurie believes he was fortunate in having an excellent navigator who would be adamant about placing the aircraft over the target at precisely the right height and precisely the right time. 'He'd been commended for his navigation,' he says. 'Sometimes he'd call me up and get me to adjust the heading a *single* degree port or starboard. A lot of them didn't bother about that.'

Some pilots, he says, were 'selfish buggers', who would give themselves more height over the target to avoid the prospect of being bombed by their own aircraft above. This itself was no rare occurrence. 'I saw it happen once, on a daylight,' Laurie remembers. He can no longer recall the target, but an aircraft lining up in front of him was directly hit by the full bomb load of another above. This time, there were no parachutes to be seen. 'I don't think anyone got out of that one,' he says. 'It was quite sickening. You didn't know whether the next bombs were going to be falling on you. I didn't tell the crew. No point in upsetting them.'

Anzac Day 1945 marked 51 Squadron's, and Laurie's, final attack of the war, on the island of Wangerooge in the Frisians. On this day, nearly 500 heavy bombers sought to destroy the coastal batteries protecting the German ports of Bremen and Wilhelmshaven. On the way in, Laurie's Halifax was hit by an anti-aircraft shell, knocking out his starboard outer engine. 'It sent a shudder through the aircraft,' he says, 'and it sent a shudder through me.' They decided to carry on to the target, but were unable to maintain their prescribed height of 20 000 feet. 'We ended up bombing way below the others from just 8000,' he says. 'I remember my bomb aimer, Joe, saying to me, "Skipper, this is too low for me!"'

As a lone straggler, Laurie knew he was in a highly dangerous position. 'If there were fighters about that day, they probably would have got us,' he says. Making it back over the sea and landing at an emergency aerodrome on the east coast of England, they were picked up by truck and taken back to Snaith. 'By the time we got back, everyone had gone to bed,' he says. It was a quiet way to end an eventful tour.

It has always bewildered me as to where, in the face of such terrible certainty of mortal danger, the men of Bomber Command found the resolve to carry on to the magic number

of thirty operations. But, as Laurie tells me, sometimes they
didn't. A story he relates from another squadron concerns a
crew bombed up beside the runway and about to go, simply
waiting for the signal to start up. 'The nervous piss, we called
it,' he says. This was the time when the crews stood around outside their aircraft, making forced conversation, careful not to
mention the target in front of the ground crew, awaiting the
order to take their spot in the take-off queue. The story goes
that the wireless operator of this particular aircraft just quietly
walked over to his captain. 'Sorry, Skip, I'm not going,' he said.

The pilot looked back blankly. 'What do you mean you're
not going? We're all ready.'

'I know that, Skip, but I'm just not going.' With no idea
what to do, the pilot fetched the flight commander who was
told exactly the same thing. The man was sorry, but simply
refused to climb into the aircraft and fly the trip. Guards were
called, the man was put under close arrest, and a spare wireless
operator was found.

Laurie tells me the man was court-martialled and sentenced
to ten years in a military prison. 'In reality,' he says, 'he would
have been released soon after the war.' The crew that took off
that night, with their spare wireless operator, was shot down
and killed. Perhaps the story is true, perhaps it is a myth, but
the fear of being seen to be LMF – 'lacking moral fibre' in the
brutal military parlance of the day – was real and dreaded by
the airmen. Even more dreaded, perhaps, than the prospect of
death itself.

Laurie seems to have found the confines of life in an
English squadron somewhat wearying. 'They were much more
class conscious,' he says. 'They would say to me things like,

"We were so glad when you colonials came into the fight."
Colonials! That's what they called us!' The Australian lack of
deference to rank irked the English as well, Laurie says, and
despite being the only officer on his crew, it's hard to imagine
his friendly, easy manner fitting in with the stifling rigidity of
the British military system. 'Once a fortnight we used to take
our ground crew down the pub for a drink,' he says. 'They
thought we were great blokes, but the English crews would
never have done it.'

Applying to the airlines upon his return to Australia in
December 1945, Laurie was told that he lacked sufficient flying hours to warrant consideration. 'I'm happy for you to train
me,' he told them. 'We don't need to,' they said. 'The air force
has trained everyone for us.' Instead, he joined the motor-car
industry and had a long career in sales. He remains an affable
and cheery man, and his memory of the war is clear, at times
vivid.

We discuss the demise of the current Australian car industry, but he accepts it as an inevitability, probably much in the
same way he accepted the drama and dangers of his tour. 'We
were young and life was different then,' he says. 'I don't recall
ever thinking I wasn't going to survive.'

Like many former airmen, he is perplexed by the sudden
interest in his part in the war, an area of his life that remained
in the shadows for decades. 'My three daughters didn't know
anything about what I'd done, not for years,' he says. 'It took
a bit of settling down, after the war, it really did. I didn't talk
about it. No-one did, really.' Laurie remains somewhat proud of
the fact that he never once used his military service to get jobs
or even get ahead. 'Oh, and just between you and me,' he adds

conspiratorially, as if about to divulge a great confidence, 'I'm actually proud of the fact that I contributed, in some small way, to the end of the war and the awful regime we were fighting. And in a way, I'm also proud that I survived.'

NAT GOULD

Role: Fighter pilot
Aircraft: Hawker Hurricane, Curtiss P-40 Kittyhawk
Posting: 17 Squadron, RAF; 75 Squadron, RAAF

Milne Bay was bloody awful.

Arthur 'Nat' Gould's war, indeed his life, would quite easily fill a book on its own. Happily, the writing of it would not be too difficult, as Nat's memory, even into his nineties, is astounding. Nor does time seem to have dulled much of the fighter-pilot spirit which took him across the globe, flying almost the entire war in numerous theatres, including one of Australia's most challenging battles.

'Was your father in the First World War?' It's one of the questions I ask all the fellows I interview. I find it helps me gain a picture of their background. About half the time, the answer is yes, but Nat surprises me.

'No,' he answers as we settle into his small but fascinatingly cluttered study in his Upper North Shore Sydney apartment. 'But he was in the Boer War.' Nat Senior, it seems, was something of an adventurer, born in London, joining up and going away to war at sixteen. He was invalided out, and found his way to the Indian Army where he broke horses, before becoming a deckhand on ocean liners, jumping ship in Australia and working for the railways in Queensland.

The apple, they say, falls close to the tree and Nat's long and eventful career as a fighter pilot continued the adventurous traditions of his father including, amazingly, a stint flying for the Russians.

You'd never guess now at Nat's humble beginnings in Brisbane. 'As a teenager I'd go around the paddocks collecting mushrooms and manure and sell them to the gardens,' he tells me. 'Whenever I had ten shillings I'd whip out to the aerodrome at Archerfield and get half an hour's flying lesson.' So enterprising was Nat that by war's outbreak in 1939, he'd chalked up thirty hours on little Taylor Cub aeroplanes and held his civilian 'A' licence.

Listening to the outbreak of war over the wireless, Nat remembers his mother's reaction. 'She was pretty upset, but I was cheering. I thought now I'd get to fly and do some travelling.' He was right about that. Joining up as soon as he could, Nat became part of the very first intake of the Empire Air Training Scheme, No. 1 Course at Archerfield in Queensland. 'That first course was all kids like me with licences, so they knew we could fly, although not very well,' he says. At Wagga, Nat was one of the first to jump from Tiger Moths to Wirraways, and it was decided he would be a single-engine pilot. 'Age came into it a bit,' he says. 'They seemed to put the older blokes into bombers. The younger ones such as me who liked doing stupid things in planes went onto fighters. We weren't supposed to be very bright!'

At this early stage of the war, the extraordinarily efficient machine into which the Empire Air Training Scheme would evolve was still in its teething phase, and had, says Nat, a somewhat ad hoc feel to it. Syllabuses and courses had yet to be worked out, and even instructors were still being sourced. Some pre-war civilian types were clearly not prepared for the role, nor the modern aircraft with which they had to come to grips. 'I had to teach my instructor how to do aerobatics in a Wirraway,' he says. 'He was terrified of the bloody things.' Nat himself didn't have much of an opinion of them either. 'The Wirraway was a bugger of a thing, actually. Hard to fly, full of vices.'

In December 1940, Nat sailed to England on a long, seven-week voyage, arriving at his Operational Training Unit at a rudimentary RAF training station close to The Wash called Sutton Bridge. With perpetual drizzle and low cloud, it was hardly the most pleasant place to spend a bleak British winter. With a cursory introduction to a clapped-out Battle of Britain–veteran Hurricane ('A bloke stood on the wing and just told me what to push and pull,' he says), Nat began training over the crowded, unfamiliar landscape of England. 'In outback Australia,' he says, 'if you saw a railway line, it'd be the only one for a thousand miles. Here, there were dozens of them.' He even had a different scale of map to deal with, every inch of which was crammed with towns and roads and rivers. 'We were stuffed,' he says bluntly.

On his second or third solo trip in the Hurricane, Nat took off from Sutton Bridge and found himself in cloud virtually as soon as he put his wheels up. Climbing up through it, he attempted to complete the cross-country exercise but his radio didn't work, and soon he had no idea where he was. Not too far off, however, he spotted an RAF Blenheim bomber. 'I thought he probably knew where he was going, so I tried to formate on him so he could guide me to an airstrip somewhere,' he says. But the closer he came to the British aircraft, the faster it seemed to speed up. 'I tried to catch him but my clapped-out Hurricane couldn't keep up with him,' he says. Eventually, Nat peeled off and did the sensible thing by going out over the North Sea to re-orientate himself with the coast and find his way home. Upon landing, he was surprised to find himself being congratulated with claps and 'well dones' all round. Little did he realise that while he'd been up, the airfield had been bombed by a formation of Junkers Ju 88s and that he had been inadvertently chasing one out over the North Sea. 'My aircraft recognition wasn't all that good at that stage,' he says. 'They all thought I was so brave, chasing down a German on just my second solo! I had no idea.'

Joining No. 17 Squadron, RAF, a famous Battle of Britain outfit, Nat's days as an operational fighter pilot would start off relatively quietly. In July 1941, he learned that his flight had been earmarked for overseas. 'We all thought we were going to the Middle East,' he says. Instead, they would head north, to the freezing and desolate Kola Peninsula in the far north of the Soviet Union.

Desperate to protect the warm-water port of Murmansk in the first few months following Hitler's invasion of Russia, Churchill agreed to give Stalin two squadrons of Hurricanes, along with some pilots and ground crew to show them how to use them. After training the Russians in these modern machines (the Red Air Force's own planes were, says Nat, somewhat 'agricultural'), they would be handed over and the RAF pilots would come home. Two squadrons, 81 and Nat's 17, were earmarked to form the new 151 Wing, under the command of the delightfully named Wing Commander HNG Ramsbottom-Isherwood, who for his devoted service to the defence of the Soviet socialist workers' proletariat would be awarded the Order of Lenin!

Initially, however, 17 Squadron's destination was a secret very well-kept, even from its pilots. In Glasgow, boarding the almost ancient aircraft carrier HMS *Argus*, Nat and his mates still believed they were heading to the sands and deserts of North Africa. 'Then when we sailed out the Clyde, instead of turning left to go to the Middle East, we turned right to go to the North Pole!' he says.

Their true destination revealed, Nat, still slightly disbelieving, endured dreadful weather as the ship ploughed north into the Arctic, knowing that he was eventually going to have to fly himself off this thing and land somewhere in Russia. 'The Hurricanes had no hooks or anything,' he says, 'so we only had one chance to take off.' Their pre-flight briefing was, at best, rudimentary. 'We couldn't use our compass up there because they all pointed north anyway,' Nat explains. 'So we were told to line the ship up with a nearby destroyer, keep on going till we hit land, turn right, look for an airfield next to a town next to a river and go down and land on it.' Somehow, the whole squadron managed to do it, although some Hurricanes which had damaged their undercarriage on the carrier's steep and unfamiliar take-off ramp were required to fly all the way with their wheels down.

For the next two months, Nat flew standing patrols and escorts in the far north of Russia on an almost daily basis. It was ostensibly a training exercise for the Russians rather than an actual combat operation, but as Nat was discovering, that detail would be lost somewhere along the way.

'Surreal' is the word he uses to describe his Soviet sojourn at Vaenga, a rudimentary airfield near Murmansk. At his first breakfast, vodka and champagne were served; RAF guards were placed on every Hurricane, then the Russians placed their own guard on them. 'It was all entirely secret, so not everyone knew what we were doing there,' he says. With the RAF airmen virtually confined to the rundown aerodrome, it was not wise to walk around the place, Nat says, without keeping a hand close to your service revolver.

Only 30-odd miles from the ground fighting of the German invasion, Nat could clearly hear the guns of the battles around Leningrad, and the aerodrome was regularly attacked by bombers. 'The Russians had no radar or anything, so the first we knew of an air raid was bombs dropping on the airfield,' he says. 'We'd have to take off through the bursts.'

In a wooden hut lacking baths or showers, Nat would occasionally dare to venture to the nearby village bath house to wash. It was not a place in which the RAF pilots felt comfortable, and the Russians in turn seemed uneasy about them. 'Some of our chaps shot down some German aircraft,' he says. 'I think it was about sixteen in total, but the Russians were strange people. They were loath to give us any real success. We never quite understood why, but we think that it was a sort of national pride; they were the ones who were going to shoot down the German aeroplanes, not these bloody Englishmen.'

On a sortie escorting a squadron of Red Air Force dive bombers, Nat would get an idea of just how strange these Russians could be. 'It was a clear day and we could see for miles. As we watched, the Russians started to dive on one of their own destroyers, which then opened up and shot down the lead aircraft! We watched them as they bailed out, just sat in our cockpits and couldn't believe what we were seeing. Honestly, the whole thing was quite bizarre,' he says.

After handing over their Hurricanes, Nat and his fellow pilots waited to hear what plans were in train to take them home. He soon realised there were none. Eventually, he and a couple of the other Australian pilots took matters into their own hands. 'We just went down to the local wharf and waited,' he says. Soon a British destroyer, HMS *Intrepid*, pulled up alongside.

'Where are you going?' asked Nat.

'Back to Blighty,' was the reply from an officer. 'Hop in.'

'So we just got on and went home,' says Nat, bringing a fittingly peculiar end to his Russian interlude. On the way back to the naval base at Scapa Flow, almost a year to the day he had sailed from Brisbane, Nat heard the news about Pearl Harbor.

From a Russian winter to the steam-bath, malaria-ridden jungles of New Guinea, Nat was transferred home to defend his own country in an entirely new war in the Pacific. Arriving back in his native Queensland in May 1942, Nat joined the already renowned 75 Squadron, a unit scratched together a few months before, and currently refitting in Kingaroy after its epic 44-day defence of Port Moresby. In this struggle, 75 had lost almost all their aircraft and many of their pilots. Soon, however, they would be heading back into action, and Nat would be joining them at their new home, a joint Australian and American base hacked from the jungle and plantations in the far-eastern tip of New Guinea, Milne Bay.

'You know,' says Nat with a slight note of exasperation, 'people know about Kokoda, but they have no idea about Milne Bay.' He's probably right, but one suspects few could be as well acquainted with this dramatic August 1942 battle as Nat. He was, after all, right in the thick of it.

Milne Bay runs roughly east–west for 18 miles and about 6 across. The airstrip, recently established on its north-western end, was simply a 1-mile strip of mud bulldozed out of coconut trees and covered with steel matting. There were virtually no facilities, and the pilots lived five to a man in flimsy army tents.

'Milne Bay was bloody awful,' says Nat. 'Never stopped raining. The mountains came straight up from the strip. When you landed it was an up and down ride. It was carved out of a coconut plantation, so if you went off the runway, which you did, you ran into a tree, which didn't do the aircraft much good.' But the Milne Bay strip was strategically important to the Japanese, and had been impacting on their plans to take Port Moresby, and therefore, New Guinea. So, in August 1942, they came to take it.

An amphibious invasion convoy carrying over a thousand experienced (mainly) naval soldiers, two cruisers, three destroyers and various transports was assembled, but spotted soon after its departure from Rabaul on 24 August. Japanese intelligence was also bad, their code had been broken, and the Australian forces defending Milne Bay were woefully underestimated.

As the invaders turned west into the long dead end of Milne Bay the next morning, the Kittyhawk pilots of 75 and 76

Squadrons were waiting for them.

'American bombers couldn't get in due to the weather,' remembers Nat. 'So we strapped two 300-pound bombs to our little Kittyhawks!' Told to go primarily for the troop transports, Nat remembers attacking in atrocious weather with visibility down to 200 feet above the water. 'The only thing you could do was skip-bomb,' he says, describing the very tricky practice of attempting to bounce a bomb off the surface of the water into the side of a ship. 'We were at nought feet and everything was firing up at us.' It was a storm of fire. Everything in the convoy opened up on the Kittyhawks at close range. Even the cruisers, he says, were firing their main naval guns to send up splashes of water underneath them. 'I was aiming at a bloody great troop ship,' he says, 'I came in, let them go and ducked back up into the clouds again.' The flak, he says, was severe, but he was unscathed.

Back at the Milne Bay airstrip, Peter Turnbull, the CO of 76 Squadron, a legend of a man who would be killed in action just two days later, congratulated Nat profusely.

'What for?' Nat asked.

'You sank that gunboat.'

Nat was perplexed. 'Gunboat? I was aiming at a troop ship,' he said.

'Well you're an awful bloody shot,' said the boss. 'You sank a gunboat!'

Nat had no idea he'd hit anything. 'The gunboat must have been close to it,' he says, 'but I certainly wasn't aiming at it.'

The battle lasted just under two weeks and was a close and vicious struggle fought at desperately close range in terrible conditions. 75 and 76 Squadrons have been freely credited by the army as being the 'decisive factor' in winning the engagement, particularly on that first day. The Japanese push towards the airfields was successful at first, but was then checked by the militia, and later Second AIF men, supported constantly by the flying artillery of the Kittyhawks.

'We'd fly ten-minute sorties,' says Nat. 'So many that we didn't even bother putting them in our logbook.' Nat tells me the pilots would be firing their guns while virtually still over the runway. 'On a couple of occasions, the Japs were just about at one end of the airstrip,' he says. To support the ground soldiers, an enemy position was determined, then the Kittyhawks' six half-inch machine guns would let loose, tearing through the jungle canopy into the unseen enemy underneath. 'Then you'd go back and land and have a cigarette and a pee and take off again,' says Nat.

Tracer was added to the last rounds of their ammunition trays, not to assist with firing, he tells me, but to indicate when they were running out. A system of flares and Very lights was used, fired by the soldiers on the ground to indicate the Japanese positions only several hundred metres ahead. 'You couldn't see them,' he says. 'Then at the next debriefing, the army would tell us that we'd killed hundreds of them.'

Nat would also attack barges, as well as Japanese troops on the beaches, who on one occasion stood waving, apparently in the belief they would not be seeing anything but their own aircraft.

Concealed snipers proved a menace, having embedded themselves in the high fronds of the coconut trees. At almost dead level, the Kittyhawks would fire into the crowns, and as the official government history later described it, 'palm fronds, bullets and dead Japanese snipers poured down with the rain'.

'I watched one of our blokes get shot down,' Nat tells me. 'Right in front of me.' When not flying, the pilots would take turns manning the Bofors anti-aircraft gun with the soldiers. 'You had to, really,' he says, 'because they couldn't tell a Zero from a Kittyhawk, they'd shoot at anything. We'd always be having to tell them, "Hang on, that's one of ours!"'

On this occasion, Nat watched from a gun pit as a Kittyhawk came tearing across the aerodrome at about a thousand feet with, he says, 'a Zero right up his backside'. The aircraft was on fire, and Nat watched the pilot, a sergeant who he knew, bail out. 'We actually saw him hit the ground, his chute didn't have time to open and he was killed right in front of us. That was Milne Bay.'

I ask Nat to give me his assessment of the Kittyhawk after his experience with Hurricanes. 'We hated them at first,' he tells me. 'We called them "bulldozers with wings", but we came to appreciate them.' The Kittyhawk was by no means a perfect fighter, particularly up against the light and manoeuvrable Japanese aircraft, but it was tough, it could take punishment, and it could handle the conditions. 'A Spitfire would have been completely useless there,' he says. 'They just didn't have the endurance for one thing. They were like dainty ballerinas by comparison to the Kittyhawk.'

Flying an aircraft the pilots knew in many ways to be no match for the enemy, Nat tells me it was understood how to deal with them. 'We were told that if you saw a bunch of Zeros above you, roll onto your back, dive and just get the hell out of there. If you're above them, however, dive and shoot and keep on going. Don't dogfight them, whatever you do, or he'll be inside you before you do half a turn. If you wanted to survive, you had to let him go. You'd hear the yelling and the screaming going on in your headphones,' he says. 'It was quite intense.'

The harshness of the conditions at Milne Bay can hardly be overstated. Photographs of the land battle show a dank and gloomy battlefield of mud-choked jungle tracks patrolled by thin, hollow-eyed soldiers clutching .303 rifles, their rotting shirts discarded as they probe warily around the next bend or clump of green. 'We all had malaria and dysentery – at the same time,' says Nat. 'At one stage we had a third of the squadron down with malaria. It was a very unpleasant place.'

The misery of illness to some extent even masked the fear. 'Honestly,' says Nat, 'you just felt too awful to be scared. You'd take off your oxygen mask and vomit all over the cockpit and poop over everything, then go back and refuel and rearm and vomit on the tailplane and do it all again. I weighed eight stone at the end of it.' There were no showers, and no decent food. 'Just cans of baked beans and bully beef, really,' he says.

At times the squadron's doctor, Bill Deane-Butcher, would attempt to intervene to give the men a chance to rest and recover. 'It was all very primitive,' Nat tells me. 'Once there were three or four of us lying in the "sick bay", really just an ordinary army bush tent on stretchers a few inches off the mud. Bill ordered us not to get up.' However, it was war, and the threat was real. Into the tent and past the doctor swept the 75 Squadron CO, Les Jackson, a difficult and controversial figure, deeply unpopular among the pilots. 'Righto, airborne,' he ordered the pilots perfunctorily, to the doctor's impotent protests.

'We were pooping and vomiting,' says Nat, 'but there was no-one else to do the job. We had no reserve and there were no other pilots coming through at that time. That was just how it was.'

Milne Bay represented the first major land defeat of the Japanese and is regarded as a true turning point in the New Guinea campaign. The airfield – now renamed Turnbull Strip after the late 76 Squadron CO who congratulated Nat on his inadvertent sinking – was spared, and in February 1944, when the war had moved on, was abandoned once again to the jungle, which quickly reclaimed it.

Nat's combat flying was also, for the time being, over. If, however, he thought the casualties would cease, he was sadly mistaken, as he was then earmarked for an even more hazardous job, training. He even penned a song about No. 2 Operational Training Unit, Mildura, a hidden talent about which I had no idea:

> At the Builders Club at 2 OTU Mildura,
> The building's run by types who think they know,
> Your ears get bashed to tatters, by a gent who thinks he matters,
> Come listen to the reams of bullshit flow.

Subsequent verses of the ditty, I'm assured, are far bawdier. 'We hated it there,' he tells me of the job he had in converting raw graduates to fighter pilots in six weeks. 'We weren't instructors,' he says, 'just "twitched up" fighter pilots who'd flown all over the world. The casualty rate was higher there than on any fighter squadron I was on, I can tell you.' His logbook attests to the dreadful accident rate of all advanced wartime training facilities under the RAAF, with 'crashed and killed' entered on page after page beside the names of young pilots who did not even get to leave their own country or earn a battle honour.

Deflection shooting, Nat says, was one of the biggest kill-
ers. 'We'd train on a lake and they'd have to fire on their own
shadow. Some just didn't leave themselves room to pull out.'
The dive-bombing range, he says, was even worse. 'They say we
left more Kittyhawks there than bombs.'

Eventually, Nat had had enough, and pressed his famous
friend, Clive Caldwell, also an instructor at Mildura, to arrange
a transfer back to an operational squadron. 'I'm going too,' said
Caldwell. 'You can come with me if you like.' So, for the final
year of the war, Nat went on to fly Spitfires with 457 Squadron
in the islands to Australia's north but, as he says, 'by that time,
the war had really moved on'.

Nat's career continued until well after the war. Taking up an
offer from the British Pacific Fleet, he accepted a commission
in the Royal Navy, travelled to England and flew off aircraft
carriers before joining Australia's nascent Fleet Air Arm. Briefly
commanding a squadron in Korea, Nat eventually rose to the
rank of commander, retiring only in 1965.

Nat seems at times curious about my interest in his past,
and unsure whether I really want to hear all his 'waffle'. 'Look,
we're going to be here all day if we carry on like this,' he says
to me a number of times during our series of afternoon conversations. When I assure him there is nothing I would rather
do than sit and listen, he seems flattered. 'Oh, well, that's fine
then,' he says. 'But maybe we should have a drink before we
keep going?' Never was I unhappy to oblige.

The malaria he picked up in the jungle continued to dog
Nat with regular attacks, he says, for fifteen years after the war.
One senses, though, that a little of the jungle has remained with
him.

While choosing not to be forthcoming about his adjustment to peacetime, the fact that Nat made the services his life for another twenty years suggests that he is a resilient character, perhaps able to throw off the lingering demons of battle more easily than others. I could not help notice, however, one or two tell-tale moments in our conversations when, describing the squalor, the sickness and the killing of Milne Bay, a deep, albeit brief weariness clouded his otherwise ebullient face. For all the impressive atmosphere of his study, surrounded by framed photographs, awards, medals and other accoutrements of a long and distinguished career in the services, there were times when his clear eyes would glaze for a moment, focusing on some best-forgotten memory of loss, comradeship, and battles long since fought and won.

REX KIMLIN

Role: Wireless operator
Aircraft: Avro Lancaster
Posting: 15 Squadron, RAF

I can't remember a single target where there was no flak.
Sometimes it was enormous.

When Rex made it known at his Initial Training School in Brisbane that he wanted to be a pilot, they simply laughed. 'Sorry, son, you've got no hope, not with your expertise in Morse. You're going to be a wireless operator.' Such was the downside of being a telegraph boy with a good speed on the Morse code key. Truth be told, he hadn't learned it for the air force at all, but simply to further his ambitions of becoming a telegraphist – in 1941 a coveted and well-paid position. In any case, like so many other boys of the era, Rex believed the war would be over before he was old enough to get involved. It didn't take long, however, for the war to come to him.

'As a telegraph boy,' he tells me as we sit on the veranda of his lovely timber home on Queensland's Stradbroke Island, 'I used to have to deliver the telegrams.' He can never forget the frozen stare on people's faces as he walked up to their front door, the distinctive cream-coloured envelope clutched in his hand. 'Sometimes they'd send a minister of religion to do it instead,' he tells me.

On one occasion, he slowly ascended the high steps of a large, well-to-do house, watched by a nervous-looking middle-aged woman standing at the top. 'I have a telegram for you,' he said, before handing it to her and retreating back down.

'Just a moment,' the woman called after him. 'There might be a reply.'

'No,' said Rex, without even turning around, 'I don't think there'll be a reply.' She opened it, read the news of a dead husband or son, and collapsed onto the steps. Not knowing what to do, Rex called her neighbour for help. 'It was a tough job for a kid,' he says.

Two years later, in May 1943 at the Melbourne embarkation depot, as he prepared to board a ship to England, Rex's was one of forty-odd names read out and instructed to stay behind on parade after the others had headed off on trucks to the docks. Instead of journeying to England, Rex was now told he would be posted to the newly opened base at East Sale in Victoria, to train on Beaufort bombers for the New Guinea campaign. He was devastated, but had no choice other than to do as he was told. Fate, however, would intervene.

A serious and mysterious flaw in some of the early Australian-built Beauforts saw an alarmingly high accident rate, which prompted the pilots in Rex's course to refuse to fly them until they were fixed. A stand-off ensued, and this very well hushed-up 'mutiny' was put down only when the pilots had their stripes ripped off them and were sent back to basic training to start their flying all over again. They were proven correct, however, when a problem with the Beaufort's trim mechanism was discovered, causing them to become uncontrollable in the air. It was eventually rectified, but in the meantime, Rex was left without a pilot. Not knowing quite what to do with him, the air force decided to wash their hands of the problem by sending Rex once more back to the embarkation depot and putting him on a ship bound for England. This time, there was no last-minute hiccup, and after a long voyage, Rex arrived in wartime Britain, almost two years since signing on.

Several months later, and after a week of trying to get to know some of the myriad faces of his fellow airmen at No. 26 Operational Training Unit in Buckinghamshire, Rex was approached by a confident-looking young man with pilots wings on his tunic, Ivan Buchanan from Geelong. 'We all called him "Buck",' says Rex. 'He was already a big wheel in the Ford Motor Company in Geelong, and continued to be so after the war.'

'You look a likely type,' Buck said to Rex. 'Would you like to be my wireless operator?'

Rex looked him up and down a bit and simply said, 'Fine.' Four more fellows were assembled, a mixture of Australians and Englishmen, and Rex had his crew, minus their flight engineer, who, as standard practice, would come later at their conversion to four-engine aircraft. For now, all they had to do was survive the next two months flying across the United Kingdom in pensioned-off Wellington bombers, which, says Rex, 'were so clapped-out that if you lost an engine at night, the rule was to bail out rather than try and land the things!' This in fact happened to one pilot Rex knew, who, after parachuting from his lame Wellington, happened to land dead centre on the runway of an unknown RAF aerodrome!

More training time was spent on 'big cumbersome old beasts' of Stirlings, then a conversion course onto Lancasters. Rex was impressed with the Lanc from the beginning. In his first ever flight, the instructing pilot cut one motor, then, to Rex's alarm, a second. 'I heard the engines cutting out,' he says, 'and went onto the intercom, just in time to hear the instructing pilot's voice saying to Buck, "Right. Now, feather engine number three." They told us that with enough height, the Lancaster could fly back home from Germany on just one motor.' During this impressive demonstration, Rex remembers watching from the astrodome as a Mosquito came up alongside, cut one of his own engines, and performed a loop right over the top of them. 'Just to say, "Anything you can do, I can do better,"' he says.

Finally, in late July 1944, Rex and his crew received their posting, to No. 15 Squadron, part of 3 Group, at RAF Mildenhall. To varying degrees, the rules and procedures differed between the several groups of Bomber Command, which normally consisted of about ten squadrons each. Rex tells me that in late 1944, it was decided that 3 Group crews would be required to complete an extra five trips on top of the standard tour of thirty. 'After D-Day, we were doing a lot of shorter daylight trips to support the army, so they reckoned we deserved a few extra!' he says. Shorter they may have been, but no less dangerous.

Rex doesn't recall the details of all his many trips, but some stand out, such as his first long night op to Brunswick. 'That's when we lost our rear gunner,' he tells me. Assuming him to have been killed by flak or night-fighter attack, I am surprised when Rex adds, 'He went LMF,' citing the 'lack of moral fibre' label thrown at those airmen whose nerves were simply not up to the stresses of operational flying. The story is extraordinary. 'It was our first real "horror op",' he says. On the run-in to Brunswick from the Dutch coast, he recalls seeing 'one great pyrotechnic display. Everything was up there: searchlights criss-crossing the sky, an occasional kite caught in the light, twisting and diving like a big moth; streams of tracer drifting up towards us, then going by as quick as lightning; every now and then a plane going down or exploding.' German night fighters too were out in force, appearing to have guessed the bombers' route to the target. 'Fighter flares' were dropped from above, exploding in brilliant magnesium iridescence, then drifting down, ghost-like, to illuminate the bomber stream, stripping away their dark concealing cloak of darkness.

'One of the flares exploded just above the rear turret of our plane,' says Rex. Instantly, Peter, the Australian rear gunner, yelled out over the intercom in a panicked voice, 'I'm blind! I can't see!'

'Have you been hit?' responded Buck, the pilot.

Alan Helyar, the laconic mid-upper gunner ('quite the opposite of Peter', says Rex), came in with a droll, 'I don't think so. The silly bugger's just been dazzled by the flare.'

Concerned nonetheless, Buck asked the flight engineer to go back to see how Peter was faring. Making his way over the difficult main spar to the rear of the aircraft, the engineer, a Liverpool Irishman named John 'Bing' Crosby, arrived at the rear turret just in time to see the gunner crawling out of it. 'I'm not going back there! I'm not going back there!' was all he could say in panic and he proceeded to lie down on the aircraft's small medical stretcher, leaving the Lancaster's tail undefended. Alan, the mid-upper, quickly went back to man it, while bomb aimer Steve Hawkins took up the mid-upper, until he had to return to his own post in the nose to get behind his bomb sight as they approached the target.

They were lucky that night. Despite the furore, they bombed and made it safely back to Mildenhall, although the atmosphere on the trip home, says Rex, was to say the least, 'very sober'. On landing, however, Peter made it easy. 'That's it, Buck,' he said, approaching the pilot. 'I'm not going back up there again, I've had it.' The next day Peter and all his possessions had been removed, as if he'd never existed. 'Nobody said much about it,' says Rex. After a short spot of leave, they were given a replacement gunner, and Peter was barely mentioned again. Rex bore him no resentment. 'I could sympathise with him,' he reflects. 'He'd been my roommate in the barracks, and we'd got on pretty well. But his nerves had just collapsed and that was that. I've often thought, There but for the grace of God go I.'

Rex managed to assuage his own fear by keeping busy, and as a wireless operator, there was a great deal for him to do. Apart from receiving regular signals from base, he would monitor radar devices, such as the fighter early-warning system, 'fishpond', and interfere with the German night-fighter radio transmissions by broadcasting on their frequencies. Rex would jam the German pilots' headphones with engine noise sourced from a microphone in one of the aircraft's engine bays, or even random taps with his own Morse key. Over the target, he would stand in the astrodome and look out for fighters or off-course British bombers. 'You saw aircraft just explode,' he tells me, either from direct hits or collisions. He has often wondered, however, if some were the victims of lax smoking rules. 'The interior of the Lancaster always smelled of petrol,' he tells me. 'Some pilots allowed smoking on board, which was bloody stupid.'

A trip flown on the last day of August 1944 is one Rex will remember simply for its audacity of scale, a 'bobby-dazzler', as he says in his own book of memoirs, penned recently for friends and family, titled *How Lucky I Was*. Assembled in the briefing room a few hours before take-off, every airman speculated on what the map behind the little curtain in front of them would reveal. The CO walked in and everybody stood. 'Sit, please,' he said, as usual. Then the curtain was drawn and Rex can still hear the audible groan that engulfed the room. The map revealed red lines of tape stretching right across Europe from their base at Mildenhall, over the North Sea, continuing across Denmark, Norway and Sweden, then a sharp swing south to the German coast. 'Well, chaps, tonight's target is Stettin,' said the boss. This long route of ten hours' flying time had been chosen to avoid as much occupied territory as possible, but the Lancasters would be flying at their capacity, their gigantic wing-tanks almost overflowing with 100-octane fuel. 'We were told that after bombing, we would have to continue to fly straight on into Germany for another 50 miles before turning and following almost the identical route back,' says Rex. It was to be a gruelling trip, flown into the face of 150 miles-per-hour headwinds. The Lancasters would need every drop of fuel they could carry.

On this trip also, a new navigational technique was tried, where in place of the standard practice of each aircraft individually navigating its way to the target, selected crews would take regular wind and speed readings, and relay them back to England where the average was calculated and then re-broadcast to the bomber stream. John Varey, Rex's 'exceptional' navigator, was one of those chosen, with Rex himself required, terrifyingly, to transmit the information by Morse, potentially exposing their position to German radar.

'Normally, the Morse key wasn't touched except in an emergency, as the Germans were listening out for your signal,' he tells me. 'On this trip I had to broadcast eleven times, all the while expecting to be blown out of the sky.'

This attack on Stettin was regarded as a success by Bomber Command, destroying residential and industrial parts of the old port and town which had escaped previous attacks. It destroyed 1569 houses and killed 1033 people, with the same number reported as wounded. Twenty-three Lancasters, or nearly 6 per cent of the force of 402, were lost, many, according to Rex, simply running out of fuel and ditching in the North Sea.

Rex very nearly 'bought it' on a daylight trip to Gelsenkirchen in the heart of the Ruhr valley in late November 1944. Becoming bolder as the war went on, particularly with the waning of the German fighter force, Bomber Command began to make forays into the industrial heart of Germany by day. On the run-in to the target, a red warning light indicating anti-aircraft radar had locked onto them lit up on Rex's panel. He advised Buck to expect flak at any moment as they flew on, straight and level, to the target. How their Lancaster, *D-Dog*, survived, is hard to imagine.

Moments after having released their bomb load, they were ringed by four accurate, simultaneous explosions. 'It was like being punched by a series of large fists,' says Rex. The pilot's windshield was blown out, and showers of Perspex and shell casings flew through the aircraft, followed by an icy-cold wind. Buck the pilot and John 'Bing' Crosby suffered cuts and had Perspex chips blown into their eyes; the bomb aimer, lying prone in the nose, received a chunk of flak to the metal release mechanism of his harness, which was bent out of shape, but probably saved his life; the two gunners had the windows of their turrets blown away and their faces blackened by the explosions, and in front of Rex, John the navigator collapsed on the floor. A piece of flak had struck him too, but his leather flying helmet had taken the glancing blow, leaving him with only a lump on the head. 'I was the only one who didn't have a scratch,' says Rex.

D-Dog, it seems, had also, miraculously, escaped serious damage, and Buck, in great pain staring into the face of the freezing slipstream, nursed them back to Mildenhall. One of the holes in the fuselage near the door was nearly 2 feet in diameter. 'When we landed, we all decided to crawl out through it,' says Rex.

The next day, they inspected their shattered aircraft in the maintenance hangar and, stunned, counted 130 holes. Buck was awarded an immediate Distinguished Flying Cross. 'It's for all of you,' he told his crew. 'Not just for me.'

Rex and his crew had only one encounter with a fighter, and were lucky it was not a closer one. Over Wilhelmshaven one night, mid-upper gunner Alan Helyar, in typical style, simply called 'fighter, port quarter above us' over the intercom, identifying it straight away as a heavily armed Messerschmitt Me 410.

'Does he look like attacking?' asked Buck. But the German for the moment seemed happy flying parallel to the bomber stream, just out of range, waiting perhaps for radio or visual confirmation of a target. 'He stooged along with us at the same height for a while,' says Rex. 'Buck just said, "Keep an eye on him."'

Alan had a better suggestion. 'I think it'll be a good idea if we just put the nose down and get out of his road.' In whole-hearted agreement with his 'avoiding a fight' philosophy, Buck gently put the nose of the Lancaster down, the aircraft slowly descended, and the German was lost in darkness.

Having survived a standard tour of thirty trips, Rex was now faced with five more, and wondered how much his luck would hold against the numbers game of operational flying. Finally trip number thirty-five arrived, on 27 November, an attack by 169 3-Group Lancasters on the Kalk Nord railway yards in Cologne, perhaps one of the 'hottest' targets in the Ruhr. They bombed using the city's great cathedral as their aiming point (it still stands today – a testament less to God's will than bad bomb aiming, says Rex) and received a few close bursts of flak, but were otherwise unharmed. The drama lasted, however, right up until the time their wheels touched down on the runway back at Mildenhall. With the crew just starting to allow themselves a slight sense of relief at having survived their tour, Buck put D-Dog into the last final approach he would ever make in oper-ational flying.

At this point, the practice was for the flight engineer to assist the pilot by lowering the undercarriage and flaps, as well as controlling the throttles, to allow the skipper to concentrate on the flying. For reasons that remain mysterious, Bing decided to cut the throttles early, when the Lanc was still 70 feet or so above the runway. Buck was nowhere near ready for this, and according to Rex, the whole aircraft 'dropped like a stone'. Buck's instincts, however, probably saved them all. He knocked Bing out of the way and slammed the throttles back open, through the 'gate', managing to lift the nose just as the wheels hit the tarmac, hard. 'We bounced about fifty feet in the air, landed on one wheel, then on the other,' says Rex. After coming to a stop in silence, then emerging from the aircraft 'quite shaken up', everyone wondered what the reaction of the pilot would be. 'He grabbed Bing, turned him around and gave him a fair kick up the arse. "You stupid Irish prick, you nearly killed the lot of us!" He was only half in jest.'

Why Bing chose to do this remained a mystery, apparently even to himself. 'Just excited to finish, I suppose,' reflects Rex. A little later, after the briefing, their chief ground engineer exclaimed, 'You call that a bloody landing?' Their tour, however, was over and the crew, after dusting themselves off, 'felt euphoric, relieved, full of life', says Rex, at just having survived.

Rex went on leave, and while dropping in on a friend in a convalescent hospital, met the visiting King and Queen, who thanked him personally for his services in the air war. Then, he boarded a ship and came home. His was one of those apparently seamless returns to peacetime, and apart from one or two bad nights, he was not adversely affected by all that he'd seen on his tour of ops. 'They talk a lot about war-related post-traumatic stress disorder today,' he says, 'but I just didn't get affected by it.' Some of these bomber boys, it seems, really were made of stern stuff.

I've enjoyed meeting Rex on the balcony of his lovely island setting amid raucous friarbirds and honeyeaters. His wife of many years, Charm, has fed and watered me, and his daughter Penny ferried me the rather long distance back and forth from the ferry terminal to his home. I wish to linger, but time, tide and timetables dictate. Rex's clarity of memory and mental alertness, I tell him, is astonishing. It seems there is a reason for this. A decade or so after the war, a chance encounter between a couple of members of his crew on a Brisbane street saw them vow to all get together, and to keep on doing so regularly. Stories were rescued from the fading abyss of memory, and preserved. Gradually, the men of his crew passed away, and today Rex finds himself the last man standing of Lancaster *D-Dog*.

The title of his memoir, *How Lucky I Was*, could hardly be more apt.

SID HANDSAKER

Role: Pilot
Aircraft: Supermarine Spitfire
Posting: 451 Squadron, RAAF

*These were the Germans, the people we were
supposed to kill. It still gets me.*

Flying your first solo in a Wirraway on your twenty-first birthday was, for Sid, one hell of a present. He was a complete natural, but a few weeks earlier hadn't dared to dream of ever becoming a pilot, convinced his modest education standard wouldn't even qualify him for the training. Instead, he put down for wireless operator / air gunner. His talent in the Tiger Moth, however, as well as his good work ethic, had not gone unnoticed. 'One day,' he tells me, 'my teacher, a pilot officer, just walked up with my form and asked why I'd put in for wireless / air gunner. I told him, but he just said, "You can do better than that. What about pilot?" So he just crossed out "wire-less / air gunner" and wrote "pilot" next it. So, a pilot is what I became.' Sid is still amazed by it today.

Being forced to then spend a couple of years flying Fairey Battles at Evans Head Bombing and Gunnery School would have driven many a budding fighter pilot to despair, but Sid didn't seem to mind a bit. He simply loved flying, and would have been happy remaining there for the duration. Eventually, however, the wheels of military bureaucracy turned and caught up with him, and with an uncommonly large number of flying hours under his belt, Sid boarded a ship and headed to England, stepping off the *Queen Elizabeth* in September 1943.

Being introduced to the Spitfire was something Sid has never forgotten. It was an aeroplane, he says, you almost felt a part of. 'With the Spitfire,' he says, 'it seemed as if you only had to think about what you were going to do and it would do it. If you thought about putting your left wing down, it went down. If you thought about doing a loop, it'd do a loop etc.'

Sid began his brief tour late in the war, arriving at the all-Australian 451 Squadron at Matlaske in Norfolk in April 1945 and completing three operational sorties. He is, however, the only pilot I have met who remained in post-war Europe for an extended period and gained a firsthand, unique insight into Germany in the immediate wake of the Nazi regime. First though, brief as it was, there was his tour to get through, and among his three trips was one that he'll always remember.

I have spoken to several bomber men who took part in the famous raid on the German island of Heligoland on 18 April 1945, where the docks, submarine pens and town were all attacked by nearly a thousand Lancasters and Halifaxes, but have never met one of their fighter escorts. In fact, no less than twenty-two squadrons of Spitfires and Mustangs were also up that day, and one of those was 451. There was no enemy fighter activity to contend with, but the flak was, as ever, accurate.

'We were sitting up at 25 000 feet, and the bombers were coming in between 10–15 000 feet,' Sid tells me. He shows me in a book some 'before and after' photographs of this rocky outcrop in a corner of the North Sea which was once in fact a British possession. During the Second World War, the Germans built U-boat pens and significant anti-aircraft defences here, which in 1945 were deemed worthy of destruction by the RAF. The attack didn't stop at the naval base or even the town. As Sid's images show, the raid reduced this pleasant rocky island to little more than a cratered moonscape. The civilian population – safe at least in natural-rock bomb shelters – were evacuated the next day. Heligoland remained uninhabitable for nearly a decade after the war.

'The bombers were hitting the submarine pens and copping all the flak, then for some reason I copped a burst underneath me,' he says. With a sickening jolt, Sid and his Spit were thrown upwards, 'like someone had kicked the bottom of my chair'. Then the five blades of the propeller of his Spitfire XIV suddenly windmilled to a stop. 'So there I was, no engine, 50 miles out from the coast with only ocean beneath me.'

Instantly, however, Sid's training kicked in. He closed down the throttle, then reached down to the awkwardly placed fuel cocks in the lower right-hand corner of the cockpit to switch off the 90-gallon drop-tanks and go onto the main. 'Then I reset everything to start the motor, put throttle and revs at a certain setting, then I had to roll her over on her back and put her nose straight down.' Sid had performed this somewhat terrifying emergency procedure countless times in practice, but never in battle, and never with a possibly damaged engine. The centrifugal force of the wind over the propeller blades would, like push-starting a car, throw the enormous Griffon engine into life. 'Well, that's what you hoped it would do, at least,' adds Sid. Luckily, it fired, coughed back into life, and as Sid says, 'bingo'.

A few days later, his logbook records, 'No more op trips. War has had it!' Sid's job, however, was far from over. Being a relatively late arrival, he was put down to accompany the squadron on its five-month stint in newly vanquished Germany as part of the British Air Forces of Occupation, where he would be based primarily at Gatow on the outskirts of Berlin. Flying over the airfields of the now defunct Luftwaffe, Sid remembers seeing 'thousands and thousands of German aircraft, 109s and Focke-Wulfs etc., all lined up. I think they just got a bulldozer and went through the lot.' He reckons he would quite like to have had a go at flying one, but one of the deepest impressions left on him was the scale of the destruction he saw.

'I really don't think I can describe what the damage was like,' he tells me with a certain awe. 'It changed my whole outlook on life.' In bombed and battered England, Sid had been taught to hate 'the Hun', but found it difficult to do so once he saw ordinary people struggling in what was left of their country. Once when playing football on the frozen ground, he slipped and broke a bone, landing him a stint in hospital. 'The German girls would come in to do the cleaning and you'd hear them harmonising as they sung,' he says. 'Just quietly so as not to wake us. It was the most beautiful thing.' This capacity to sing when around them lay ruins left a deep impression on the young man from Newcastle. 'At the airfield, there were hundreds of them working on it. At the end of the day, I'd sit in the window and listen to them singing perfectly as they went home.'

At night, he would sometimes ride with his fellow pilots to a club or bar through the shattered Berlin suburbs in trucks. 'On a clear night, you could ride through these streets and all you'd see were gaunt, burned-out walls of buildings with the moon shining through them,' he tells me. Only very occasionally, the glow of a single kerosene lamp from a cellar would indicate evidence of life.

'There were signs as you came into the city saying "No fraternisation", but if you had chocolates or cigarettes,' says Sid, 'you were a millionaire.' On the post-war black market, a single Lucky Strike cigarette could fetch about five marks. The Americans would give Sid cartons of them. 'At the market you could give someone a carton and people would be fighting to give you money in these great wads of banknotes,' he says. 'I never counted it, but they were always scrupulously honest,' he says. For those who wanted to take advantage of it, exploiting the defeated Germans was easy. Women greatly outnumbered the men, and few of them had very much of anything, let alone luxuries.

'They didn't even have things like soap,' Sid tells me. 'People think I probably took advantage of that, but I didn't drink and I didn't smoke and I was engaged back home to be married. I was probably a bit sanctimonious, I suppose.'

Coming out of a club, the conquering airmen were always followed by small children, requesting treats, cigarettes, anything. 'The smokers would throw a butt their way and there'd be a scramble for it,' says Sid. 'They'd open them up and make fresh cigarettes out of them. It was pitiful.'

A moment that stays with Sid to this day is being discharged from hospital. On crutches, he hobbled towards a village which was under a foot of snow. As he made his way along the frozen pavement, he saw standing ahead of him a sole German private, in uniform, missing his right arm. As he passed, the German recognised Sid as an officer, stood to attention, and gave him a solemn left-arm salute. 'I had to recover from the crutches to return his salute,' he says. 'I can't tell you why but that really shook me.' Reaching the village, he saw, perhaps for the first time, thin children, boys, girls, women, but very few men. Suddenly he saw his own family in their faces, his brothers and sisters; nieces and cousins. 'These were the Germans, the people we were supposed to kill. It still gets me, thinking of it,' he says. Sid couldn't bring himself to enter the village, and turned back.

Berlin, like the rest of Germany at war's end, was divided into zones of jurisdiction under the four victorious Allied powers, as it would continue to be for decades. While there was little distinction between the French, British and American zones, the Russian sector was a different story. 'I used to see them using oxen to pull carts down the streets of their zone,' Sid tells me. It was also not a place, at the dawn of the Cold War, to find yourself uninvited. 'You had to be careful taking off,' he continues. 'As soon as we pulled up our wheels we were over the Russian zone and they'd fire at you!'

It took a while for Sid to break the habit of constantly scanning the skies for German fighters that were now confined to the ground, but he settled into a routine that was little more, he says, than 'keeping our hand in'.

Flying once or twice a week to show the flag to both the defeated populace and, increasingly, the Russians, Sid would do the odd bit of practice bombing or strafing, but it must have seemed an anticlimax after the stress of operations. But there was still the weather or accidents to claim you, even though the guns were now silent.

Flying through cloud on one occasion, Sid did his best to stay in close formation to his section leader who had his eye on his instruments. Soon, however, all he could see was white. Knowing there was, somewhere in the area, a high mountain range, he climbed as high and as quickly as he could. At 10000 feet, he was hopelessly lost. Then, beneath him, a break in the cloud. If he put his nose down and emerged from the bottom of it, he might get a clue as to where he was. Down and down Sid now went, watching his altimeter drop away rapidly. At an alarmingly low 1500 feet, he realised that the gap was far closer to the ground than he'd thought. 'When I came out of the cloud base,' he says, 'I was so low I can remember making out the details of a *single fern tree*.' Once again climbing, Sid did the sensible thing and radioed base for a bearing.

Sid arrived back home in May 1946, after four years and one month in the air force. His adjustment, he says, was a difficult one. 'I had an ulcer that I didn't get rid of for twenty years, just from the stress. And I'd gotten used to the air force way of life. For four years they told you what to do, gave you your food, your clothes and you didn't have to think for yourself.' As almost all of the airmen I have met have told me, after the war, nobody wanted to know about what they had gone through. Few questions were asked and almost none were answered. People simply wanted to move on.

Sid's healing came much later, after nursing the demons of what he'd seen and felt in post-war Germany, when a re-injury of the ankle he'd broken while on the squadron proved a catalyst to recovery. As well as qualifying him for a war-related injury, his doctor suggested he tackle the depression which had visited him regularly since the war. 'They told me I should see a psychiatrist,' he tells me. 'It was a bit like a red rag to a bull at first, but it turned out to be the best thing I ever did.' The pride that had prevented him from contacting Veterans Affairs abated, and he came to see that he was in fact thoroughly deserving of the modest help a free and grateful society should offer men such as he.

Recently, Sid was asked to talk to a professional group about his experiences flying Spitfires, and it proved to be a revelation. 'They couldn't get enough of me,' he says. He's now given a number of talks, all to fascinated responses, and the experience of doing so has been positive. A trip back to England in 2009 was less successful, rekindling the stress of war which for decades had, as is the case with so many of the men who flew, lain dormant in his memory.

DICK DAKEYNE

Role: Wireless operator
Aircraft: Consolidated B-24 Liberator
Posting: 319 Squadron, US 5th Air Force

*I believed I was helping keep the
Japanese out of Australia.*

As a young man, Dick had every intention of following in his
father's footsteps in joining the army, even bringing his dad
along with him to the recruiting depot to join up in downtown
Sydney, in January 1942. But when he told the officer behind
the desk that he was 'just eighteen', the response was a patron-
ising, 'Well, son, of course we won't be sending you anywhere
until you're nineteen.' Affronted, Dick walked straight out and
joined the air force, who were happy to take him immediately.
'We were all *that keen* to get into the war, you see,' he tells me
today with some amazement.

Dick is a lively and engaging man with a crystal clear memory which, thankfully, he's keen to demonstrate. I look around his airy retirement unit in Coffs Harbour at an array of books and framed maps, accompanied by a somewhat incongruous collection of African tribal art. Books on geography stand next to gaudy carved statuettes of people with grotesquely enlarged mouths and faces. 'I taught in Kenya after the war for nine years,' he tells me, as I take it all in curiously.

At No. 2 Initial Training School at Bradfield Park, Dick was disappointed not to be categorised as a pilot, but didn't take it too personally. 'At that stage of the war,' he tells me, 'the air force simply had enough pilots.' Dick became instead a wireless / air gunner. Months later, in a gymnasium, an NCO made a sudden announcement to the hundred or so 'WAGs' assembled in front of him. 'Right,' he began, indicating one side of the big room. 'We want fifty of you blokes over here to go to Canada.' An immediate stampede of young men shook the building, spurred on by the idea of action and a free trip overseas.

'I wasn't quick enough,' says Dick, 'and missed out.'

The sergeant, however, wasn't quite finished. 'Right, now I want fifty of you over here to go to Maryborough.'

No. 3 Wireless Air Gunners School at Maryborough, Queensland, sounded nowhere near as exciting as Canada, but Dick turned to a friend. 'I've never been out of New South Wales,' he said.

'Neither have I,' his mate replied. 'Let's go!'

Initially slow on some of the basics such as Morse ('I struggled to get the minimum twenty words a minute,' he tells me), Dick was nevertheless regarded highly enough to be one of

just eight men selected to undergo a special three-week training course to serve with the mysterious-sounding 'Section 22
of General Headquarters', a secret radio counter-measures unit
known more simply (to those few who knew it at all) as Section
22. Set up in late 1943, this multi-national, multi-service organisation comprised specialised personnel from all branches of the
US armed forces as well as British, New Zealand, Dutch and
Australian wireless experts.

'As well as carrying out bombing missions, my job was to
help find out what the Japanese ground radar was all about,'
Dick says. 'The frequencies they were using, the range at which
they could pick us up, and most important, their location.' Dick
would operate the advanced American SCR-587 radio set,
learning all he could about ultra high frequencies (UHF).

A further surprise awaited Dick in Darwin when he learned
that instead of applying his skills at an RAAF squadron, he
and another sergeant, Joe Holohan, were to be sent to fly with
the Americans, specifically the US 319th Squadron, currently
based at lonely Fenton airstrip in the red dust and scrub near
Katherine in the Northern Territory. Flying as a radio counter-measures operator was an exacting job, requiring hours of
intense concentration, hunched over a radio receiver with a
set of headphones, twiddling knobs in a cramped and awkward
makeshift niche above the bomb bay. 'They hadn't provided
anywhere in the aircraft for us radio counter-measures people
to sit,' he says, 'so we had to improvise one.' Even more vital
than the ability to work in a confined space, however, was the
need for absolutely perfect hearing – and in both ears.

'We used two dipole antennas on either side of the aircraft,' Dick tells me. 'I had to continually switch from right to

left on the receiver.' When picked up by Japanese radar, Dick would hear the signal as stronger in one ear than the other. He would then instruct his pilot to 'turn gently' to the left or the right, into the line of bearing, which would be logged by the navigator. Using the code word 'snark', he would immediately transmit the latitudes, longitudes and frequencies of the Japanese position. Other aircraft would do the same, and the location of the Japanese radar could be reasonably triangulated. 'Anything with the prefix "snark" was top secret,' he tells me. It sounds somewhat rudimentary now, but these were the beginnings of electronic warfare.

Straight away, Dick liked the Americans, and they in turn seemed to take a shine to him. Some Australian airmen I have met have little good to say about 'the Yanks' but Dick won't hear of it, citing them as brave, well-trained and highly professional. Some minor cultural hurdles had to be negotiated, but once Dick had become inured to chilli con carne for dinner and pancakes and maple syrup for breakfast, everyone settled into their outback tent-camp home. Dick, however, managed a few surprises of his own. 'They couldn't believe that I didn't know how to drive a car, or that at nineteen, I was still a virgin,' he tells me.

On 30 May 1943, Dick's adapted B-24D was ready for operations, and he and Joe Holohan flipped a coin to see who would complete their first mission. Dick won the toss, and as luck would have it, on that first trip, he picked up a Japanese radar station in the vicinity of Surabaya, East Java. 'As far as I know,' he tells me, 'this was the first bit of radio counter-measures intelligence in this part of the south-west Pacific theatre.' Luck was with him too, when a lone Zero flew alongside them, at a distance of about 800 yards, just beyond the range of Dick's guns, but for reasons that remain a mystery, chose not to attack. 'I think he was just amazed to be seeing these great big Liberator bombers for the first time,' he says.

The first, and most deadly, Japanese air raid on Darwin of February 1942, in which nearly 600 people were either killed or wounded, is well known. Less so are the more than sixty subsequent air attacks on Australian territory, which continued until November 1943. One of these, number fifty-five, Dick remembers as the most dramatic moment of his war.

In the middle of June, Dick was part of a group of enlisted men sent to Darwin to unload some of the newly arrived US 380th Bomb Group's equipment, which had been delivered by ship. After a few days, the job was done, and at around ten o'clock on the morning of 20 June, Dick remembers contemplating his first stint behind the wheel of a truck to head the 80 or so miles back down to Fenton. 'I'd only ever been in a car once or twice in my life,' he tells me. 'One of the American sergeants said to me, "Well, Aussie, you've gotta drive one of these home so get in there and learn!"'

After a quick lesson in double de-clutching, Dick and the convoy dispersed around the Winnellie football field, near the present-day Darwin Airport, waiting for the order to go. 'It was a Sunday morning,' he remembers. 'We were standing around having a game of softball with some of the blokes from a camp across the road, and an alarm went off.' The slow *beep-beep* was unfamiliar to everyone. 'Just a yellow alert, don't worry about it,' someone said, and the game continued.

'We were all as green as grass,' Dick says, shaking his head. 'None of us had had any experience with air raids at that stage.'

About a quarter of an hour later, a second alarm sounded, this time faster and more urgent. Dick looked to the sky and saw the pale undersides of a perfect formation of high-level Japanese 'Sally' bombers. This time, the game stopped. 'That's a red alert!' someone shouted, and everyone scattered.

Fortunately, some rudimentary slit trenches about 18 inches deep had been dug after a previous attack, and Dick and an American air gunner, 'Stoney' Markey, made for one of them. 'It was a little L-shaped trench,' he says. 'I dived in one side, and Stoney jumped in the other.' Moments later, there was a long, single, gigantic explosion, 'one enormous sound, all together', as Dick puts it. The Japanese formation of about twenty medium bombers had pattern-bombed the area with high explosive and anti-personnel bombs, spraying jagged pieces of shrapnel just above the ground. As green as he was, Dick had remembered the adage to always carry your tin hat, and had the sense to put it on his head. 'If I hadn't had that tin hat, I would have been killed,' he says.

As soon as the din had passed, Dick heard the urgent voice of Stoney. 'Dick, Dick, my leg!' Dick looked to see the man's leg, all but severed by a piece of shrapnel, 'just hanging on by a piece of skin'. Once again, Dick's foresight paid off. In the eighteen months spent between signing on and being called up for training, he'd decided to complete a St John Ambulance first-aid course, and so when the time came, he knew immediately what to do. The amount of blood told him that the man's femoral artery had been severed, and that in a minute or two he would most likely bleed to death. 'I used my belt as a tourniquet, then found a rock to put pressure on the wound and stop the bleeding,' he says.

As Dick was saving the man's life, a parked truck began to catch fire a few feet away, raining flaming grass and other debris on top of them. Emerging from the trench, Dick dragged the wounded man along the ground to the shelter of some drums. 'Pretty stupid,' he tells me, 'as they were most likely filled with petrol!' Then, five minutes after the attack, it was the turn of the Japanese fighters to come in and strafe. 'That really was scary,' says Dick. 'We were all out of our trenches by then and there was nothing we could do but lie down flat.'

Three men were killed on this attack, and eleven wounded, including Dick himself. He shows me his hands, where scars are still evident. 'I couldn't understand it for a while, but I think I had my hands over my tin hat during the attack.' He and Stoney were carted off to hospital, Dick with lacerations to his fingers, but considering himself lucky to still have them, Stoney losing his leg. 'If we hadn't been just that little bit below ground level, we'd have been all killed,' Dick tells me. 'We could have dived anywhere. I just happened to go to one side, and Stoney went to the other. How do you explain it?'

Dick was off duty for six weeks. 'In hospital, I couldn't get my hands wet, so when I had a shower, the nurse at the hospital just told me to "hold them up!"' he laughs. When he returned to Fenton, he wore his tin hat that had saved his life, complete with the dint at the front of it, with pride.

As well as a specialised radio operator, Dick was also a gunner, and when not in his cramped radio compartment, he climbed down to man the Liberator's right-hand 50-calibre waist gun. As his tour progressed, he found there would be a good deal to shoot at. While carrying out bombing attacks on Japanese-occupied islands in the Dutch East Indies, Dick's

Liberator was attacked by Japanese fighters on around twelve separate occasions. Some of his American crewmen would often yell excitedly down the intercom, 'There's one, coming in nine o'clock high!' etc. Dick's co-pilot, however, was always a picture of calm, simply telling the men to stay cool and get ready for them. Once, it was a Zero float plane which, Dick says, came up 'low and from the front'. His was the only gun that could bear on it, and after firing, he noticed it begin to smoke, before going into 'a bit of a spin' and disappearing. However, as he didn't actually see it crash or blow up, Dick modestly refrained from claiming it as a kill.

Once they were sent to attack a newly built Japanese air-strip, Langgoer, on an island just west of New Guinea. Dick recorded it in his logbook, with the note 'hot interception by 25 aircraft'. 'That was the hottest fight I was ever in,' he tells me. 'The Japanese were all over us, good pilots and all very keen.' Their attack shot down at least one Liberator and knocked out engines in several more. One new American pilot on his first mission limped his aircraft back to Australia, but made the fatal error of attempting to get all the way back to Fenton. 'He should have gone in at Darwin, and he didn't,' says Dick. Just a couple of miles short of the runway, he ran out of fuel and crashed, killing the entire crew. 'Yes,' he reflects, 'that was a scary day.'

Whether fighters showed up or not, Japanese ack-ack could always be relied on to appear, particularly during the two-minute bomb run to the target when the aircraft was required to fly straight and level for the 'bombardier' (as the Americans termed their bomb aimer) to set his sights and press the release. Much of the fire was extremely accurate. After one trip Dick noticed two corresponding holes on both sides of the fuselage, just a metre or so in front of his position, and reflects that this was probably his closest call in the air. 'I still don't know if it was a bullet from a fighter, or anti-aircraft,' he says. 'It's actually quite amazing how little we were hit.' Some of his friends were not so lucky.

Operating one of the waist guns on a large mission to attack a major Japanese base at Penfui in Timor, Dick's Liberator flew alongside that of his friend with whom he'd tossed a coin a few weeks earlier, Joe Holohan, flying just his second mission. 'Over the target,' Dick remembers, 'Joe's plane was hit by ack-ack and one of its engines started to smoke.' The Japanese fighters, 'and there were plenty of them', says Dick, swarmed onto this 'lame duck'. 'The pilot tried to ditch, but she exploded just before hitting the water. There were no survivors.'

In August, the squadron attacked the oil-refining town of Balikpapan on Borneo on two nights in succession. Half the aircraft were ordered to target the town, the rest to 'skip-bomb' the ships in the harbour. 'We were told to go for the biggest ship we could see,' says Dick. However, having no previous experience of this technique in which the bombs are 'skipped' at low level like stones across a pond into the sides of the ships, Dick's bombardier overshot and they missed everything.

A month later, a similar technique was attempted at Makassar on the island of Sulawesi. Dick was not on that trip, but his friend and tent neighbour Lieutenant Dave Lippincott, and his crew of Liberator *The Red Ass*, was. 'That was a really tough one,' says Dick. After counting all the Liberators home, everyone waited on the airstrip for the one missing 'ship'. 'I can remember we were all standing around waiting, saying, "They must be coming home, they must be coming home." Then, you look at your watch and realise their petrol's gone. It's a terrible feeling.' It was believed that Dave's aircraft was hit by the explosion of its own bomb. There were four survivors, but they were picked up by the Japanese and beheaded.

'You're bringing all these memories back to me now, that have been out of my mind for so long,' Dick tells me after a deep silence.

Dick made life-long friends with his American crew and kept in touch for years after the war. In an extraordinary coincidence, he even met, in the 1960s, on an academic tour of Japan, a former anti-aircraft gunner. 'Where were you based?' asked Dick.

'Oh, a little out-of-the-way place you've never heard of on the northern tip of New Guinea called Manokwari.'

Dick certainly had heard of it, having bombed it on four occasions. 'You were terrible shots,' Dick told the gentleman good-naturedly through an interpreter. 'Didn't come anywhere near us.'

'Well, you weren't too crash hot yourself,' the man replied. 'After you'd dropped all your bombs in the bay, we'd send boats out to collect the dead fish for our dinner!' The two men stayed in contact for years.

Dick describes his return to civilian life as a relatively untroubled one, taking advantage of the government's offer of free university education to study, then teach geography. But he didn't talk about the war. 'From 1946 when I got out, till about 1989, I didn't even think about the war,' he tells me, nor were his children particularly interested. He believes his Christian faith, found not long before he began his training, became an enormous help in wartime. 'I believed I was helping keep the Japanese out of Australia,' he tells me. 'I had a feeling that if I was killed, well, I'd be going to the right place.'

POSTSCRIPT

I still recall sitting down for my very first interview with an airman, in his living room in a leafy suburb in my home city of Melbourne. I was aged about thirteen. I had no idea it was going to be an interview at the time of course, but that's what it turned out to be. The man I had come to see was Arnold Easton, a former 467 Squadron navigator who had completed a full tour of operations on Lancasters during a period of horrendous losses for Bomber Command in 1943 and 1944. Arnold was a tall man, and striking, with pale, intelligent blue eyes and remains still in my memory as one of the quietest and most gentle men I have ever met. It occurred to me only recently, as I completed the final interview in this book, that Arnold would have then been, in the mid-1970s, roughly the same age I am now, somewhere in his early fifties.

We'd met by chance through a friend of my mother's at a theatre function to which I was reluctantly dragged, but towards the end of the evening, the two of us struck up a brief conversation about his wartime flying. How the subject ever came up I have no idea. My parents, long inured to my obsession, no doubt rolled their eyes and left us to it. A week later, I presented myself at his doorstep, having accepted his invitation to talk further.

He was prepared for my visit, as his niece had recently completed a school project on her quiet airman uncle, and he had it out ready to show me. He probably thought our discussion would be similar to the one he had recently conducted with his niece: answering some general questions, explaining some technicalities, and giving a generalised overview of the great air war in which he had participated. But he was wrong. The school project was spread across a dining room table on several sheets of fine white cardboard, covered with tidy, spidery writing and cut out pictures of aeroplanes, annotated diagrams and tables of figures. As soon as I saw it, I was drawn instead to a small bunch of shiny metallic strips sticky taped to a corner. 'Now I just want to tell you what this is,' he began, but before he could finish the sentence I simply said, 'window', recognising instantly the aluminium foil strips dropped by the ton by the bombers to confuse German radar. He stopped and looked at me anew. 'How did you know that?' I shrugged my shoulders like a typical thirteen-year-old.

For some reason, Arnold ended up telling me more that day than he'd ever considered telling his niece. For me, it was a revelation, the first proper conversation with someone who had lived an obsession which, even then, I had carried in my head for years. Navigators were special. Highly intelligent, meticulous, sensitive. 'The brains of the aircraft', as many of their grateful crew described them. Their responsibility in guiding their bomber across a hostile, blacked-out continent to a pinpoint target and back again, using nothing but a map, a wristwatch and mental arithmetic was almost incomprehensible. I kept asking Arnold questions, endless questions. Some he ignored, or skirted around, so I would ask him again. I made him describe to me all he could remember about the Lancaster, the colour of its interior, and its smell. I forced him to recall faces, conversations, voices. We spoke about aeroplanes, the art of navigation, the men he knew and the base, at Waddington in Lincolnshire where he was stationed. 'The strangest thing was flying into a battle, with aircraft going down around you, flak exploding, thinking every second you were about to die, then coming back and waking up in clean sheets in the middle of the English countryside with rabbits darting in and out of the hedgerows,' he said.

As he spoke, the quieter and the paler he became. Gradually I stopped asking, and just listened. Regrettably, I have now forgotten much of what he said, and in the end my presence was an irrelevance anyway. His eyes fixed on the centre of a table, he began, unprompted, to speak about the wrenching, unbearable stress of his tour, of watching faces he knew around him gradually disappear, and the nightmares that visited him still. He thought, he told me, about the bombing itself, about what was happening on the ground, underneath his Lancaster, as tons of high explosives cascaded onto factories, houses, hospitals, apartment blocks, God knows what.

He showed me his Distinguished Flying Cross, still in its case, its liquid, silver arms fashioned poetically to resemble propeller blades under a ribbon of diagonal blue and white stripes. He was proud of it, but I remember also an awkwardness, as if he himself didn't quite know what to make of it. I remember wanting to take it out of the box and handle it, but he said something and closed the lid, returning it to its home in the bottom drawer of a desk.

He then passed me an old blue cloth-bound book with a small RAF wing and crown embossed on the cover. 'Air Navigation, Vol 1', said the title, and on the inside cover 'His Majesty's Stationery Office, 1941. For Official Use'. Its pages were creamy and smooth and filled with myriad intricate, diagrams, charts and tables. Its chapter headings included, 'The Theory of Dead Reckoning Navigation', 'Astronomical Navigation' and 'Wireless Direction Finding'. This was, Arnold told me, his navigator's text book, the bible from which all navigators learned the craft of getting an aeroplane from A to B. I was taken with it immediately and began asking him to explain some of the details, many of which he could still recall without hesitation, while others had been long forgotten. Something then tripped me up, a quote at the beginning of the first chapter, not, as one might expect from the king or some figure of influence concerning duty or responsibility, the first words young navigators read were, bizarrely, those of Lewis Carroll:

> *'Of course the first thing to do was to make a grand survey of the country she was going to travel through. It's something very like learning Geography, thought Alice.'*
>
> Alice Through the Looking Glass

'Hang on to that if you like,' Arnold told me, and I did.

At the end of our conversation, he was exhausted, and politely suggested it was probably time for me to leave. I caught a train home, and never saw him again, a regret I carry to this day. Arnold passed away many years ago, but I doubt if a month has gone by that I haven't thought of him, or the book he gave me.

The people who fought in the great and dreadful conflict of the mid twentieth century are all but gone, a fact almost entirely lost amid the rigid hysteria of the Anzac centenary, a spectacle which the airmen I spoke to, almost to a man, found repellent. 'Anzac Day used to be a day of mourning, a national ordeal,' one of them told me. 'But even then I didn't march in the bloody thing.' He was proud of it, too.

I am profoundly thankful to the many men who spoke to me about their war. I am thankful for their generosity, their dignity, their humour and their modesty. I am thankful for what they did, and their nobility amid the ghastly ignobility of war. And as I too close this long chapter of my own life, begun as a child talking to a middle aged former navigator about events before my time, I will miss them, all of them, beyond words.